Recommendat

The Most Reverend and
Cottrell, Archbishop of York.

"Robin Gamble has been an inspiration to hundreds of clergy and lay leaders through Leading your Church into Growth. In this book he offers us 100 thoughtful, challenging and insightful reflections on Jesus. Dig deeper with Robin into what it means to lead a Jesus-shaped life."

Canon Gordon Dey, Founder of 'Jesus Shaped People'

"In these strange times I believe Robin Gamble's new invitation to take '100 Days to find, follow, and become like Jesus' is a brilliant recipe for many, both for people who've lost time and energy for taking time out each day for prayer and bible reading, and for those who just need something different and significant to refresh their Christian journey. He shares it with us, having tried and tested it for himself:

'Then I came to a change of direction in the road. I decided to find out as much as I could specifically about the man Jesus and to copy him. To make him my hero, my model, my mentor. To literally try and do it his way.......this 'doing it his way' personal revolution has transformed my life and ministry.'

Robin's choice of scripture readings is excellent - and his insights and questions give us additional tools that enable us to connect today with what Jesus said and did in the 1st century AD. His capacity to include 'ordinary people' is impressive - and there may well be some for whom the use of '100 Days' will be the spur they need to make a new beginning with Jesus."

The Right Reverend Philip North, Bishop of Burnley

"This book is a chance not just to meet the most amazing person the world has ever known, but to begin a relationship with him one that will change your life in the most amazing and unpredictable ways. If you are a searcher looking for answers, or a Christian seeking refreshment, Robin Gamble's engaging and rich reflections will open up the Gospels for you in a completely fresh way. Start now, and in a hundred days' time, anything could have happened!"

Reverend Simon Ponsonby, international author and speaker. Pastor of Theology at St Aldates, Oxford.

"I know no-one who has spent more time studying Jesus and more time speaking of Jesus than Robin Gamble.

He has devoted his life to Jesus, and over four decades of ministry helped people to discover Jesus.

Through this set of 100 fresh, exciting, provocative studies, one of England's most effective evangelists invites us all, wherever we are, to "Come to Jesus, come back to Jesus, come closer to Jesus"

Reverend Neil Short. Vicar of St Michael's Blundellsands Diocesan Missioner, Liverpool Diocese.

"Robin asked me to read the first few days to give him my verdict. I loved it.

- *I have since used the whole book for my own quiet times.*
- *I have decided to encourage our congregation of St Michael's, Blundellsands to buy and use it for their own quiet times.*

- *I have chosen one day out of every five to use as the basis for the sermon the following Sunday.*
- *I have taken a second one out of every 5 to use as the basis for the weekly Bible study.*
- *In my role working for Liverpool Diocese I sent it out to seven clergy colleagues, four of them are going to use it.*

In my view 100 days with Jesus provides a great opportunity to encourage any congregation into a deeper walk with our Lord."

Reverend Matt Woodcock, author of 'Becoming Reverend' and Radio 2 contributor, said:

"I love Jesus 100! Reading about the life of Jesus in this way has become a really important part of my own personal quiet times and also a crucial resource for our small-group gatherings.

Robin has such a tremendous and rare gift of being faithful to the teachings and way of Jesus but putting it across in such a relatable, contemporary and refreshing way. This book presumes no prior knowledge of anything Christian but is suitable for anyone at any stage of faith. I can't recommend it highly enough.

I've been plagiarising Robin for years - and this book gives me even more rich and engaging material to 'borrow' from! Buy it. Use it. Enjoy it."

Canon John Young, Author of the classic 'The Case Against Christ'.

"Robin is in the Premier League of communicators: he is charismatic, clear, funny, encouraging and challenging."

JESUS 100

100 days to find him
100 days to follow him
100 days to become like him

Robin Gamble

Grosvenor House
Publishing Limited

This book is published by
Grosvenor House Publishing Ltd
Link House
140 The Broadway, Tolworth, Surrey, KT6 7HT.
www.grosvenorhousepublishing.co.uk

A CIP record for this book
is available from the British Library

ISBN 978-1-83975-833-1

Jesus

Stable to cross

Unknown boy to misunderstood man

Galilee to Jerusalem

Crucifixion to resurrection

Dust to dust

Light to light

Glory to glory

Then to now

Introduction

Jesus

He started out as the peasant child of unmarried parents. He lived in a tiny, dusty village in an 'up North' part of an obscure and disliked country on the extreme edge of a great empire.

He was active for between eighteen months and three years. He didn't do any of the things that make people famous: didn't fight any battles, didn't build any great cities, write any books or make any discoveries. All he did was spend time amongst his own people, teaching them about God, healing the sick, giving peace to the disturbed, gathering a handful of followers. He died a criminals' death and...

And today he is the most loved, well known and influential celebrity on the world stage. He has transformed more lives, inspired more world changes and humanitarian movements than anyone else in human history. Music has been composed, pictures painted, books written and cathedrals and cities built, all in his name.

Even in a modern secular state like Britain where we don't quite know what to do with him, he is still the most remembered, admired and respected person in our shared culture and memory.

So how did the obscure 'Jesus of Nazareth', become 'Jesus Saviour of the World'? How did Mr Nobody become the friend of everybody?

100 Steps

So this is the plan. 100 days to 'Journey with Jesus'.

From reading the four gospel stories about him I have picked out 100 readings to take us from birth and boyhood, into maturity and ministry and finally to crucifixion, resurrection and ascension. Actually it is not so much a 100 passages to just read, more like a 100 miles or steps to travel. You see it is not just about his life but ours too. It is not enough to read a bit a day, put the book down and then get on with life. Here we have the opportunity to open the windows of our soul on to a whole new life. To discover the path that he trod and still treads, breathe the peace that he gave and still gives and love the love that he shared and still shares.

Perhaps you are reading this as a curious explorer, or as a new Christian, or as someone who has already spent years faithfully following Jesus. Here you have a 100 days to find him for the first time, or for the first time in a long time. A 100 days to change your life journey, to follow his path. A 100 days to actually become more like him.

Now be honest with yourself. Have you ever thought, 'life could be so much better', 'I could be happier', 'there could be more purpose, more direction, more joy'? If you haven't, then I am truly sorry for you because somewhere along the way you have lost it. If you have thought these things then you need to spend 100 days in the company of the greatest life-changer the world has ever known. And then another 100, and another 100 after that.

Pouring over the gospels and reading a pile of 'Jesus books' over the years, I have come to the conclusion that there are 10 key marks to the man Jesus:

- He was a Northerner
- He came from the 'working class'
- He battled with demonic evil
- He came up against the religious leaders and establishment
- He combined words (proclamation) with works (healing and exorcism)
- The common people loved him and knew that he was unique
- He honoured and made special room for women
- He created a new style of companionship amongst his followers
- He had a very strong sense of Jerusalem as his destiny
- Jesus had a unique self-awareness. He saw himself as the Saviour of people and as the Son of God.

These 10 marks or themes will keep appearing and re-appearing as you follow Jesus in these 100 readings. They are like silken threads, woven together to form an unbreakable cord that is both soft to the touch and steel-like at the core.

Hopefully, every one of these 100 readings will give a challenge or invitation to find, follow and become. But just to help you, I have picked out occasional signposts along the way. I have also included various thoughts, suggestions, and questions and written some special prayers to help you to both understand him and to journey alongside him.

100 Stories About Jesus

We find out most about who Jesus was, what he did and why things happened as they did by reading the gospels. The four gospels are best described as collections of short stories forming one long story of Jesus' life. The first three, Matthew, Mark and Luke are remarkably alike. Together they tell the story of Jesus rambling around the Galilee area then travelling down the Jordan Valley to the great climax in Jerusalem. Here we see him gather his disciples, heal the sick, teach parables and talk lots about being the Son of Man and about the Kingdom of God. In John's gospel the story is a bit different. He seems to bounce back and forth between Galilee and Jerusalem. There are still disciples and miracles, but not quite as many. Instead of calling himself the Son of Man he coins the 'I Am' expressions and instead of the 'Kingdom of God' we have 'Eternal life'. The four gospels then fall into a three and one package.

Here I have picked out 100 of these short stories, to form a sort of Matthew, Mark, Luke and John combined version. You could see it as a 'greatest hits' of Jesus, but I prefer to think of it as a flowing together of the four greatest streams of literature that the world has ever produced. It jumps about a bit, as do the originals, and some of the stories are grouped together under headings such as, 'parables' or 'people he met', this happens in the originals too.

Some people will read these stories in a very disciplined fashion, one a day for just over 14 weeks. Others will miss the odd day, but that's ok as long as you pick it up again. Some will make the major mistake of reading two or three at a time, like doing two- or three-days walking in one day. The point is, it is not just about the time to read, it is about the follow up time to think about, ponder and assimilate the reading.

Matthew, Mark, Luke and John can best be understood as collections of eyewitness records remembered and written down by the people who were there. They were the ones who actually saw and heard. Unlike them, I myself, have never physically seen, felt, heard or touched Jesus, neither have I met anyone who has (this despite all the language people loosely use about Jesus speaking and showing). But I am still a witness. I am a sort of 'testing him out and finding that he is really there' witness. I have searched, read, explored, made decisions and followed.

Some years ago I made a radical change to my life. Up until that point I had been living as a Christian and working as a vicar and evangelist on the rough basis of trying to be and do all the normal Christian stuff.

I listened to God talks, read God books and had God conversations and sort of tried to do and be it all. My life, ministry and evangelism were ok, but only ok. Then I came to a change of direction in the road. I decided to find out as much as I could specifically about the man Jesus and to copy him. To make him my hero, my model, my mentor. To literally try and do it his way. Today I view the place where I live as my Galilee, I try to base my daily life of relationships, work and prayer on him. The way I wander around, share the good news and pray for healing is an attempt to do it his way. This 'doing it his way' personal revolution has transformed my life and ministry.

So as a sort of 'deep thought and life-style witness' as opposed to an 'eyewitness', I stand in the witness box, make my oath to speak the whole truth and nothing but the truth, and then declare that to follow the path of Jesus is to live in a bigger, deeper, richer, fuller and more alive way than any other.

Who is this slight, bearded man,
Walking through the early morning mist,
Coming down from the hills,
Down from his prayers?

His face, his eyes, his lips,
The song of his talking,
The shape of his walking.

He knows where he is going.
And those who know
Are following him.

That's all the preparatory info. Now we are ready
to begin this life changing 100 day journey.

1. Silent Night

Luke 2: 1–7

¹ In those days a decree went out from Emperor Augustus that all the world should be registered. ² This was the first registration and was taken while Quirinius was governor of Syria. ³ All went to their own towns to be registered. ⁴ Joseph also went from the town of Nazareth in Galilee to Judea, to the city of David called Bethlehem, because he was descended from the house and family of David. ⁵ He went to be registered with Mary, to whom he was engaged and who was expecting a child. ⁶ While they were there, the time came for her to deliver her child. ⁷ And she gave birth to her firstborn son and wrapped him in bands of cloth, and laid him in a manger, because there was no place for them in the inn.

Day one, the story begins. In secret, in obscurity, in silence, Jesus is born.

Ninety-nine more days to go.

We are so familiar with this story. We have seen it on a thousand Christmas cards and watched children acting it out in dressing gowns and tea towels at school nativities. So have we lost sight of what a strange and mysterious story it really is?

The names and places set the stage. First, we see the mighty Empire, with decisions made by its emperor in Rome. Jesus is going to be born on the distant edge of this world. He is irrelevant to it, a nobody. Second, Mary and Joseph appear living in Nazareth, a tiny village 'up North'. Think not of a nice attractive modern village but of grinding poverty, insecure lives, ignorance and superstition, a poor diet and a hot dusty terrain. Jesus is born dirt poor, he is a peasant, at the bottom of the pile. Third, we read of Bethlehem, city of Kings. There is a bloodline between the great King David and Jesus. A new King is being born.

A baby is born –   an irrelevant baby – on the edge of
                    the Roman Empire
                    a poor baby – to Mary and Joseph
                    a royal baby – into Bethlehem

Yes we know the story, but actually we know so little about it. It is so familiar, but the rich details are elusive. We know the outline, but most of us have never 'coloured it in'. So at the beginning of our 100-day journey we will spend a full week at the very beginning of what is usually referred to as 'the nativity'. Angels and prophets, shepherds and kings, light and dark, we shall meet them all on this crowded little stage. As we look again at these familiar tales we shall be starting out on a holy trek, a pilgrimage and following in the footsteps of the greatest human being who has ever lived.

There is of course a hidden away little thought in all this. If this is how the story of Jesus entering the world began, how did the story of Jesus entering your world begin? Where and when is your Bethlehem? Or perhaps that story has not yet fully begun, perhaps your own private world is still at the 'pregnant with possibilities stage'. Maybe you are still a searcher, not yet a follower.

Most of us have got our own deep centre. Much of it we keep hidden away for most of the time. It holds memories of the past and plans for the future. There regrets float around, along with hopes and dreams. It is here at our centre, in our deepest, most 'me' place that we need a stable and a crib. It is here that Jesus needs to be 'born' in us.

Back to the emperor for a second little thought. If Jesus has been born into your world, whether it was ten weeks or ten years ago, who is at the centre, who is the emperor, who issues the big decrees in your empire? Who gives the orders? Is it your boss, your children, your bank manager, your partner or you yourself? Or possibly you are trying to make Jesus your emperor?

Dear Lord Jesus
As you entered then
So may you enter now.
As you entered there
So may you enter here.
Beginning small and growing,
Beginning in my inner place and spreading out to
my whole life.
Amen.

2. Mother Mary – Let It Be

Luke 1: 26–38

26 In the sixth month the angel Gabriel was sent by God to a town in Galilee called Nazareth, 27 to a virgin engaged to a man whose name was Joseph, of the house of David. The virgin's name was Mary. 28 And he came to her and said, "Greetings, favoured one! The Lord is with you." 29 But she was much perplexed by his words and pondered what sort of greeting this might be. 30 The angel said to her, "Do not be afraid, Mary, for you have found favour with God. 31 And now, you will conceive in your womb and bear a son, and you will name him Jesus. 32 He will be great, and will be called the Son of the Most High, and the Lord God will give to him the throne of his ancestor David. 33 He will reign over the house of Jacob forever, and of his kingdom there will be no end." 34 Mary said to the angel, "How can this be, since I am a virgin?" 35 The angel said to her, "The Holy Spirit will come upon you, and the power of the Most High will overshadow you; therefore the child to be born will be holy; he will be called Son of God. 36 And now, your relative Elizabeth in her old age has also conceived a son; and this *is the sixth month for her who was said to be barren. ³⁷ For nothing will be impossible with God." ³⁸ Then Mary said, "Here am I, the servant of the Lord; let it be with me according to your word." Then the angel departed from her.*

Over the next three days we are stepping back a bit to see what was happening in the lead-up to the stable birth. It's basically three readings filled with angels, prophets and shepherds.

Angels are everywhere in the nativity stories. They are the chorus line to the central characters of Jesus, Mary and Joseph. In our imagination they are beautiful, strong, shining, humanoid looking beings with eagle wings. In the Bible they are messengers, God's postmen and postwomen.

So how did it happen, the greatest of all angel stories? Did it come swooping down out of the night sky, a massively brilliant apparition? Did it all happen in a dream? Perhaps it was all much more matter of fact as Mary was sweeping the floor or pounding bread at the table.

Angels seem to be all the rage these days in our 'sort of spiritual, new age culture'. Some people seem to have an extra sight and see angels everywhere. Me, I have never seen or knowingly experienced a single one. I have met a few people who have, but not many. That is the point. Angels are not everyday, everywhere. They are very special and this is a very special birth. Angels are God's messengers, his announcers. They are heaven's heralds and occasionally they come to earth.

Why Mary? Because God saw more than an ordinary peasant girl, he saw the inner Mary. He looked not on the outside but on the inside. He saw purity, faithfulness, godliness in her inner core.

Mary is pregnant with Jesus who will be Son of the most high, the new David. That's quite a lot for the son of an unmarried, teenage, peasant girl. 'How can this be?' said Mary. Hence the song *'Let It Be'*. The Beatles of course, got their theology a bit mixed up. It is not Mother Mary who appears to us when we are alone and in trouble, but her son. Nevertheless, they are still great words of wisdom to discover. Who would have thought an absolute rock anthem, a classic, a Lennon and McCartney standard all goes back to the young girl, Mary. She was nervous, full of self-doubt and lacking in confidence. She had no idea what she was letting herself in for, the troubles ahead and the demands it would all make on her. Yet still she uttered the words 'I am your servant, so let it be, according to your word'. This is trusting acceptance of God's word and obedience at the deepest level.

Pregnancy is a wonderful experience. It is all about life. Life burgeoning, life coming. As the mother's belly grows so does the potential; the future hope; the expectancy. But pregnancy is also a nervous, vulnerable time. There is always the danger of miscarriage, accident or still birth. And as all mothers know, birth comes through pain.

At the beginning of your 100 days with Jesus there is a pregnancy in your mind, in your soul. Something or someone has planted a seed; a new spiritual life is happening within you; there is expectancy of a growing relationship. There could be problems. It may all come to nothing. But if all goes well there will be a birth. So here are a couple of big questions to keep thinking about throughout the day: how and when will your finding and following of Jesus be fully born? And have you yet managed to say to the messenger, *'Let it be'*?

> **Lord**
> **I am your servant**
> **So let it be.**
> **Let it be in me,**
> **Through me, for me,**
> **According to your word.**
> **Amen.**

3. Joseph and the Angel

Matthew 1: 18–25

18 Now the birth of Jesus the Messiah took place in this way. When his mother Mary had been engaged to Joseph, but before they lived together, she was found to be with child from the Holy Spirit. 19 Her husband Joseph, being a righteous man and unwilling to expose her to public disgrace, planned to dismiss her quietly. 20 But just when he had resolved to do this, an angel of the Lord appeared to him in a dream and said, "Joseph, son of David, do not be afraid to take Mary as your wife, for the child conceived in her is from the Holy Spirit. 21 She will bear a son, and you are to name him Jesus, for he will save his people from their sins." 22 All this took place to fulfil what had been spoken by the Lord through the prophet: 23 "Look, the virgin shall conceive and bear a son, and they shall name him Emmanuel," which means, "God is with us." 24 When Joseph awoke from sleep, he did as the angel of the Lord commanded him; he took her as his wife, 25 but had no marital relations with her until she had borne a son; and he named him Jesus.

This is a typical little soap opera story. Mary and Joseph are betrothed. They are saving up to get married, and then she tells him she is pregnant. They are both godly people, her being pregnant is a disgrace. Times were much more conservative then. This is such a very human story of a very human situation. Then suddenly, we go from the very human to the ultra-cosmic and mysterious.

I know all about angels from a hundred nativities. In fact I know nothing about angels; they are of a different order from a different type of universe. They are as knowable as quantum mechanics, chaos theory and black holes all rolled into one. Gabriel, that is the one who appeared to Mary, described himself as 'I stand in the presence of God'. God is a bit like the sun, get too close and you get burnt, and so what sort of creature stands in the presence of God? How weird and wonderful is this? Despite all this not understanding of the truly mysterious, I like angels (and I bet you do too). They just have a good feel to them. I would like to find out more about them. On one occasion a very good friend of mine who is much more tuned in to angels than I am, came to my church. It was at a very low point in my life when I was suffering from a lot of depression and found leading a church service very difficult. He told me afterwards that all the time that I was leading the service he could see an angel by my side, supporting me.

Robbie Williams touched everyone's pulse with his great *Angels* song.

> 'And through it all, she offers me protection
> A lot of love and affection'.

I like Joseph too. He has a sort of modest, salt of the earth, solid goodness to him. He doesn't strike me as one of life's great thinking, deeply reflective souls. He is a northern man who works with his hands and who likes to do the right thing. Joseph is not the sort of man to have deep, mysterious dreams of sacred angels. He probably dreams of timber and footings, nails and screws, hammers and saws. It is the angel, a real creature not a dream creature, who takes the initiative and steps into his dream. Joseph is not dreaming up an angel, the angel is coming to find and talk to him.

The child is given two names. First 'Jesus' as saviour and secondly 'Emmanuel' meaning God is with us. These are massively deep ideas. How much of this did Joseph fully grasp, how much did he really understand? I suspect that most of it just left him gasping. Nevertheless, he accepted and trusted in a sort of 'beyond understanding' obedient humility.

Finding Jesus is far deeper than understanding. It is about 'seeing' or perhaps we should say just glimpsing something of God. Our glimpsing is not the first thing, the first thing is his sending, communicating, appearing. The glimpsing is the tiniest opening of the door. It's the beginning of thinking, seeing and responding. In our modern world we are obsessed with the need to understand. What is happening to Joseph is far beyond the world of rational thought and intellectual analysis. So don't expect to fully understand all of the things of God, but do expect to find, or to be found. Expect him to come to you and respond by opening your door slightly; to catch a glimpse of light.

> Lord God
> As you are finding me, help me to find,
> As you are speaking, help me to hear,
> As you are appearing, help me to see.
> That I might awaken and do as you command.
> Amen.

4. The Story Begins with Promises

Matthew 1: 22–23

[22] All this took place to fulfil what had been spoken by the Lord through the prophet: [23] "Look, the virgin shall conceive and bear a son, and they shall name him Emmanuel,".

Luke 1: 55

[55] "according to the promise he made to our ancestors, to Abraham and to his descendants forever."

Isaiah 53: 3–6

[3] He was despised and rejected by others; a man of suffering and acquainted with infirmity; and as one from whom others hide their faces he was despised, and we held him of no account. [4] Surely he has borne our infirmities and carried our diseases; yet we accounted him stricken, struck down by God, and afflicted. [5] But he was wounded for our transgressions, crushed for our iniquities; upon him was the punishment that made us whole, and by his bruises we are healed.

*⁶ All we like sheep have gone astray; we have all
turned to our own way, and the LORD has laid on
him the iniquity of us all.*

Time to travel back in time. Where does the Jesus story
actually begin? Follow the river backwards and you
find its source is a tiny spring. Follow the deep and wide
flow of Jesus' miracles, teachings, crucifixion and
resurrection back to its source and you pass through his
childhood, nativity, shepherds and angel messengers.
Eventually you get right back to a few prophets living
hundreds of years before Jesus.

Daniel, Micah and Isaiah were around in Old Testament
days. They were prophets. Their eyes were fixed on what
was going on around them, seeing the corruption, the
injustice, the failed religion. Their hearts and minds were
rooted in God, in his truth, his teachings, and his plans.
They had a deep conviction that God was all loving and
in control and armed with this awareness they peered into
the misty future to try and pick out God's ultimate
intentions. They looked beyond the struggles of their own
days to a future time when God would send a special
person. The coming man will be a chosen by God 'new
King David', a second 'Moses-like leader', a 'Messiah'.

In Jesus' day the Jews were desperate for the arrival of
this promised one. They had been waiting for hundreds
of years. They imagined him to be a conquering hero, a
new king sent to reign on David's throne. They had
never fully understood the prophecies of a servant, a
son of man, one to shine a spiritual light, one destined
to suffer, one born to give.

They wanted one who would conquer
He came as one to suffer
They were looking for a lion
He was coming as a lamb
They wanted someone to force out the Romans
He was the sent one to drive out the demons
They wanted power
They got peace
Wanted victory
Got humility
Wanted an empire
Got a kingdom.

Like all parents, God the father had a special hope or purpose for his son. He wanted him to change the world, but he wanted even more. He planned for, not just a servant person but a whole servant people. When we align ourselves with the promised Son of God, we become a part of the promised people of God, we become servants, lantern-bearers and world-changers with him.

Lord God
Help me to become like Jesus.
You sent him to this world,
To be a servant
To bring peace
To shine a light
So send me to my world
To serve
To pacify
To shine
For you
Amen.

5. Shepherds

Luke 2: 8–20

⁸ In that region there were shepherds living in the fields, keeping watch over their flock by night. ⁹ Then an angel of the Lord stood before them, and the glory of the Lord shone around them, and they were terrified. ¹⁰ But the angel said to them, "Do not be afraid; for see – I am bringing you good news of great joy for all the people: ¹¹ to you is born this day in the city of David a Saviour, who is the Messiah, the Lord. ¹² This will be a sign for you: you will find a child wrapped in bands of cloth and lying in a manger." ¹³ And suddenly there was with the angel a multitude of the heavenly host, praising God and saying, ¹⁴ "Glory to God in the highest heaven, and on earth peace among those whom he favours!" ¹⁵ When the angels had left them and gone into heaven, the shepherds said to one another, "Let us go now to Bethlehem and see this thing that has taken place, which the Lord has made known to us." ¹⁶ So they went with haste and found Mary and Joseph, and the child lying in the manger. ¹⁷ When they saw this, they made known what had been told them about this child; ¹⁸ and all who heard it were amazed at what the shepherds told them. [19] *But Mary treasured all these words and pondered them in her heart.* [20] *The shepherds returned, glorifying and praising God for all they had heard and seen, as it had been told them.*

After the Old Testament prophesying and angel-promised pregnancy we are back at the stable. This is a classic 'royal birth' story. A king's son is born in the palace; heralds are sent out to the city and nation to announce the event; the rich and famous come to offer their presence and presents. Except here the palace is a stable, the heralds are angels and the rich and famous are the 'bottom rung of the ladder' shepherds. God's version of the world is so different from ours. His way of seeing and valuing people turns our status, class obsessed world upside down. This birth as a homeless person into insecurity and poverty and his welcome by the shepherds all point to Jesus' future. His life and his ministry will all be lived out amongst the poor and the struggling, they are the ones who will respond to him. He will not be centre stage, he will not have political or religious power and authority, wealth with all its supportive relationships to other wealthy people will be denied him. He will live, operate, minister and work on the edge.

After all the excitement of the birth, the announcements and the visiting, the angelic host return to heaven. The 'New David' lies in the manger in the royal city of Bethlehem. The shepherds become, in effect, the first evangelists as they share their story and amaze their listeners. Joseph is stolidly in the background. Mary sits and ponders all.

The story is so well known to us that it loses its importance and sense of mystery. Each detail is loaded with significance but we often miss it.

So perhaps we should be like Mary and (as one translation puts it) ponder over everything. To ponder means to weigh, to balance, to reflect on. It involves deep thinking; going over something time and time again; not necessarily coming to quick conclusions. Pondering is a gradual business involving lots of remembering and reflecting. Spiritual people are all great ponderers. So ponder on all these birth stories. Stable, angels, shepherds, what did they mean then, what do they mean to you now.

I can still remember when Jesus was born into the inner heart/stable of Robert. It was my first job as a clergyman, my wife and I were doing lots of youth work and Robert was the leader of the pack. Cleverest at school, strongest personality, best at football and cricket and most indifferent to God, he was the leader.

After months of just playing footie and listening to loud rock music he had eventually started sniffing around the Jesus end of our youth ministry. Gradually he started attending on a Sunday night, joining in the discussion and asking questions.

Six months later we saw him stand up and open up. He invited Jesus to come and be born in his heart – he has never looked back.

Pondering or deep spiritual thinking is like slow cooking. We like fast food, microwave '2-minute' dinners, even better if someone delivers it to our house. Slow cooking takes patience, but has a deeper, richer flavour.

So slow down, find some room and think deeply in a ruminating sort of way, pondering, rolling it around, about what is happening inside your stable. Allow space for the spiritual expectancy in your inner place to grow slowly. Stop, ask questions, talk to God, talk to a friend, practice slow cooking deep in your soul.

> 'The heavenly babe you there shall find
> To human view displayed.
> All meanly wrapped in swaddling bands
> And in a manger laid'

So, here are the questions for today:

What are you pondering right now?

How far advanced is the slow cooking?

> **Lord God, Heavenly Father**
> **As you sent your son into the world**
> **Send him into my life.**
> **As he was born into a stable**
> **Enable him to be born into my heart**
> **And as Mary pondered**
> **Slow me down that I might ponder.**
> **Amen.**

6. Wise Men Come

Matthew 2: 1–12

 ² *In the time of King Herod, after Jesus was born in Bethlehem of Judea, wise men from the East came to Jerusalem,* ² *asking, "Where is the child who has been born king of the Jews? For we observed his star at its rising, and have come to pay him homage."* ³ *When King Herod heard this, he was frightened, and all Jerusalem with him;* ⁴ *and calling together all the chief priests and scribes of the people, he inquired of them where the Messiah was to be born.* ⁵ *They told him, "In Bethlehem of Judea; for so it has been written by the prophet:* ⁶ *'And you, Bethlehem, in the land of Judah, are by no means least among the rulers of Judah; for from you shall come a ruler who is to shepherd my people Israel.'"*

 ⁷ *Then Herod secretly called for the wise men and learned from them the exact time when the star had appeared.* ⁸ *Then he sent them to Bethlehem, saying, "Go and search diligently for the child; and when you have found him, bring me word so that I may also go and pay him homage."* ⁹ *When they had heard the king, they set out; and there, ahead of them, went the star that they had seen at*

its rising, until it stopped over the place where the child was. [10] When they saw that the star had stopped, they were overwhelmed with joy. [11] On entering the house, they saw the child with Mary his mother; and they knelt down and paid him homage. Then, opening their treasure chests, they offered him gifts of gold, frankincense, and myrrh. [12] And having been warned in a dream not to return to Herod, they left for their own country by another road.

Who were these wise men and why did they take all this trouble in coming to Jesus?

- They were wise men, so that's why they took the trouble to come and find Jesus.
- They came and found Jesus, that's what made them wise men.

We live in a world full of clever people. We are university educated, scientifically aware, technology rich. Information is just a screensaver away. All knowledge can be 'googled' in less time than it takes to make a cup of tea. But what about wisdom? Wise people are much more than just clever or well-informed. They possess wisdom in their deepest place. Clever people are often so aware of what they know, of their academic achievements. This cleverness brings its own sense of accomplishment and often a preening pride. Wise people are quiet and peaceful in their understanding of life, of how much more there is still for them to learn. Clever, bright people have arrived, proud of their achievements, waiting for others to come to them for help. Clever people think they know it all, wise people are aware of how little they know. They find a delight and an excitement in the search for truth.

> Wise people are searchers,
> they go on journeys,
> they look to other people,
> they ask questions,
> they want to discover.

The Wise Men came out of Persia. They were skilled in the arts of astrology, medicine and philosophy. They were teachers and debaters, readers and thinkers. These men were wise; they were searching for a special one. They had read the signs, seen the stars and in their wisdom they realised that one greater than themselves had been born. They needed to find and worship this 'greater than themselves' King. All this, the realising, the searching, the offering of gifts, the being overwhelmed with joy, the worshipping, this is all true wisdom.

Every now and then I come across wise men and women. Sometimes they just turn up at church and don't quite know why they are there. Maybe they have been invited by a friend or work colleague or seen something in a Christian's life that they want for themselves. Occasionally they come looking for help or possibly for a baptism and then stay on afterwards asking questions, absorbing the full worship experience. They are looking for something more than money, comfort and instant enjoyment. Their searching is a spiritual thing, they are looking for something more, something deeper, richer in life. What makes them wise is not their cleverness but their awareness that something is missing and their determination to search for it. They are searching, that is what makes them wise.

So enough of the wise men, what about Herod? Herod, the King, is not actually the true King. Jerusalem, the royal city, is not actually the royal city. The chief priests are not actually the true priests. They are the King, capital and priests of this world, but not of God's. They are power-holders and controllers. They have no sense of humility, wonderment or searching. Their position is threatened, that is all they can see. They are too full of themselves to make space for any others. They are certainly not going to move over and make space for Jesus.

> 'They call me the Seeker
> And I've been searching high and low'
> – The Who

I love this song. Partly because I love 'The Who' and partly because I have always been a seeker. Always seeking that something extra, feeling there are bits of my life missing, thinking that I could always be a slightly better man.

Every now and again. Sometimes in worship, sometimes in bible study or personal prayer. Just every now and again I feel I might be a bit of a finder.

So here is today's big question: - How is your wisdom-fuelled search going?

Wise people are
Journeying people.
Looking, seeking, not there yet people.
They ask questions, gaze up at the stars,
Think about the past, wonder at the future.
They know there are bits missing
And are searching for them.
Wise people are searching for God people.

Lord God
Help me to see the star
To follow
And to find
That I might be with you
Amen.

7. Massacre of the Innocents

Matthew 2: 13–23

¹³ *Now after they had left, an angel of the Lord appeared to Joseph in a dream and said, "Get up, take the child and his mother, and flee to Egypt, and remain there until I tell you; for Herod is about to search for the child, to destroy him."* ¹⁴ *Then Joseph got up, took the child and his mother by night, and went to Egypt,* ¹⁵ *and remained there until the death of Herod. This was to fulfil what had been spoken by the Lord through the prophet, "Out of Egypt I have called my son."*

¹⁶ *When Herod saw that he had been tricked by the wise men, he was infuriated, and he sent and killed all the children in and around Bethlehem who were two years old or under, according to the time that he had learned from the wise men.* ¹⁷ *Then was fulfilled what had been spoken through the prophet Jeremiah:* ¹⁸ *"A voice was heard in Ramah, wailing and loud lamentation, Rachel weeping for her children; she refused to be consoled, because they are no more."*

¹⁹ *When Herod died, an angel of the Lord suddenly appeared in a dream to Joseph in Egypt*

and said, ²⁰ *"Get up, take the child and his mother, and go to the land of Israel, for those who were seeking the child's life are dead."* ²¹ *Then Joseph got up, took the child and his mother, and went to the land of Israel.* ²² *But when he heard that Archelaus was ruling over Judea in place of his father Herod, he was afraid to go there. And after being warned in a dream, he went away to the district of Galilee.* ²³ *There he made his home in a town called Nazareth, so that what had been spoken through the prophets might be fulfilled, "He will be called a Nazarene."*

It is often referred to as the 'Massacre of the Innocents'. The title says it all. This one incident seems to spoil the whole nativity narrative, so much so that these days we usually drop it from the story. Why is it in there in the original? Because it is one way of saying, 'welcome to the real world Jesus'.

Herod was a tyrant. He lived opulently and spent extravagantly, building elegant palaces and cities on the backs of a peasant workforce. He murdered, assassinated and so silenced most of his family and close supporters. Though history calls him 'Herod the Great', some Jewish voices called him 'Herod the Monster'. Joseph Stalin, Pol Pot, Adolf Hitler, Mao Tse Tung we have had plenty of Herods in our modern world so why not one in Jesus'? All the questions that we ask about suffering, war and injustice; about the triumph of the wicked and the pain of the poor are right there at the heart of the birth of the Saviour. Historians today estimate that about 20 baby boys were involved in the

Massacre of the Infants. Jesus was baby 21, but he didn't escape death, for him and his parents, it was delayed. On the cross Jesus became the 21st of the Bethlehem boys to die. It is because of his death that the other 20 have a chance.

I have a personal stake in all of this because my daughter, Zoe, is part of the 'Massacre of the Innocents' which runs continually throughout human history. She has profound and multiple learning difficulties. Something happened when she was a baby, or perhaps when she was born. It is all very unfair and painful. There is no individual Herod in Zoe's story; rather it feels like the meaningless result of the blind tragedy of children suffering. A tragic tale that has run through the centuries. A tragic tale that has touched millions. Bethlehem's babies needed a saviour, so do lots of other children who have lived and struggled and often died so young. I don't think Herod's massacring of the innocents and the perpetual, on-going story of the suffering of children can ever be fully explained. However, I sort of feel that there is something very deep here. That in a way that is beyond words, this story somehow locates Jesus right at the heart of infant mortality, abuse, murder, pain and disability. Don't ask me to explain this. It is something that I sense and hope for, rather than see and understand.

Jesus the escapee becomes a refugee. The story and flight to Egypt is carefully shaped to depict Jesus as the new Moses, and Herod as the new Pharaoh. The Old Testament book of Exodus shows us the Pharaoh as a murdering tyrant in his attempts to stamp out God's people, now Herod is doing exactly the same. No matter what happens it is vital that Mary and Joseph protect the life of the baby Jesus, not for his own sake, but for the sake of all those who are going to need him.

> One born to suffer – To be with the suffering
> One born to bleed – To befriend the bleeding
> One born to weep – To be alongside the weeping
> One born – So that after the suffering, the bleeding and the weeping
> All might live.

Lord God
Though I live in a rich and peaceful place
Help me to listen to the poor.
Open my eyes to the places of distress
Remind me especially of the children,
The vulnerable, the aged.
Help me to make this a more peaceful world.
Amen.

8. In the Beginning

John 1: 1–5

[1] *In the beginning was the Word, and the Word was with God, and the Word was God.* [2] *He was in the beginning with God.* [3] *All things came into being through him, and without him not one thing came into being. What has come into being* [4] *in him was life, and the life was the light of all people.* [5] *The light shines in the darkness, and the darkness did not overcome it.*

John 1: 10–14

[10] *He was in the world, and the world came into being through him; yet the world did not know him.* [11] *He came to what was his own, and his own people did not accept him.* [12] *But to all who received him, who believed in his name, he gave power to become children of God,* [13] *who were born, not of blood or of the will of the flesh or of the will of man, but of God.*

[14] *And the Word became flesh and lived among us, and we have seen his glory, the glory as of a father's only son, full of grace and truth.*

It comes as a bit of a shock to many readers to discover that of the four gospels only Matthew and Luke include the birth stories of Jesus. Mark opens with him as a thirty-year-old man starting his ministry in Galilee. Meanwhile, John is different again, beginning his story of Jesus with this hauntingly majestic overture cum prologue.

It takes us back to before the angels, before the prophets, before human history, to the big-bang of creation. This is divine cosmology, mystical physics, quantum mechanics from before the dawn of time. The prologue is the New Testament's Genesis; both open up with the same three words,

'In the beginning'

In the beginning was 'The Word'. Here the idea of the word has got two distinct but overlapping meanings and to understand fully John's idea of 'the word' we have to know a little bit about both the Greek and the Jewish world into which Jesus was born.

1) Most people in the ancient world 'thought' in Greek. It was the language of the educated and the intellectual. The Greeks believed that there was a rational principle or law that governed and organised the whole of creation and through which everything came into existence. The governing principle, a bit like our understanding of gravity, was impersonal; it was just there, just a force. They called it the 'word' or 'logos'.

2) As well as entering into this 'Greek thinking' world Jesus was also born into the 'Jewish believing' one.

The Jews believed that things existed and worked because the personal, creative God spoke them into existence. God's 'word' ran the Universe.

'God said let there be light,
And there was light.'

So this introduction to John's gospel, with its announcement of 'the Word' is loaded, stuffed with truth, insight and revelation. It combines the Greek and Jewish ideas on creation, the world and the universe. It is philosophical, poetic, mystical, profound and very beautiful. The book of Genesis meets Plato, meets Stephen Hawkins, meets Star Trek. Creation, big-bang, evolution and even black holes, Jesus is in it all. He is alone 'in the beginning' with God and was God. Creator of creation, life of life, light of all lights. He is both the great and rational mind/logos behind the Universe and at the same time the creative, personal word of God.

And now for the second part of this 'beyond understanding, so just sit in awe' prologue. The 'with-God-before creation word' has entered the world, taken on flesh and become an ordinary human being. Invisible, untouchable beautiful divinity has become physical, sweaty, dribbly, humanity. Evolution has born its ultimate fruit.

In the beginning has suddenly leapt forward over 14 billion years to the second beginning. Jesus has been born. The cosmic moment has become a common man.

I recently came across a T-shirt design which said, 'For those who are too stupid for science try God'. The message is a simple, condescending cliché, clever people are atheistic, science based whilst believers are...

It occurred to me that you could turn the message around, 'For those who are too stupid for God try science'.

For this 'In the beginning' overture, we get both God and science together in balance and in the right order.

> **Lord Jesus**
> **I need a beginning**
> **A new beginning**
> **Another beginning.**
> **May you be my**
> **'In the beginning'**
> **Amen.**

9. A Growing Boy

Luke 2: 40–52

40 The child grew and became strong, filled with wisdom; and the favour of God was upon him.

41 Now every year his parents went to Jerusalem for the festival of the Passover. 42 And when he was twelve years old, they went up as usual for the festival. 43 When the festival was ended and they started to return, the boy Jesus stayed behind in Jerusalem, but his parents did not know it. 44 Assuming that he was in the group of travellers, they went a day's journey. Then they started to look for him among their relatives and friends. 45 When they did not find him, they returned to Jerusalem to search for him. 46 After three days they found him in the temple, sitting among the teachers, listening to them and asking them questions. 47 And all who heard him were amazed at his understanding and his answers. 48 When his parents saw him they were astonished; and his mother said to him, "Child, why have you treated us like this? Look, your father and I have been searching for you in great anxiety." 49 He said to them, "Why were you searching for me? Did you not know that I must be in my Father's house?"

[50] But they did not understand what he said to them. [51] Then he went down with them and came to Nazareth, and was obedient to them. His mother treasured all these things in her heart.

[52] And Jesus increased in wisdom and in years, and in divine and human favour.

Very little is said about Jesus as he grows up. All the fascinating details about his playing out with friends; relating to his parents; getting along with brothers and sisters to say nothing of teenage rebellion and acne, nothing. One minute he is a baby and the next, a thirty-year-old healer and teacher.

Actually it is not complete silence. There are a few snippets to point us in the right direction, but before looking at them we have to know one or two things about his background.

So here are three pointers to the world in which Jesus grew up, and the influences which helped to shape him. Firstly it was an agricultural world of tiny villages. Nazareth probably had a population of about 400 living in small half cave half house dwellings. This was a desperately poor world where Jesus' family and everyone else in the village struggled to survive. They were the underclass. Secondly, his was a Jewish world, where the teachings, songs and characters of the Old Testament were inscribed in his memories. A world of special foods, of the Sabbath and of the Jerusalem Temple. Thirdly, Jesus grew up in a strong family world. Mary and Joseph, four brothers and several sisters and

Jesus all held together by love and loyalty. So, Jesus was born into... A village world

A Jewish world

A caring family world.

Back to Jesus. Twice here we read of him as a boy growing physically, intellectually and spiritually in strength, wisdom and grace. Sandwiched between these two verses we have the captivating little story of his visit to the Temple.

Mary and Joseph losing Jesus is not quite as crazy as we might think when we realise that men and women often travelled in large caravan type groups. They were long straggly people convoys wandering there and back to Jerusalem. Sometimes the boy Jesus would have hung on to the men's group and sometimes to the women's group. There was a big crack for him to fall down.

Suddenly the Temple, and not Nazareth, is his natural setting. He needs to be not with his mum and dad, but in his father's house. He is hungry to learn and explore with all the other spiritual teachers. He is a child prodigy of spiritual awareness. For the first time we glimpse a space, a difference and a breakdown in understanding between him and his family. Mary and Joseph did not understand, he is odd, different, not normal; he is Jesus.

As we have seen Jesus was living in a poor village, Jewish, tight family world. That was his setting, his context, his place. That was his outer world. He also had an inner world. This 'inner world' of a father, temple, spiritual learning world. This was his inner context, his inner place. As we journey with Jesus we shall keep seeing him stealing away to special places. Empty, silent places away from the crowds, where he can be with the Father.

Jesus is still a young boy, he is not yet ready, much preparation lies ahead, but he is getting there. He is 'growing in favour with God and man'.

Here are a big couple of questions for you to think about and maybe discuss with someone:

> How much have you grown?
> Are you still growing?

Lord Jesus
Help me also to find a place in your fathers' home
Help me to find my own place
Help me to find a place in my life with you
That I too might grow in favour with God and man.
Amen.

10. John the Baptist

Mark 1: 2–8

> [2] *As it is written in the prophet Isaiah, "See, I am sending my messenger ahead of you, who will prepare your way;* [3] *the voice of one crying out in the wilderness: 'Prepare the way of the Lord, make his paths straight,'"*
>
> [4] *John the baptizer appeared in the wilderness, proclaiming a baptism of repentance for the forgiveness of sins.* [5] *And people from the whole Judean countryside and all the people of Jerusalem were going out to him, and were baptized by him in the river Jordan, confessing their sins.* [6] *Now John was clothed with camel's hair, with a leather belt around his waist, and he ate locusts and wild honey.* [7] *He proclaimed, "The one who is more powerful than I is coming after me; I am not worthy to stoop down and untie the thong of his sandals.* [8] *I have baptized you with water; but he will baptize you with the Holy Spirit."*

Jesus has gone from baby to boy to man and is about to launch out on his great mission. Before that however, there are three preparatory stepping stones for us to think about. These are the stories of his temptation and baptism, but first, John the Baptist.

John the Baptist was Jesus' cousin. As with Jesus, his birth was announced by angels, made a huge impact on his parents Elizabeth and Zechariah (Luke 1: 5); and was commemorated by a great early Christian hymn (Luke 1: 67).

The supply-line of prophets in Israel had dried up years ago. Suddenly there was a new one, and a great one too. He was a young man in his mid to late 20s, living an austere lifestyle, a righteous, non-compromising man. Calling a spade a spade and a sin a sin, John travelled around the towns and villages of Judah, which was in the south. With great passionate eloquence he called people out to be baptised in the River Jordan and out they came by the truckload. There was something in all of this of a return to the great days of Moses and the escape from Egypt. There was to be a new purified people of God, a new Exodus, Israel would be a newly cleansed promised land and his baptism and 'soaking' was the new crossing of the Red Sea.

John was the forerunner, preparing the way for the 'one who was coming'. He was not the Messiah, but Jesus was. He was like a 'road builder cum herald cum people get ready warm-up act'. The 'one who is coming' will be far greater, more powerful and far more holy so that John will not even be able to fasten his sandals for him. John is baptising in water, but the coming one will baptise in spirit and fire.

John's holiness was rugged, hard, lonely. Jesus' would be just as deep and passionate, but would be more human, warmer, friendlier and gentler.

John took people back to their past, Jesus led them to their future. John directed people to their sinfulness; Jesus took them beyond that to their deep inner needfulness. John asked the questions but it was Jesus who pointed to the answers.

So here we see these two great spiritual leaders. They are cousins, they are both servants of God, sent to his people, but one is greater than the other. They are a bit like the moon and sun with the dawn breaking just as the moon is waning.

John was able to take people on a journey. It was a journey to the river. Jesus was to take them on from there deep into a new land on the other side of the river and even to the gates of Heaven itself.

Now here is a final thought, a teaser. Suppose this passionate, demanding John the Baptist was to wander into your life, listening to your words, watching the things you do and don't do, picking out all the dirty washing, the stuff in the basket and the stuff just left on the bedroom floor. Suppose Jesus was to follow him into the house of your mind and soul, and in a rather warmer way was to say something like, 'yes it is a bit of a mess, but let me help you to clear it all up.' To say, 'let me wash it for you.' What do you think would be the stuff that they would both be focusing on?

Dear Lord Jesus

> Your light exposes my darkness
> Your purity highlights my sinfulness
> Your love contrasts with my selfishness
> So may your truth point to my failing
> Call me to repentance
> And wash me in forgiveness
> And may I emerge from the water Newer
> > Cleaner
> > Better
> > For you

Amen.

11. Jesus' Baptism

Matthew 3: 13–17

¹³ *Then Jesus came from Galilee to John at the Jordan, to be baptized by him. ¹⁴ John would have prevented him, saying, "I need to be baptized by you, and do you come to me?" ¹⁵ But Jesus answered him, "Let it be so now; for it is proper for us in this way to fulfil all righteousness." Then he consented. ¹⁶ And when Jesus had been baptized, just as he came up from the water, suddenly the heavens were opened to him and he saw the Spirit of God descending like a dove and alighting on him. ¹⁷ And a voice from heaven said, "This is my Son, the Beloved, with whom I am well pleased."*

What is it about the early morning shower? It is cleansing, energising and even quite enjoyable. So why do I always feel there is a preventative little barrier stopping me jumping in? Why do I keep putting it off whilst drinking endless cups of tea? John's baptism of people was just the same, cleansing, energising even enjoyable, but always there were barriers and hesitations. Essentially, baptism then as now, was about spiritual beginnings, that's why there are always things that get in the way.

The Jews had first used baptism as the entry point for Gentiles who wanted to begin to follow the Jewish faith. John used it as a point of renewal calling the urban sophisticates out of the all-powerful Jerusalem, to turn from their sins, be washed clean and make a new start with God.

So how strange to see Jesus coming to baptism. He had no sins to repent of and no need of renewal or rededication. No wonder John is a bit embarrassed by Jesus coming to him, he thinks it should be the other way around. Jesus, however, was the last person to stand on ceremony filled with a sense of his own importance. His respect and admiration for John added to his own humility and modesty leads him happily into the water.

Jesus had travelled south from the Galilee to Judea. There he had lived and worked with John and his disciples. He saw the crowds coming out, watched John baptising and listened to his great prophetic messages. Soon the time came for the student apprentice to become the master. Baptism is essentially about new spiritual beginnings. This baptism of Jesus is his big beginning. He goes into the water to mark the end of his preparation; his great human and spiritual gestation period of 30 years is over. He comes up out of the water, empowered and affirmed, ready to launch out on his great ministry.

Here at Jesus' baptism we see one of the great Trinitarian set pieces in the Bible. That is to say, we get a clear view of the three-in-one Godhead. God the Son (in human form) is in the water; the dove-like God the Holy Spirit descends and rests on him (a sort of laying on of divine hands); and the creative voice of God the Father speaks out. The Father's voice speaks from Heaven, the Son is on Earth below, and the Spirit descends from Heaven to Earth to join the two.

What about us and our big beginnings? Some people seem to gradually become followers of Jesus but for most of us the becoming will involve one or more decisive moments. Moments when we decide, change direction, say 'yes' and launch out in a new life or a new phase of our life. These are baptismal moments of new beginnings.

> Baptisms
> Beginnings like birthings
> New beginnings
> Old beginnings
> Beginning again
> And again
> Beginning of beginnings
> Beginning in baptism.

You may be looking at, pondering such a launching out moment yourself. Perhaps you have already taken that big initial step of following or are actually in the middle of it right now. So this could be your first or your twenty-first new beginning moment. The thing to learn from Jesus' baptism is that it is not all just about us. There is also the voice of our Father, speaking from Heaven, saying how pleased with us he is. He is positive, joyful and excited about our decision to step out onto the journey. Not only a voice of God from Heaven, but also a Spirit of God from Heaven descends and touches each one of us when we set out to serve and follow him.

> **Lord God**
> **Lead me into the water**
> **Bring me out on the other side**
> **Take pleasure in my new beginning**
> **And lead me onward.**
> **Amen.**

12. Temptation in the Wilderness

Matthew 4: 1–11

¹*Then Jesus was led up by the Spirit into the wilderness to be tempted by the devil.* ² *He fasted forty days and forty nights, and afterwards he was famished.* ³ *The tempter came and said to him, "If you are the Son of God, command these stones to become loaves of bread."* ⁴ *But he answered, "It is written, 'One does not live by bread alone, but by every word that comes from the mouth of God.'"*

⁵ *Then the devil took him to the holy city and placed him on the pinnacle of the temple,* ⁶ *saying to him, "If you are the Son of God, throw yourself down; for it is written, 'He will command his angels concerning you,' and 'On their hands they will bear you up, so that you will not dash your foot against a stone.'"*

⁷ *Jesus said to him, "Again it is written, 'Do not put the Lord your God to the test.'"*

⁸ *Again, the devil took him to a very high mountain and showed him all the kingdoms*

of the world and their splendour; ⁹ and he said to him, "All these I will give you, if you will fall down and worship me." ¹⁰ Jesus said to him, "Away with you, Satan! For it is written, 'Worship the Lord your God, and serve only him.'"

¹¹ *Then the devil left him, and suddenly angels came and waited on him.*

Living our busy lives, the best that many of us can manage are brief God gaps. A quick few minutes, perhaps between shower and breakfast, a thought and prayer whilst driving the car or a hurried reading and prayer before sleep. Jesus lived a different way, he made space for God or to put it better, he made space for himself to be with God.

He is coming out of the decisive launching experience of his baptism. He is about to begin his great world changing ministry. So much to do, so little time to do it. But before beginning, or rather, as a way of beginning, he goes off alone into the wilderness, 'the empty lands' and spends 40 days just himself and God.

He is on retreat, fasting, praying, pondering and planning. Suddenly his blessed times of contemplation are interrupted, the enemy seeks him out. The devil has been waiting for Jesus for a long time. He has prepared the ground, baited his traps. In the next two- or three-years Jesus and the devil will be locked in a salvation or damnation struggle, and it begins here. Jesus came out to find God; the devil came out to find Jesus.

It is difficult to say exactly who or what the devil is. In the Jesus story he seems to be the anti-light and anti-life candidate, the personification of all that is evil. Just as God wants to create and protect, the devil wants to destroy and condemn. In our times we have become used to evil people with their hungry lusts for greed, fame, influence and power. These same lusts here take the form of temptation. Jesus knows the sort of Messiah that his Father called him to be, here the devil wants to take him down another road. Jesus could become the ultimate materialist who fills himself with food and drink, gold and treasure. Jesus could throw himself off the Temple and being seen by many to be saved by angels, could become a massive religious celebrity, a sort of *X-Factor* winner amongst spiritual leaders. Finally, he is tempted to look out from the mountain top and imagine himself to be the ruler of the world. Or he could stick on track and follow the way prepared for him by God.

'I can resist everything apart from temptation,' said Oscar Wilde.

Fortunately for us, Jesus was a bit stronger than Oscar. He went into the desert, 'the deserted place', to meet with God. I'm sure he did meet with God and whether or not he expected it, he met with the dark enemy too. The devil spoke and wormed his way into his mind and heart. For 40 days he tempted him, offering him these three different ways of being Jesus. Every time, and every day he rejected the devil's temptation and followed the divine template.

He went into the wilderness, led by the Spirit, having just offered himself for the publicly, decisive experience of baptism. He had begun. Now he was ready, stronger, feet set firmly on the 'Father's' path to faithful Messiahship.

He has been 30 years in preparation, he is now ready to launch. We have just spent 11 days with him in his preparation, are we ready to follow him as he comes out of the wilderness?

Finally, we began this day thinking of our little 'God Slots', why not follow the path of Jesus and find some serious sort of 'God Space'. Discover your own little wilderness, even if it's only a walk with the dog, or 15 minutes in your favourite chair. He says no to the alluring, fabulous and compelling temptation of the devil. He must have been exhausted, hungry and empty at the end of it. Actually, not empty, but filled with a sense of knowing and doing what was right, filled with a sense of victory, of having passed the first great test. Now he is ready.

Time to find and be found; time to get yourself on his path.

> Lord Jesus
> Where is my wilderness?
> Whose is the tempting voice I hear?
> What is the temptation that draws me?
> Will you help me overcome it?
> Amen.

13. Galilee – 'Up North'

Matthew 4: 12–17

12 Now when Jesus heard that John had been arrested, he withdrew to Galilee. 13 He left Nazareth and made his home in Capernaum by the sea, in the territory of Zebulun and Naphtali, 14 so that what had been spoken through the prophet Isaiah might be fulfilled:

15 "Land of Zebulun, land of Naphtali, on the road by the sea, across the Jordan, Galilee of the Gentiles 16 the people who sat in darkness have seen a great light, and for those who sat in the region and shadow of death light has dawned."

17 From that time Jesus began to proclaim, "Repent, for the kingdom of heaven has come near."

Jesus has been spending time down in Judea (southern Israel, near to Jerusalem) with John the Baptist. Perhaps he has been a quiet observer on the edge of his movement, watching and learning.

John's arrest means it is time for him to step out on his own mission and so he returns to his northern roots.

Luke tells us that Jesus was 30 years old when he began his work and that he was led on this northern relocation by the Spirit. Rather like England today, Galilee had a strong 'Up North' feel to it, filled with people speaking with a strong northern accent. It was poorer and more working class than Jerusalem and Judea to the south. It lacked the money, influence and metropolitan sophistication of Jerusalem. It lacked the temple, the priests and the Pharisees. To use a certain phrase, 'It was rough up North'. Not only that, but Galilee was not actually seen as 'kosher' territory. For hundreds of years it had been a 'non-Jewish' wilderness. The Jews had started re-colonising it just a few generations before Jesus but there were as many (and bigger and richer) Roman and Greek towns in Galilee as there were Jewish. It really was seen as the place of the Gentile. For most Jewish spiritual leaders it was a place to be avoided, for Jesus it was his beloved homeland. The place he grew up in and felt proud of. It was to become his new mission field. Jesus clearly has a very strong sense of roots and place, he shuns Jerusalem and its Temple, the centre of Jewish faith, and begins out on this northern edge that he calls home. Nazareth is actually in the south-west of Galilee, and so he moved to Capernaum, a much more central base standing on the lake itself.

This then was the setting, the stage for most of Jesus' great missionary work.

At the beginning of 2009 I started a new job as vicar of an 'Up North' church in Bradford. I had been out of parish or local church ministry for 15 years. Not only was I 're-entering' the life of a local church I was also 'returning' to my home town of Bradford in Yorkshire, the multi-cultural, multi-ethnic 'Bradford of the Gentiles'. I decided to shape the whole of my ministry, and that of my church, around that of Jesus. So, I returned to my northern roots, to a missionary way of operating. I decided to see the parish (or local area in which the church is set) as our Galilee. Our calling then was to go around doing everything in our Galilee that Jesus did in his. Meeting and greeting people, proclaiming the Good News, offering prayer for healing, attempting to replace demons with inner peace.

It is not just churches that have a 'Galilee Context'. Every individual Christian has got a place where they live and a whole network of family, friends, work colleagues etc. Add the place you live in to the people you live with and you have your own personal Galilee. Most of the people who inhabit our own little world are living in darkness. That is not to say that they are great sinners but rather that they occupy a time and place where no-one has got round to turning on the great 'Jesus light'. His message, his life, his healing has not yet reached them. Just like Jesus our 'Galilee' is our 'mission field', our stage, and like his ours too will probably contain lots of Gentiles. The great challenge is for us to shine the light, in our Galilee and amongst our people.

> To meet and befriend
> To go into people's villages and homes
> To heal and to drive out demons
> To invite and to proclaim
> To scatter seed and to grow fruit.

Lord Jesus
As you walked the roads of your Galilee
May you now walk the paths into mine.
Come and visit my family and friends
Meet my people.
Bring your healing and Good News into my
human village.
Amen.

14. The Big Idea

Luke 4: 16–21

> [16] *He went to Nazareth, where he had been brought up, and on the Sabbath day he went into the synagogue, as was his custom. He stood up to read,* [17] *and the scroll of the prophet Isaiah was handed to him. Unrolling it, he found the place where it is written:*

> [18] *"The Spirit of the Lord is on me, because he has anointed me to proclaim good news to the poor. He has sent me to proclaim freedom for the prisoners and recovery of sight for the blind, to set the oppressed free,* [19] *to proclaim the year of the Lord's favour."*

> [20] *Then he rolled up the scroll, gave it back to the attendant and sat down. The eyes of everyone in the synagogue were fastened on him.* [21] *He began by saying to them, "Today this scripture is fulfilled in your hearing."*

Every time there is a general election in the UK the various parties begin by publishing their manifesto, their ideas, promises, their big plan for what they will do when they are elected. Here in Nazareth, the town where he grew up, and still at the beginning of his ministry it is as if Jesus is putting out his manifesto. It has been thirty years in preparation. That is thirty years of listening to God, looking around at the state of people's lives, thirty years of conversations and studying the scriptures. Now he is ready to go and this is:

> His manifesto
> His declaration of intent
> The statement of his goals
> Of who he is and what he is all about
> This is his big idea
> The mission statement
> His Jesus plan.

The words he actually uses however are not his own creation they are the five-hundred-year-old words of Isaiah 61: 1–2. He makes them his own however by saying, 'at last now is the time, I am the one, the Spirit is on me, I am anointed and this is what I am going to do'.

When we read his 'what I am going to do list' we can see it falling into two major zones of thought, almost as if his plan has got two major thrusts. One is all about addressing people's immediate and physical needs, whilst the second idea responds to their eternal spiritual needs.

Jesus is going to reach out to the poor, release the captives, give sight to the blind and free the oppressed. At the same time he will bring good news and proclamation. He is going to touch their bodies and reach into their souls, give them help and hope.

Having read out Isaiah's amazing prophetic and promise words he calmly sits down, everyone's eyes are on him and he says, 'today this scripture is fulfilled'. Wow, we have lift off.

Jesus makes the words of Isaiah his two pronged or twin zoned mission statement. Today if we are serious about following him it should be ours too. The problem is we find it very difficult to follow two tracks at the same time. There have clearly been times in the churches history where it has been all proclamation and very little helping of the poor. In today's church we seem to have got it the other way round, lots of helping the poor, getting involved in social community issues and raising grants but not much proclamation of the Good News. Jesus did both and made them part of the one whole mission.

Here then is a big question for us all. Looking at our own individual mission and that of our church have we got a well-balanced 'holistic' mission in the way Jesus had? Are we becoming like him or are we doing it our way?

Interestingly, Jesus retained all of Isaiah's words except for one about 'proclaiming the day of God's vengeance'. It looks as though Jesus planned to be more into forgiveness than Judgement.

> **Lord Jesus**
> **Help me to do it your way**
> **To share your words**
> **And to show your works.**
> **To offer good deeds**
> **And to proclaim good news.**

To bring help
And to offer hope
That my world might be transformed by your
love.
Amen.

15. Calling the Disciples

Mark 1: 16–20

16 As Jesus passed along the Sea of Galilee, he saw Simon and his brother Andrew casting a net into the sea – for they were fishermen. 17 And Jesus said to them, "Follow me and I will make you fish for people." 18 And immediately they left their nets and followed him. 19 As he went a little farther, he saw James son of Zebedee and his brother John, who were in their boat mending the nets. 20 Immediately he called them; and they left their father Zebedee in the boat with the hired men, and followed him.

A bunch of spiritually minded young men becoming disciples to some learned teacher or rabbi was a common enough happening in Jesus' world. Usually it was the students who chose their teacher, thus they would listen to various rabbis before deciding which one to follow. The big difference here is that rather than the learner choosing their teacher, in the way that our young people apply to the college or university of their choice; here it is the rabbi doing the choosing.

Two pairs of brothers, Simon and Andrew, James and John, catchers of fish. Jesus sees something in them, values them, sees a more vital and important future for them and suggests that they use their lives to catch people. The great missionary is seeing, calling and offering to lead and teach other missionaries.

Was this the first time they had seen each other? Did it all happen in a few spontaneous minutes? Or had these men already been listening to the new preacher? Had they been 'pondering' for a while? Had they already stood or sat in the listening crowd and heard something special in him? And as they listened, had he seen something a bit special in them, something particularly responsive and motivated? Had they already had some initial chats, had they already been drawn closer to him?

This might have been a one off 'he saw them, they heard him' call and response. Or it might have been the decisive 'make your mind up' call after a period of thinking and discussing. Some of us are, 'yes, now' quick decision people while others are 'I have thought about this for a while, and am gradually following him' people. The key point here is that Jesus calls and they drop their nets.

This is their first step on the path of discipleship, they are no longer considering, feeling and thinking about it. They are now mind made up, they have still got questions but they are committed and stepping out on the way. They are no longer just listening to Jesus, they are following him.

In our church we have lots of new attenders. They come, look around, feel welcomed, notice other people, listen and take part. Some leave after a while, others remain but are fairly uninvolved whilst others move into a deeper commitment. They are a bit like the initial crowds who gathered to listen to Jesus. This first step of coming and listening, of being part of the crowd is a wonderful first step. But that is all it is just a first step. These fishermen brothers of Simon and Andrew, James and John have taken a second step. They have stepped out of the crowd to become followers and disciples. In stepping forward they leave something behind, the nets are the part of their old life that are not going to figure in the new one.

Whoopy Goldberg in 'Sister Act' gets it just right.

> 'Love him, I love him, I love him
> And where he goes I'll follow, I'll follow, I'll follow
> I will follow him, follow him wherever he may go
> There isn't an ocean too deep
> There isn't a mountain so high it can keep me away
> He is my destiny.'

Watching Jesus change the world is one thing, but following him and becoming like him while he does it and then going on to do it with him is quite another.

Lord Jesus
You are the world changer and life transformer.
Help me to step out
To follow you
To change one life.
To change one person's world
To change your world.
Amen.

16. Searchers then Disciples

John 1: 35–51

[35] *The next day John again was standing with two of his disciples,* [36] *and as he watched Jesus walk by, he exclaimed, "Look, here is the Lamb of God!"* [37] *The two disciples heard him say this, and they followed Jesus.* [38] *When Jesus turned and saw them following, he said to them, "What are you looking for?" They said to him, "Rabbi" (which translated means Teacher), "where are you staying?"* [39] *He said to them, "Come and see." They came and saw where he was staying, and they remained with him that day. It was about four o'clock in the afternoon.* [40] *One of the two who heard John speak and followed him was Andrew, Simon Peter's brother.* [41] *He first found his brother Simon and said to him, "We have found the Messiah" (which is translated Anointed).* [42] *He brought Simon to Jesus, who looked at him and said, "You are Simon son of John. You are to be called Cephas" (which is translated Peter).*

[43] *The next day Jesus decided to go to Galilee. He found Philip and said to him, "Follow me."* [44] *Now Philip was from Bethsaida, the city of*

Andrew and Peter. ⁴⁵ Philip found Nathanael and said to him, "We have found him about whom Moses in the law and also the prophets wrote, Jesus son of Joseph from Nazareth." ⁴⁶ Nathanael said to him, "Can anything good come out of Nazareth?" Philip said to him, "Come and see." ⁴⁷ When Jesus saw Nathanael coming toward him, he said of him, "Here is truly an Israelite in whom there is no deceit!" ⁴⁸ Nathanael asked him, "Where did you get to know me?" Jesus answered, "I saw you under the fig tree before Philip called you." ⁴⁹ Nathanael replied, "Rabbi, you are the Son of God! You are the King of Israel!" ⁵⁰ Jesus answered, "Do you believe because I told you that I saw you under the fig tree? You will see greater things than these." ⁵¹ And he said to him, "Very truly, I tell you, you will see heaven opened and the angels of God ascending and descending upon the Son of Man."

Great though the works of John the Baptist had been, here comes Jesus to do a much, much greater work. So we see John point beyond himself to Jesus the Lamb, and then we see two of his disciples move on to become followers of Jesus.

In the previous reading we saw how Jesus turned the usual rabbi type of procedure on its head by taking the initiative in searching out and then calling his disciples. Here we see the opposite of that. These two are already on the spiritual journey. They have certainly arrived at a good place with John, but they are not yet where they need to be. They are a bit like our old friends, the 'Three Wise Men'. Like them they are searching.

When they see Jesus and feel the encouraging words of their mentor they begin to follow. And when I read this story it feels as if I have become one of these searcher followers. As if Jesus turns around, looks me in the eye and says, 'So then, Robin Gamble, what exactly are you looking for?' – then waits for an answer. Whether you and I are at the, 'trying to find, learning to follow, or working to become like him stage' still he asks us what are we looking for? So what would your answer be?

It is likely then that the full movement of these four becoming disciples was a two-way movement. They were searching for Jesus, Jesus was searching for them. And John the Baptist? Well he seems to have been the middle man helping the one to find the other.

In calling him teacher, they are in effect, saying 'we are your pupils'. We want to bow our heads, lower our own self-pride and learn from you.

In asking 'where are you staying?' they are, in effect, saying 'we need to be with you, your place must be our place'. So often today when people get close to Jesus they expect him to move into their place, this picture of the disciples shows all the movement going the other way.

In saying 'come and see', Jesus was effectively drawing them in, pulling at their curiosity. Gently, lovingly he was landing the fish.

Andrew brings Peter. The next day back in Galilee Philip brings Nathaniel. In these two stories all the key steps to discipleship are laid out for us: -

- The searching for more
- Jesus turning and beckoning
- Searching becomes following
- Jesus draws us in
- The searchers turn and beckon their friends.

Here we have seen Jesus beginning to gather disciples. The mission has gone from one man to a community. The movement has begun. In fact the movement still goes on. The fact that you are reading this book right now probably points back to an Andrew or a Philip introducing you to Jesus. It might have been years ago in your childhood or perhaps just a few weeks ago. Now it is your turn to become part of the great missionary movement of Jesus.

Lord Jesus,
Rabbi, teacher, leader.
I am still searching
Still following
Still wanting to become like you.
So may you help me today on my journey.
Amen.

17. From Now On

Luke 5: 1–11

[1] *Once while Jesus was standing beside the lake of Gennesaret, and the crowd was pressing in on him to hear the word of God,* [2] *he saw two boats there at the shore of the lake; the fishermen had gone out of them and were washing their nets.* [3] *He got into one of the boats, the one belonging to Simon, and asked him to put out a little way from the shore. Then he sat down and taught the crowds from the boat.* [4]*When he had finished speaking, he said to Simon, "Put out into the deep water and let down your nets for a catch."* [5] *Simon answered, "Master, we have worked all night long but have caught nothing. Yet if you say so, I will let down the nets."* [6] *When they had done this, they caught so many fish that their nets were beginning to break.* [7] *So they signalled to their partners in the other boat to come and help them. And they came and filled both boats, so that they began to sink.* [8] *But when Simon Peter saw it, he fell down at Jesus' knees, saying, "Go away from me, Lord, for I am a sinful man!"* [9] *For he and all who were with him were amazed at the catch of fish that they had taken;* [10] *and so also were James and John, sons of Zebedee, who*

were partners with Simon. Then Jesus said to Simon, "Do not be afraid; from now on you will be catching people." [11] When they had brought their boats to shore, they left everything and followed him.

This is the third of our 'recruiting or calling the disciples' stories, there is one more to come when Jesus meets Levi. There are also quite a few 'teaching or training' and finally 'sending out' of the disciples readings. The reason I am including so much about Jesus and the disciples is because this theme forms the very essence of the finding him, following him and becoming like him journey that we are on.

The disciples mentioned in Luke, chapter 5 have done quite a bit of initial listening and watching. They probably started out as mildly interested before becoming 'wanting to find him searchers'. They are now moving from the finding to the following part of their journey.

Daniel has been gradually 'coming to Jesus' over the last couple of years. It started with a curious visit to church; then I visited and chatted to him and his wife in their home; then a few more visits to church punctuated by lots of absences. After a while I persuaded him to come on an enquirers' course and eventually he ended up helping to lead one. And he is still not yet at the point of 'fully following' Jesus. Maybe it was like that for these first fishermen followers. Several meetings, a thinking about it period and a few calls before they did actually fully and for all time 'leave their nets'.

Back to Luke, chapter 5, the key movement or shift in the story happens when Jesus looks away from the crowd of the mildly interested and into the eyes of the hungrily searching and calls them to follow him. In the previous story from Mark the Greek wording used means 'to invite', here in Luke it is a bit stronger implying 'to summon'. This is not a forced recruitment. It is warm and invitational but Jesus is definitely looking deep into their eyes and souls and beckoning these first disciples.

The other big difference between this and the Mark story is that here Luke adds on the amazing catch of fish and the conversation between Jesus and Peter. There are two little insights or thoughts that I want to pick out of their talk. Both of them strike me as 'telling details' and set me off thinking deeply about my own relationship to Jesus.

Firstly, Peter knows everything there is to know about fishing. He can thread a hook, cast a line and gut a fish in his sleep. He has got the wind in his beard and the fish scales under his finger nails. Jesus is a preacher and perhaps before that he was some sort of jobbing labourer with his father. Peter lives by the sea; Jesus was brought up in the hills and valleys. Peter spends his life catching fish; Jesus spends his eating them. So why does Peter, the big confident fisherman, listen to and follow the advice of Jesus when he tells him how to do his job? What does Jesus know about deep water and bulging nets?

Peter has clearly seen and heard, perhaps over several weeks, something in this Jesus which leads him to put all his own thoughts to one side and follow him. In fact he has become so trusting of Jesus that he follows him not just with his religious ideas and persuasions, but in the practical details of how he is doing his job. Jesus tells a fisherman how to fish, the fisherman listens.

Jesus is not just a religious guru interested in our Sunday morning thoughts and prayers; he is interested and wants to be involved in all the seven days a week, practical aspects of our lives. Maybe, just maybe, he knows more about some of the lifestyle issues of your life than you do. Home improvements, career moves, child care and money management are not usually seen as spiritual issues but then neither is fishing. John and Lorraine were new Christians, considering moving house but not quite sure. When I suggested that they pray and ask God to guide them, it was a completely novel, even 'spooky' idea. Up to that moment they had thought God was just about religion and not ordinary life. Our lives become better, happier, and richer when we learn to listen to and trust in him.

Secondly, I love the phrase, 'from now on'. As one of life's grey melancholics I have an inborn inclination to look back at my life negatively. I look back at mistakes I made, things people said and did to me that still leave a mark, things I said which I wish I hadn't and opportunities missed. When Peter met Jesus he met a completely looking forward, let's start a new life sort of leader. Jesus leaves the past, looks to the future and says, 'from now on'. He invites Peter to start a new chapter, to begin again with a whole new optimism and vision of what his future life can be about.

'From now on' is a blue sky, lift your vision above the horizon, bump up your spirits to number 10, let's all believe something good is going to happen, type of statement. It acknowledges the past with its regrets and disappointments but takes us forward. It is as if Jesus is saying, 'Yes, I know what has happened in recent years, I know why your heart has developed a bit of a limp. I know why some of your 'young man dreams' never quite worked out. But, and it is a very big 'but', 'from now on things can be very different". 'From now on' is the big new start, the new beginning, the turning of the page in a man or a woman's life story.

Here then is a big question for you, 'What does his 'from now on' to you feel like?'

> In the beginning
> Follow me.
> From now on
> Choose the narrow path.
> Be born again
> Jesus is big on new beginnings.

Lord Jesus
I hear you calling me
Calling me to a crossroads question
To a 'from now on' decision.
Help me to follow you
And to become like you
This day
Amen.

18. First Impact

Mark 1: 21 – 28

²¹ They went to Capernaum; and when the Sabbath came, he entered the synagogue and taught. ²² They were astounded at his teaching, for he taught them as one having authority, and not as the scribes. ²³ Just then there was in their synagogue a man with an unclean spirit, ²⁴ and he cried out, "What have you to do with us, Jesus of Nazareth? Have you come to destroy us? I know who you are, the Holy One of God." ²⁵ But Jesus rebuked him, saying, "Be silent, and come out of him!" ²⁶ And the unclean spirit, convulsing him and crying with a loud voice, came out of him. ²⁷ They were all amazed, and they kept on asking one another, "What is this? A new teaching – with authority! He commands even the unclean spirits, and they obey him." ²⁸ At once his fame began to spread throughout the surrounding region of Galilee.

At thirty years of age Jesus comes out of the harbour of preparation, steers his boat onto the wide waters and hits Galilee like a landing craft hitting a D-Day beach. It begins in a small village synagogue in Capernaum and finishes with his fame sweeping out over the whole area.

A synagogue was rather like a small village church. Except, it was Jewish not Christian, and more of a gathering of local people than a building made out of local stones. The synagogue members probably met together in an outdoor area or perhaps in a rich member's large house if they were lucky enough to have such a person. They met on the 'Sabbath', their restful, holy day. A sort of combination of our Saturday and Sunday.

The faithful met to study their religious writings, to say their prayers and to catch up on local gossip. Jesus had grown up in just such a 'small village synagogue world'. He knew the ropes and the sorts of people who pulled them, he was confident and assured in this place. Here he makes his first impact. He begins as a new and astounding type of teacher and then moves on to become a 'driving evil out' type of saviour:

> His teaching is truly authoritative
> His salvation is totally amazing

Here begins the Kingdom struggle, the great epic clash between goodness and evil, Jesus and the devil, light and dark, life and death; it has started.

In a land alive with teachers, Jesus stands out. Every time he opens his mouth people know straight away that he is different. He carries a certain authentic truthfulness. He is fresh, relevant; he is one of them. He understands the ordinary people, their lives and their struggles. He understands the extraordinary God, His love and His salvation. In a word, he has 'authority'.

I must have listened to hundreds of scribes or religious teachers over the years. Most of them have been ok to quite good. They all had an ability to open the book, read the book, understand and explain the book. Every now and again I have listened to a teacher who didn't just open the book, he opened me, my life, my pain and hopes, my inner place. Great teachers have the ability to take a deep insight into the heart of God and plant it deeply in the human heart. Jesus was just this sort of teacher, 'What is this? A new teaching – with authority?'

Jesus wasn't just a teacher, he was a professor; not just another guru, but an absolute genius; not so much a life coach as a life transformer.

He talks, they listen, a single voice, an attentive silence, and a place of peaceful thought. Suddenly an almost satanic shrieking breaks the calm.

Now I have to confess that I am never quite sure what an 'unclean spirit' otherwise known as a demon actually is. Is it a sort of dark, underworld 'fallen-angel'? Is it an illness? A psychological weakness or a deeply buried hurt or fear that somehow takes over or grips our inner heart? What I do know is that unclean spirits are always dark and destructive and are as prevalent and real today as they were in Jesus' day. *'Alien'* the movie comes pretty close to the truth, in its image of a hungry, devouring presence living inside a human 'host'.

The unclean spirit is powerful, more powerful than the man he lives in, but not as powerful as Jesus. The spirit knows this. The spirit whom everyone fears is instantly fearful of Jesus, 'Have you come to destroy us?' When Jesus calls the darkness to come out there is a huge struggle. The spirit has got its hooks into the man, but Jesus' voice has got its hooks into the spirit and he commands/drags it out of him.

Jesus the teacher becomes Jesus the 'liberator', the 'driver-outer'. These twin themes of teacher and saviour have begun, soon they will be running like spring hares. 'His fame began to spread throughout the surrounding region of Galilee'.

Jesus the Teacher speaks to our brain, our intellect, our thinking. Jesus the Saviour reaches deep into our heart, our memories, our 'inner-me'. Brain and heart; intellect and emotion; thinking and feeling. Never just brain or just emotions, but always the whole me.

So what is the big thing you want to learn about and what is the inner bit of darkness you want to be rid of?

Lord Jesus
As you teach my mind
And excite my intellect
May you also reach into my heart
Cleanse my soul
And set me free. Amen.

19. Jesus Praying

Mark 1: 35–39

> *35 In the morning, while it was still very dark, he got up and went out to a deserted place, and there he prayed. 36 And Simon and his companions hunted for him. 37 When they found him, they said to him, "Everyone is searching for you." 38 He answered, "Let us go on to the neighbouring towns, so that I may proclaim the message there also; for that is what I came out to do." 39 And he went throughout Galilee, proclaiming the message in their synagogues and casting out demons.*

This is Jesus praying, but perhaps not as we know it.

When I was a young boy one of my jobs was going to the fish and chip shop. Every Saturday morning I would queue up in a warm, battery, fishy, sizzling atmosphere, then when my turn came I would lean against and peek over the tall counter and present my list of what everyone wanted. It has often occurred to me that this is just like much of our praying. Queuing up in a prayer meeting or privately at home and presenting our list of what we want God to serve us up with.

Here in Mark's Gospel Jesus shows us a very different picture of prayer. No queue gathered, no list presented, just a simple man and his Father. Jesus is being with his Father. Actually, I suspect there probably was a list of hopes and fears somewhere, but there will also have been lots of silence and listening; breathing and dreaming; a baring of his deepest inner soul; a looking to the days ahead; a simply being in the presence, Son and Father together.

This is one of my favourite and most significant stories of Jesus. Sadly, I find that many pass over it quickly, their attention on all the fast-moving action stories that come a bit later. Here is a little stillness hidden away in the 'rushing around' of the Galilee ministry. It is clearly not a one-off but part of a regular pattern in Jesus' lifestyle. It comes after Jesus' first burst of demanding ministry and just before an even bigger and more exhausting one. Healing the sick, driving out demons and preaching the good news must have drained his tank. I see this as an emptied Jesus filling up at the petrol station before the next phase of giving out.

Time and space, space and time, how valuable but elusive they are. Jesus is a very busy person with lots of people making demands. He lives in a crowded village and probably in a very crowded house. Does any of this feel familiar? He could have simply operated as a very busy and stressed person, always thinking of the next job to be done, but here we see him getting away from demanding people and schedule. He makes time and space for God, and of course, God makes time and space for him.

Time and space. I wonder if the real reason that I am so drawn to this little story is that it crystallises the big deficiency in my life. It highlights everything that I aspire towards but never actually get a hold of. You see, I am by nature an activist. I rush around, talk too fast and overfill my diary. Writing a sermon (quickly), checking my emails, chatting on the phone whilst making a list of tomorrow's jobs and then dashing out (five minutes late) to a meeting – oh, I hate it and love it all at the same time. Frankly, I am just too busy to spend time with God. And therein lies my problem, I am too busy. And it is not just my diary but my constantly buzzing brain that are both suffering from 'non-slowness', 'non-peaceful oasis', 'non-God-time'. In our crazy world we elevate those clever folk who can multitask. Why don't we turn it round and focus instead on the value of non-tasking? In the case of Jesus, it was because he was so busy that he knew he had to make time for God. With so many demands about to made upon him, he had first to make some demands on his father. He faces a long day giving himself to other people; first he had to spend some time with his 'other God'. This is not his 'me-time', it is his 'me and thee time', not so much chill-out as warm-up.

Everyone needs time and space, even you. Are you a busy, 'get out of my way, I'm on a mission to change the world' activist or a gentle, swan-like, 'I'm in a special place to pray for the world' contemplative? How much time do you spend rushing around after others, be they children, parents or friends? How much time is there left for you? Perhaps you have got the balance just right like Jesus. Prayer followed by action, action followed by prayer. Early in the morning, in a silent house with a cup of tea and the Bible open; out alone walking the dog whilst talking to God; sitting in your favourite armchair simply thinking about your life and turning it inside out to let God in, where is the time and space for you?

We live in a crazy, over-busy, over-working, over-rushing world. But God doesn't really do quick fixes. He is not a fast-food, drop you a quick text, catch you later kind of God. He is more of a 'be still, for the presence of the Lord, the Holy One is here – let's spend some time together God'.

> Time and Space
> Help me Lord
> Help me to turn off the telly
> To turn off the car radio.
> To slow down
> To sit down.
> To come down
> From all my flying around.
> Help me Lord
> And come to me as I come to you.
> Amen.

20. Springtime in Galilee

Matthew 4: 23–25

23 Jesus went throughout Galilee, teaching in their synagogues and proclaiming the good news of the kingdom and curing every disease and every sickness among the people. 24 So his fame spread throughout all Syria, and they brought to him all the sick, those who were afflicted with various diseases and pains, demoniacs, epileptics, and paralytics, and he cured them. 25 And great crowds followed him from Galilee, the Decapolis, Jerusalem, Judea, and from beyond the Jordan.

At the time that I am writing about this story of Jesus there is civil war in Syria. Refugees are fleeing south, as what started out as part of the 'Arab Spring' becomes the latest killing fields. Syrians were also on the move in the first century, early in the mission of Jesus.

Then it was the 'Galilean Spring', a sort of spiritual revolution based entirely on one man and his earliest band of followers. They were drawn like desperate moths to a brand-new light. Syrians came from the North, Jerusalemites (who were normally so disdainful of the Galileans) came from the South, Jordanians from the East, and the people of the Decapolis, the 'ten towns' from the beyond the Jordan Gentile world came as well.

It has something of the feel of that *'Sound of Music'* moment when Maria wanders through the spring flowers and sings 'The hills are alive with the sound of music'. Here the hills and valleys are alive with the sound of Jesus.

This is a big summarising story. There are lots of individual stories of teachings and personal encounters to come but here we have a big brushstroke trying to encapsulate all that was happening, a big picture type of story. At the heart of it we see the triple impact 'Galilean Spring-time' ministry of Jesus as he proclaims the good news, heals the sick and drives out demons.

In today's church, clergy, pastors, ministers, lay and youth workers of all types are often keen to become better trained and equipped. This desire often sees them going for more degrees, MAs and doctorates etc. There is of course nothing wrong with this; education is a very good thing, although it can get a bit out of hand and derail the mission itself. I always advise young people launching out in ministry to do a PhD in Jesus studies. To learn how to:

> P - Proclaim the Good News
> H - Heal the sick
> D - Drive out demons.

Note that I said, 'learn how to', not 'learn about'. I love book-learning. That is why I am writing a book to help people learn. Doing a PhD in Jesus studies might start off in the library but it quickly takes us out into the real world. Ultimately we have to learn by watching other people doing it, by doing it ourselves, by trying it, by failing and then by succeeding. By sometimes getting it wrong and occasionally getting it right. That is how the disciples learnt. Here we see them just beginning their learning process. They watch and listen as Jesus proclaims, heals and drives demons out. In a few weeks' time they will be doing it themselves. Following is about watching, seeing, reading, thinking and then doing.

Of course doing a PhD in Jesus studies is not just for pastors and vicars, youth workers and evangelists. It is for all of us who want to be followers and learners, servers and doers. It is for all of us who want to see a Galilean springtime in our own little world, in our life, our family, our network of friendships, our church and community. So, what would it feel like if the good news was proclaimed, a bit of healing was prayed for and some of the darkness was driven out of your world?

> Are you looking for him, trying to find him?
> Are you finding him, trying to follow him?
> Are you following him, trying to become like him?
> Maybe you are sick, wanting to be healed by him?
> Possessed, wanting to be set free by him?

We have all got so much to find, to learn, to do and to be in him.

> Lord Jesus
> Proclaimer, healer, driver out of demons.
> As you brought a wave of springtime then,
> May you bring it today through my words, my love, my actions.
> May you bring your springtime to my world and to my people.
> Thank you
> Amen.

21. Water into Wine

John 2: 1–12

^{1} *On the third day there was a wedding in Cana of Galilee, and the mother of Jesus was there.* ^{2} *Jesus and his disciples had also been invited to the wedding.* ^{3} *When the wine gave out, the mother of Jesus said to him, "They have no wine."* ^{4} *And Jesus said to her, "Woman, what concern is that to you and to me? My hour has not yet come."* ^{5} *His mother said to the servants, "Do whatever he tells you."* ^{6} *Now standing there were six stone water jars for the Jewish rites of purification, each holding twenty or thirty gallons.* ^{7} *Jesus said to them, "Fill the jars with water." And they filled them up to the brim.* ^{8} *He said to them, "Now draw some out, and take it to the chief steward." So they took it.* ^{9} *When the steward tasted the water that had become wine, and did not know where it came from (though the servants who had drawn the water knew), the steward called the bridegroom* ^{10} *and said to him, "Everyone serves the good wine first, and then the inferior wine after the guests have become drunk. But you have kept the good wine until now."* ^{11} *Jesus did this, the first of his signs, in Cana of Galilee, and revealed his glory; and his disciples believed in him.*

12 After this he went down to Capernaum with his mother, his brothers, and his disciples; and they remained there a few days.

Matthew, Mark and Luke all follow a similar path. Jesus leaves the scene of his baptism and temptations down in Judea and moves north for his main ministry in Galilee. John's Gospel gives a different shape and order to things. It describes some of Jesus' early visits to Jerusalem that the other three do not mention and provides new stories such as him meeting the woman at the well and the turning of the water into wine.

Weddings are massive, though quite intimidating events. For many they are the biggest day of their lives. Food and drink, early morning nerves and late-night revels, wedding dresses and best outfits, tears and laughter all combine in these love celebrations and launching into new lives.

So John's story is about a big fat Jewish wedding day. It can be brilliant or it can be a disaster, whichever it is it will certainly be big. This tale has always struck me as a real embarrassment for all those rather grey, anti-drink, anti-fun, overly religious folks who are not keen on people having a good time. Of course alcohol and partying can get out of hand. For several years we ran an AA group in our church, it opened my eyes to how booze wrecks so many lives and families. For many, however, they are part of what it means to live a good and full life. The company of others, good food and drink, greeting and meeting, celebration and laughter, music and dance, praise and prayer, poetry and rock 'n' roll are all colourful parts of God's colourful world. Here then is Jesus, half-way through a wedding celebration, they have already drunk quite a lot of wine, and he is turning water into even more of the stuff. Only Jesus could get away with it. This is a great life affirming, let's have a party moment.

My understanding of the story took on a whole new relevance a few years ago when a friend asked me to give the talk at his wedding. I eventually found myself standing before Matthew and Anna, a beautiful and 'want to do it God's way' couple. I made a couple of jokes about Matthew's disreputable past and how Anna was far too good for him, both sets of parents nodded in agreement. Then I told the story of water into wine and looking deep into their eyes asked the question, 'So do you want your marriage, your friendship, your romance, love-life, running of a shared home and walking with God to be like water or wine?' Water is ok, it does the job and quenches the thirst, but it's a bit thin and flat. On the other hand dark red wine, full of taste, warmth and inner mystery, well, it is of another dimension.

Here at the beginning of Jesus' ministry, there is a story of a real wedding, but it takes on an added symbolism. It is in effect a sign, a signpost to Jesus' heavenly impact. Here we see Jesus touching lives, be they married or single, young or old and his touch turning them from water into wine. And there are lots of other little details in the story for you to think about, such as 'on the third day' (echoes of the resurrection), the appearance of Mary (we don't see her again in John until the crucifixion), the obedience of the servants and the use of 'purification jars' (where is the purification in our lives?)

Now I am no wine expert (although even I can tell the difference between water and wine). I do, however, have a rough idea that to produce good wine you need three things.

> First, plenty of juicy fruit.
> Secondly, hours and hours of glorious sunshine.
> Thirdly, lots of patience.

So where is the fruit, the sunshine and the patience as your years, character and lifestyle go from water to wine?

I always think wine is a great symbol. Life and love, fruit and friendship, long meals and late nights. They are all there in every glass. The symbolism flows throughout the ministry of Jesus. Here water is turned into wine, later on we will all be welcomed as branches into his vine, and there will be talk of new wine in old wine skins. Later still, we will read of tenants stealing the profits of the master's vineyard, and finally before his death he will share the one cup of wine with his disciples.

> **Dear Lord Jesus**
> **As you turned the water into wine**
> **So may you turn the water of my marriage,**
> > **of my singleness,**
> > **of my love affair, of my**
> > **sexuality,**
> > **of my hopes and dreams,**
> > **of my past and future,**
> > **into wine.**
> **Take the ok greyness of my life and transform it**
> **with your sunshine and warmth.**
> **Help me to be patient as the fermenting goes on.**
> **That I might be filled and changed by your touch**
> **Amen.**

22. At the Back of the Queue

John 5: 1 – 8

¹ After this there was a festival of the Jews, and Jesus went up to Jerusalem. ² Now in Jerusalem by the Sheep Gate there is a pool, called in Hebrew Beth-zatha, which has five porticoes. ³ In these lay many invalids—blind, lame, and paralysed ⁵ One man was there who had been ill for thirty-eight years. ⁶ When Jesus saw him lying there and knew that he had been there a long time, he said to him, 'Do you want to be made well?' ⁷ The sick man answered him, "Sir, I have no one to put me into the pool when the water is stirred up; and while I am making my way, someone else steps down ahead of me." ⁸ Jesus said to him, "Stand up, take your mat and walk."

'The blind, the lame and the paralysed', whatever we call them, are a sad bunch of people. In the chaotic scrambling around for money, position and security that we call living, they are at the back of the queue. When the cards were dealt they were given a bad hand.

If they were born disabled or disadvantaged then they have probably never fully taken part in the great game of life. If they became disabled during life then they were, as the army calls it, 'invalided out'.

Not only is this poor man at the 'back of the queue' because he is disabled, he is even at the back of the 'back of the queue'. The others can push in front of him, get to the water, be a bit more noticed and maybe even find healing. This poor man is left behind in the dark shadows of the porticoes. He is at the back of the back of the queue, but for the first time in his life he shakes a double six. For the first time in his life there is someone to help him. Jesus has noticed him and is going to do something. Jesus has looked not at the front but at the back of the queue, and rather than help the man into the healing pool he is going to do something far more wonderful. He is going to help the healing pool into the man.

This man has been in this poor state for 38-years. So the chances are that he was either born this way or had some sort of disabling accident or illness as a young boy. In a strange, unlooked for, sort of way, I seem to have lived with disability for most of my life. When I was a young boy my father was a very physically able middle-aged man. He worked as a labourer and when not working was usually in his garden, decorating or doing odd jobs around the house. Football, cricket and rugby were his great pastimes. One day he fell off the top of a lorry that he was loading up and he never worked or lived in a fully able-bodied way again. (However this physical disability seemed to open spiritual doors for him and he blossomed in his walk with God).

Later on in life disability struck again with the birth of my daughter Zoe. Today Zoe is over thirty, delightful and beautiful, but she is completely dependent on others. She can never get herself to the edge of the pool, she has to be helped there.

> There are lots of people at the back of the
> queue.
> There are those
> Who are just not big enough?
> Popular enough
> Confident or lucky enough.
> Some do not earn enough
> Were not good enough at football as a kid
> Failed their exams as a teenager
> And are not particularly good looking.
> Many just don't seem to have the knack of
> building friendships
> Or have simply been unlucky in love, unlucky
> in life.
> There are plenty of people at the back of the
> queue
> Who just do not have enough of enough?

The back of the queue people are usually the most ignored, but in this story, this man is the most noticed, the first to be spotted and picked out as special. With Jesus the back became the front of the queue. The last really were the first and the first became the last. Where are you in the queue? Front, back or middle? Front of the middle, or back of the middle? Front of the back, or back of the front?

Lord Jesus
Give me your eyes to see
Your heart to feel
Your hands to touch
That like you I might
See the people at the back of the queue
And help the helpless
In this needy world
Amen.

23. I Am the Bread of Life

John 6: 27–35

27 Do not work for the food that perishes, but for the food that endures for eternal life, which the Son of Man will give you. For it is on him that God the Father has set his seal.' 28 Then they said to him, "What must we do to perform the works of God?" 29 Jesus answered them, "This is the work of God, that you believe in him whom he has sent." 30 So they said to him, "What sign are you going to give us then, so that we may see it and believe you? What work are you performing? 31 Our ancestors ate the manna in the wilderness; as it is written, 'He gave them bread from heaven to eat.'" 32 Then Jesus said to them, "Very truly, I tell you, it was not Moses who gave you the bread from heaven, but it is my Father who gives you the true bread from heaven. 33 For the bread of God is that which comes down from heaven and gives life to the world." 34 They said to him, "Sir, give us this bread always."

35 Jesus said to them, "I am the bread of life. Whoever comes to me will never be hungry, and whoever believes in me will never be thirsty."

'I am the bread of life'

When I was a kid, bread was bread. Mother's Pride, Wonderloaf and Hovis. Today it is ciabatta and croissants, bagels and baguettes, naan and (Peter Kay's favourite) garlic bread. Suddenly lots of us are non-wheat, or gluten free eaters. Back then we all simply ate and filled up on it. Bread and jam, bread and dripping, we even had bread and butter and tinned fruit. In Jesus' day it was bread and wine.

In John's Gospel we find the seven 'I am' sayings where Jesus takes seven pictures or metaphors to describe who he really is and how he deeply impacts on our lives.

> I am the bread of life (6: 35)
> I am the light of the world (8: 12)
> I am the gate (10: 9)
> I am the good shepherd (10: 11)
> I am the resurrection and the life (11: 25)
> I am the way, the truth and the life (14: 6)
> I am the true vine (15: 1).

In all these 'I am' sayings there is a subtle reference back to the occasion in the Old Testament when Moses asked God what His name was and He answered, 'I am who I am' (Exodus 3: 14). So Jesus is both talking about seven ways in which he touches human lives and at the same time saying here are seven ways in which I am just like God.

Unique in the Bible and world literature. They are seven mysterious truths. Powerful and personal; prophetic and poetic; human and divine. They are statements that become promises. In each one of them they represent Jesus saying, 'this is who I am, and this is what I can do for you'. In saying something about Jesus, they also say something about us. If he is the shepherd then we are the sheep, if he is the way we are the lost and if he is the bread then we are the hungry.

Bread has always been one of the staples of life, a fundamental building block in our diet and the first thing most people spend their money on. Alongside potatoes, rice and pasta, bread is a hole-filler, an energy-giver, a daily foundation to build everything else on. At the feeding of the 5,000 Jesus multiplied the loaves. In the Lord's Prayer he teaches us to pray for bread. He knows the importance of bread.

So when Jesus says, 'I am the bread of life', what is he saying to you right now? Where are you hungry, where do you need energy, building up, something to keep you going? Where and what is the biggest hole in your life that needs filling?

Jesus' disciples were known as his companions (Luke 24: 33). I love that word. It resonates with friendship, help and mutual support. It means more than this, however. To be a companion is to be a 'sharer of bread' (as in the French 'pain' for bread). Together we journey; sharing with and in both our daily bread and in our bread of life.

Today is the 23rd day on our journey. Are you a searcher trying to find Jesus? Have you found him and

are now trying to follow him? Or perhaps you are a
follower wanting to become like him?

A thought for the day. Stop. In your mind visualise Jesus
as a great big crusty loaf, tear a slab off and eat. Fill the
hole. Tear off another chunk and fill the hole some
more. Think about the idea of feeding on him several
times a day, every day. Now you are ready to journey
onwards as one of his companions.

> Lord Jesus
> If you are the bread of life
> Then I am one of the hungry ones,
> As I live I get hungry
> When I serve you I get hungry
> No matter how much I eat
> I keep getting hungry.
> So may you be my daily bread
> My daily bread of life.
> Amen.

24. Disciples and Discontent

John 6: 60 – 66

> [60] *When many of his disciples heard it, they said, "This teaching is difficult; who can accept it?"* [61] *But Jesus, being aware that his disciples were complaining about it, said to them, "Does this offend you?* [62] *Then what if you were to see the Son of Man ascending to where he was before?* [63] *It is the spirit that gives life; the flesh is useless. The words that I have spoken to you are spirit and life.* [64] *But among you there are some who do not believe." For Jesus knew from the first who were the ones that did not believe, and who was the one that would betray him.* [65] *And he said, "For this reason I have told you that no one can come to me unless it is granted by the Father."* [66] *Because of this many of his disciples turned back and no longer went about with him.*

Sadly it is a feature of virtually all spiritual movements and organisations. It eats away at the foundations, causes disunity in the framework and ultimately prevents the building reaching its full stature. It is 'discipleship discontent', grumbling, complaining, and conversations in corners. It happened to Moses in the Wilderness, it will happen to Paul on his journey and here it happens to Jesus. It has happened to me in every church I have been involved with, and it is something, sadly, that I have contributed to when I should have been a better follower. So if you're ever a leader of a church, children's project, admin team or house group, and the members are grumbling, then at least you know that you are in good company.

Most of us start out imagining that the disciples in the New Testament were very special, very different from us, very much better than us. They live next to Jesus and have been preserved in a million stained-glass windows. We often imagine Jesus' disciples as being wonderfully together, resolute and deeply spiritual whilst seeing ourselves as shallow and second rate. In fact the truth is that they were much like us, broken and human. Equally truthful is the realisation that we ourselves are often much more faithful than we give ourselves credit for.

Even worse than 'disciple discontent' is 'follower fall-out'. Some time ago I arranged to meet Sarah in a Costa Coffee shop. Sarah was a bright 18-year-old member of our church and youth group. Full of enthusiasm, keen to help, learning to read her Bible, Sarah is great, except we hadn't seen her for a while, well not at church anyway. On the odd occasion that she had been there she had developed a sort of bored looking, not engaged, facial expression.

It turned out to be a very painful conversation as Sarah explained her situation. Actually she didn't explain, she had no explanation of why she had suddenly 'had enough of it all'. Sarah had grown up, grown out of or just moved on from church, God, 'the whole thing'. The sad thing was looking at her and seeing that a sort of light or flare had disappeared out of her eyes. I remembered how alive and smiling she had been a year or so earlier when she told me about how the Holy Spirit had touched and moved her, about how she was reading her Bible and getting involved. Suddenly the joy, the enthusiasm and the interest in other people as well as God had gone.

I have to confess that sometimes I rather envy the 'can't be bothered crowd' and could easily join them. So what stops me? I think it is my love of life, of reality, my need for a purpose and meaning, my hunger for joy, my love of light. Ultimately the 'Spirit' has so set me alive that I keep on wanting to live.

I wonder what it felt like for Jesus when 'many of his disciples turned back'? These were not simply members of the crowd, but real disciples. My guess is he must have felt at least two things. Firstly, a sadness for them, that they are losing something very special. It is the classic story of the person who throws away their lottery ticket, only to discover a few days later that it was a winner.

Secondly, Jesus must have felt a bit of a failure, that somehow he had not done a proper job in discipling them. As leaders and discipleship builders, we are never supposed to take it personally, but we all do, and I suspect Jesus did too, because in 'turning back' they no longer 'went about with him'.

When I became a disciple I made a decision to follow him. I am free to go on following him or to follow myself. Over the years I have known so many who have lived great lives of faithfully following the one who has the words of eternal life. I have known quite a few who have given up on Jesus and gone back to an earthly life. I have never known one who Jesus himself gave up on.

Lord Jesus
It sometimes feels
Like it is too easy to give up
And too hard to keep going
But in you I have found the words of eternal life
In you I have placed my belief
And have come to know
That you are the Holy One.
So help me this day
To lift my head to see,
Lift my heart to believe,
Lift my feet to follow.
Amen.

25. Eternal Life

John 6: 67 – 69

> [67] *So Jesus asked the twelve, "Do you also wish to go away?"* [68] *Simon Peter answered him, "Lord, to whom can we go? You have the words of eternal life.* [69] *We have come to believe and know that you are the Holy One of God."*

Our previous reading had us thinking about people giving up on Jesus. Today let us be a bit more positive. If the giving up of some disciples perhaps left Jesus feeling a bit of a failure, in complete contrast, what sort of massive hit did Jesus feel when Peter said, 'you have the words of eternal life'. Joy and satisfaction, because here was a disciple who clearly must have been tempted to join the leavers but who came through stronger and deeper and closer. 'We have come to believe and know'. Something is deeply rooted inside Peter and the remaining disciples. They did not make a quick, ill thought through decision. It sounds like there had been a gradual, interior journey involving lots of thinking and pondering. Firstly they believed and then they began to know who Jesus was.

John's gospel has a different feel to Matthew, Mark and Luke. In these first three, known as Synoptic Gospels, the big phrase is 'Kingdom of God and Heaven'. In John it is 'Eternal Life'.

We have already come across 'eternal life' in Jesus' meeting with Nicodemus and with its partner phrase 'believe'.

'For God so loved the world that he gave his Son so that everyone who believes in him may not perish but may have eternal life (Jn 3: 16)

I remember when I first started trying to find Jesus it was the 'coffee-like smell of the words eternal life' that drew me. I had already discovered that life was not as good as it could be, more than that, death struck me as a really bad idea, something to be avoided at all costs. Then I came across this picture of eternal life in John's gospel. At first it struck me in a fairly one-dimensional way as everlasting life, life after dying, life that went on forever, not as something that was wrapped up by death and then buried like so much fish and chip paper. Later on as I began to explore, learn and to follow Jesus I discovered other dimensions to 'eternal life'. That it has a quality, an experience in the here and now as well as in the future. It is not just life after death but a whole new way of living before death. That the person living eternally is more alive in the present moment than anyone else.

> Flesh
> Spirit
> Word
> Eternal
> Life.

This is a little word chain that runs through the early parts of this story. There is a missing link in my chain; it is the word 'believe'. It is believing which opens the way to eternal life. Most of the people I meet are quick to tell me how they 'believe in God'. What they mean is that they believe he exists. True belief is far more than this, it means that we believe in him as a personal being not just an idea. It means that we are drawn closer, following him, basing our life on him.

In John 6 we see three different types of belief/response to Jesus. There are those who clearly do not believe. They believe he exists, but they don't believe in him as a person to be followed, trusted and accepted. Then there are those who stop believing in him, who 'no longer went about with him'. Finally there are those who are so drawn to him, to his words, to who he is, that they cannot not go on believing. They are the disciples.

They believe in him, because he first believed in them.

> 'You were my strength when I was weak
> You were my voice when I couldn't speak
> You were my eyes when I couldn't see
> You saw the best there was in me
> Lifted me up when I couldn't reach
> You gave me faith 'cause you believed
> I'm everything I am
> Because you loved me.'   Celine Dion.

Lord,
You are the giver of eternal life
You give it today and tomorrow.
So help me to so believe in you
That I might live in you
        follow you
        remain with you
This and everyday.
Amen.

26. Let it Flow

John 7: 37 – 39

37 On the last day of the festival, the great day, while Jesus was standing there, he cried out, "Let anyone who is thirsty come to me, 38 and let the one who believes in me drink. As the scripture has said, 'Out of the believer's heart shall flow rivers of living water.'" 39 Now he said this about the Spirit, which believers in him were to receive; for as yet there was no Spirit, because Jesus was not yet glorified.

> Let anyone who is thirsty, come to me
> Let the one who believes in me drink.

Water does three things. It cleans the body, quenches thirst and gives life in a dusty place. I think of these three things every time I carry out a baptism whether it is an adult or a small child. In fact, not only do I think of them, I talk about them. They represent three of life's simplest, most basic and essential needs. We all need to be clean, to drink and to live. All organic life, plants and crops, birds and insects, animals and human beings, we all have these same three basic needs for water.

Jesus lived in a dry, dusty land. There is a rainy season but the water soon disappears, the streams dry up and the spring flowers wither. His was a land of hot stones, barren hillsides and brown wispy grass. He knew the importance of water. He knew its freshening, cleansing effect at the end of a hot day, it's wonderful thirst quenching inner rush on a thirsty day, knew it's life greening impact on a scorching fading away day.

He experienced all of this in his own watery baptism in the River Jordan. What he wants for his people is not just that they get into the river, but rather that the river gets into them.

John who baptised Jesus said, 'the one who sent me to baptise with water said to me "He on whom you see the Spirit descend and remain is the one who baptises with the Holy Spirit".'(John1:33)

Here Jesus uses the imagery and the instant understanding in his listeners' minds of the importance of water to talk about the Holy Spirit. The water is the Holy Spirit and the Spirit is Holy Water – cleansing, refreshing, producing life in the desert.

God's great plan is that after Jesus' glorification (this is John's way of talking about the crucifixion and resurrection of Jesus) the Spirit will come, it will be God's gift, the rain, the flow, the river of life. In Luke's gospel, chapter 24, verse 49, after his death and resurrection (his glorification) Jesus told the disciples to wait in Jerusalem 'until they are clothed with power from on high'. It is another reference to the Holy Spirit, God's water of life. The great tap was turned on at the day of Pentecost (Acts 2: 1) and the Spirit flowed.

The vital connection or inflow that enables the watery Holy Spirit to flood into us is here described by Jesus in two phrases.

> Let anyone who is thirsty come to me
> Let the one who believes in me drink.

The key ideas are coming and drinking.

As a man in his late sixties, whose best years are behind him, struggling still to be a good husband and father, living in the middle of a sea of worldly unbelief and overcast every day by melancholia, I am a thirsty man. I am needing to drink of the Spirit of cleansing, refreshment and life. So for me, first coming to the river and then drinking in of the cool water are great pictures.

In fact, the more I look at other people, the more I get the impression that there are lots of us, and men in particular, who need to come and drink. Charles was a working-class man, he worked long hours, never had much money but he provided for his wife and family. It was when he first met men at his local pub from the local church who were filled with the Spirit that he realised how thirsty he was. Norman was a bellringer, a long-time faithful member of the Church of England but he had never actually bobbed his head under the surface and drunk the water. Nick had been a great Christian youth leader, he knew lots of Holy Spirit songs but he had not actually drunk for years. And then there are all the others who come to church, come to the edge of the river but who run a mile when it comes to opening up in worship, going deeper in prayer or joining a sharing group. How thirsty many of us men are.

The water in which I baptise splashes on the surface of the head and body. No matter how much I use, it is still on the surface and quickly dries up. Here Jesus is talking about a different water and a different baptism. This is Spirit water and Spirit baptism. This is water of the Spirit on the inside and Spirit water which never dries up.

Man or woman, how thirsty are you?

> Lord Jesus
> Help me to come to the water
> Open me that I might drink of the water
> Baptise me in your Holy Spirit of life.
> Amen.

27. A Night-Time Visitor

John 3: 1 – 10,16

¹Now there was a Pharisee named Nicodemus, a leader of the Jews. ² He came to Jesus by night and said to him, "Rabbi, we know that you are a teacher who has come from God; for no one can do these signs that you do apart from the presence of God." ³ Jesus answered him, "Very truly, I tell you, no one can see the kingdom of God without being born from above." ⁴ Nicodemus said to him, "How can anyone be born after having grown old? Can one enter a second time into the mother's womb and be born?" ⁵ Jesus answered, "Very truly, I tell you, no one can enter the kingdom of God without being born of water and Spirit. ⁶ What is born of the flesh is flesh, and what is born of the Spirit is spirit. ⁷ Do not be astonished that I said to you, 'You must be born from above.' ⁸ The wind blows where it chooses, and you hear the sound of it, but you do not know where it comes from or where it goes. So it is with everyone who is born of the Spirit." ⁹ Nicodemus said to him, "How can these things be?" ¹⁰ Jesus answered him, "Are you a teacher of Israel, and yet you do not understand these things?

¹⁶"For God so loved the world that he gave his only Son, so that everyone who believes in him may not perish but may have eternal life."

What an intriguing story? An encounter story between Jesus and Nicodemus. It is night-time so there are shadows, mystery, hiddenness and secrecy all wrapped together. Nicodemus was a Pharisee (one of the good ones), Jesus was on a visit to Jerusalem. Matthew, Mark and Luke's gospels only mention Jesus coming to Jerusalem right at the end of his ministry but John's gospel tells of various earlier visits. It may well be its author had discovered some different stories of Jesus that the others were not aware of and this is one of them.

Nicodemus has perhaps watched Jesus from a distance, listened to some of his talk and met other people who have been changed by him, he's getting very interested. Unlike the other Pharisees, he does not see Jesus as a threat and nor does he have a patronising sense of superiority towards him, in fact, quite the reverse. Nicodemus is a genuine searcher. He knows that Jesus is a very special sort of teacher, one who can work miracles. He wants to know more. He is aware, however, of the tense politics between the Jerusalem based Pharisees and the 'new man from up north', so he comes at night.

Like all serious searchers, Nicodemus is gradually being drawn closer, but he has got lots of questions and things he does not really understand. If you are searching, may I ask, 'how intent are you on your search?' Nicodemus makes a big effort in coming to see Jesus at night. How much effort are you making? He steps out of the crowd of Pharisees and goes it alone. Have you stepped out of the crowd yet? And what are your questions? And are you really searching for Jesus or expecting him to search for you? And are you coming in the day or the night time?

The intense and deep conversation centres around three issues:

- Rebirth; the ultimate making a new start, or starting out afresh in life; being born again from above; born of water and Spirit.
- Spirit; a spiritual search should lead to a spiritual birth; the spirit is God's spirit. He is as free as the wind and as part of the new birth God wants to breathe his Spirit into our lungs. A new type of living, living in us.
- Belief; to believe is to begin the new life; so far everything has been words, talk theory; believing is the first part of the doing. Nicodemus' search has brought him to a doorway, in believing he puts his hand on the door handle twists and gives it a big shove.

Rebirth, Spirit, Belief. Yes, I know this is a story about Nicodemus, two thousand years ago, and his great spiritual search, but it's also a story about you and me today. A story about anyone who has two or three key questions that they would like to put to Jesus.

Nicodemus appears twice more in John's story (7: 50 and 19: 39) and it looks as if his shadowy approach led to a sort of life changing rebirth. He sheds his timid searching in the night-time to become an openly supportive follower of Jesus. He steps out into the daylight of belief.

> Searching for Jesus,
> Asking questions,
> Coming to him,
> Listening.

These are like stepping stones on a journey.

> **Dear Lord Jesus**
> **This is my journey**
> **My search**
> **From an old life**
> **To a new life.**
> **From an old way of thinking**
> **To a new way of thinking, learning and believing.**
> **From an old me**
> **To a new me.**
> **From an old birth**
> **To a new birth.**
> **May you be my gateway, my pathway, my**
> **shepherd.**
> **Amen.**

28. The Sermon on the Mount

Matthew 5: 1–2

> *¹ When Jesus saw the crowds, he went up the mountain; and after he sat down, his disciples came to him. ² Then he began to speak, and taught them,*

In our following of Jesus' journey we have come to one of the great treasures or mountain top moments. It is the 'Sermon on the Mount'. We could spend endless time in these next three chapters of Matthew, but because we have to keep moving we shall spend only five sessions dipping into them. The well we are dipping into, however is a deep well and holds much rich and cool water. The whole thing can be summed up in three sentences: -

> This is how you live a good life.
> This is how you live a Godly life.
> This is how goodness and Godliness live in you.

I think it is quite important before diving into the contents of the Sermon on the Mount to work out who is it for. Who is Jesus preaching to? Who are the listeners?

It looks in these verses as though Jesus specifically leaves 'the crowds' behind and takes his disciples or committed followers up the mountain for a sort of teaching, commitment and bonding session all in one.

In the gospels the 'crowd' are often seen as those who are drawn because they want something from Jesus, as if he was some sort of 'all welcoming, healing, sweet shop type person'. In the gospels followers or disciples are those who step out of the crowd and into a commitment to find out more, to follow, to serve, to change their lifestyle and life direction around Jesus.

The distinction between 'crowd' and 'disciples' gets a bit more complex when we realise that out of what was probably a fairly large bunch of disciples Jesus chose 'the twelve'. Luke has a story of Jesus' great sermon as well, except his shorter version begins with Jesus spending the whole of the previous night in prayer before picking out this inner group (Lk 6: 12–13). These were the ones who seem to have given up their jobs and walked away from their daily lives to accompany Jesus on his wandering mission. So there were, what we might call, 'stay at home disciples', continuing with their normal family and village life, but doing it all the Jesus way. And then there were the twelve, the 'on the road', footing it and doing it alongside Jesus, disciples.

Here is the interesting thing about the receivers or listeners to the Sermon on the Mount; they begin as a group of disciples leaving the crowds behind to follow him up the Mountain. At the end of the sermon however, we read about the crowds being astonished at his teaching (Mt 7: 28). It looks then as if some of the crowds also found their way up the mountain and were drawn towards becoming real followers themselves.

So what is the best sermon you have ever heard? Who was the preacher? Man or woman? Young or old? Did it feel like a deep, traditional, sermon, or was it sort of cool, edgy and contemporary? And what about you as a listener? Were you really open, working hard, or were you waiting to be entertained? And what about the big truth factor? Did it set you free? Did it challenge your lifestyle? The way you relate to other people? The way you cling on to money and possessions? This great sermon that you heard recently, did it make you laugh or cry, fill you with rejoicing or regret. More than anything else did it draw you closer to God and make you want to be more like him.

Chapters 5–7 of Matthew's Gospel show us Jesus leading a retreat, giving big and deep teaching all about goodness and Godliness. Jesus inspiring people to follow him and adopt his attitudes and ideas. The teaching is given to both the 'stay at home' and the 'on the road' disciples and beyond them to the crowd who were curious, hungry and searching. The ones who were being drawn deeper and closer.

We seem to be back with the searcher follower movement. Here it looks like:

Curious in the crowd
Stepping out to find more
Seriously listening
Responding to what he is saying
Following and doing.

Big Question, 'Which of these five stepping stones are you on?'

Lord Jesus
Call me out of the crowd
Draw me up the mountain.
Call me out of the crowd
Open my ears, my mind, my heart.
Call me out of the crowd
And into your inner circle of disciples.
Call me and help me to follow you.
Amen.

29. The Beatitudes of a Truly Blessed Life

Matthew 5: 3–12

3 Blessed are the poor in spirit, for theirs is the kingdom of heaven.

4 Blessed are those who mourn, for they will be comforted.

5 Blessed are the meek, for they will inherit the earth.

6 Blessed are those who hunger and thirst for righteousness, for they will be filled.

7 Blessed are the merciful, for they will receive mercy.

8 Blessed are the pure in heart, for they will see God.

9 Blessed are the peacemakers, for they will be called children of God.

10 Blessed are those who are persecuted for righteousness' sake, for theirs is the kingdom of heaven.

11 Blessed are you when people revile you and persecute you and utter all kinds of evil against you falsely on my account. 12 Rejoice and be glad, for your reward is great in heaven, for in the same way they persecuted the prophets who were before you.

They stand out like pure true trumpet calls. They are like a series of nine truly great paintings. They are beacons, greatest hits in the entire series of world literature. They are poetic and prophetic, realistic and idealistic. As soon as you read them, you just know that they are utter truth, but utterly unreachable. You know you would like to live like this but you are quite sure that you will never manage it. They are the Beatitudes.

Beatitudes are about attitudes. So many of us today are stuffed with attitude much of it is aggressive, arrogant, uncaring and selfish, and often ignorant. We suck in attitude, from watching *EastEnders*, from reading the *Daily Mail* and listening to bigoted gossip. We plug in to not very intelligent politicians, trading their prejudices and it fills us with attitude. The hallmark of modern attitude is that we are right and others are wrong. Attitude is a thousand miles away from beatitude.

A beatitude is a 'great blessedness', a bestowing of peace and joy. I like to think of a great blessing as being rather like the falling of the softest of rain on a hot and sunny summer's day. Together the refreshing water and the warming sunshine fall on our head and shoulders and soak through to our mind and heart.

In these nine statements of God's values and promises, Jesus is basically taking the world with all its tacky, shallow and materialistic values and turning it upside down. You see the world's beatitudes or blessings are all for:

The rich and famous
The good looking and healthy...
Those who are good at sports and career
fulfilled
The successful, the powerful
And all those with lots of family and friends...
They are for those who live in a big house
And drive a nice car...

But Jesus goes for:

The poor
Those who mourn
The meek. The righteous
The merciful. The pure
The makers and keepers of peace
The persecuted
The 'put upon'.

When you look at this list you can easily come to the conclusion that Jesus is actually describing himself. This is what he was like as a person, this is how he lived, and how other people treated him. Jesus the beatitude teacher is in effect Jesus the beatitude man. He lived meekly, purely, vulnerably and for the sake of others.

This then is the upside-down bit. The people who will be most blessed, most enriched and most warmed to the core, both in this world and then on into Heaven itself, will be the Jesus-type people. That is not to say that we will be as purely perfect, as always meek, as peace-making as Jesus was. But it is to say that we are trying to find him, to follow and be like him.

Jesus lived God's way. His beatitudes form the right attitudes about how to be a 'proper human being'. More than this they are promises and assurances about comfort and inheritance, filling and mercy, childhood and gladness. Now it is vital to realise that this is not a big morality tale, 'do this and you will be rewarded with that'. Rather, it is a big promise or 'grace tale', not so much about living a good life but more about receiving a God blessing. In the words of Tom Wright this is not so much, 'good advice as good news'.

Now here's a final thought, if you mashed together the words 'beautiful' and 'blessed' you might end up with something like 'beatitude'.

> O Lord God
> May your blessing on me
> So touch my heart that I might be a blessing to others.
> May your meekness make me meek
> Your righteousness make me hunger
> Your pureness purify me.
> So that this day
> I might live as one of the blessed ones.
> Amen.

30. Salt and Light

Matthew 5: 13–16

13 "You are the salt of the earth; but if salt has lost its taste, how can its saltiness be restored? It is no longer good for anything, but is thrown out and trampled under foot.

14 "You are the light of the world. A city built on a hill cannot be hid. 15 No one after lighting a lamp puts it under the bushel basket, but on the lampstand, and it gives light to all in the house. 16 In the same way, let your light shine before others, so that they may see your good works and give glory to your Father in heaven."

So when did Britain become such a foody nation? Who was the first person to put great, modern food on the telly? Was it baby-faced Jamie, foul-mouthed Gordon, or delectable Nigella? Speaking as a non-chef and pretty much non-kitchen person, I have this old-fashioned view that salt is about taste. Good food should taste good and a bit of salt brings up the taste. So salt is important, and as for light, who wants to live in a world without candles. These days people can't even go to a pop concert, remember an old friend or even have a bath without lighting a few. So when

Jesus talks about salt and light he is scratching where we itch.

The word gospel means 'Good News'. Most of the time Jesus lays it on thick about God drawing close to us, caring for us, rescuing and forgiving us and pouring out his eternal love and life. All of this, God's generosity and love beyond love, we call Grace. It is undeserved yet given gladly. Every now and again however Jesus makes it clear that he expects his followers to do a bit of giving themselves.

He expects us to be salt, to give our taste, our quality, our value to the world. As a follower of Jesus who is trying to become like him, I ought to have a certain honesty, integrity, compassion for others and sense of justice. Well I can simply keep all this to myself living a sort of smugly puritanical lifestyle, or I can share it with my world. My country, my city, even my local community, they all need saltiness. My workplace, social club, school and family are all like unsalted bags of crisps. Once upon a time packets of crisps used to contain bright blue, little bags of salt. Only when the salt was broken open did the crisps become truly tasty.

So where will I scatter my salt today? Or to put it a bit better, amongst whom or over which people will I scatter my salt today?

- Someone at work
- Friends at church
- A member of my family
- The person who I have stopped talking to.

The same applies to light. Light shows up the truth, illuminates the right path, helps people feel secure, and makes the world a more colourful place. Well it does when it is lifted up. Jesus saw himself as the light of the world (Jn 8: 12). When he was born the star and angels laid on a great lightshow, when he died a great darkness came over the land (Mt 27: 45). Cosmic sunrise to black hole all in one lifetime.

Today we are the lightshow. So using the language of verse 15 ask yourself:

- What or where's 'your house'?
- Who else lives in the house?
- How are you shining light on them?

Salt and light are about lifestyle and character as well as words and image. They are about who we are, what we do, and how we speak. Later on in the Sermon Jesus takes this double image or metaphor and applies it to our anger management (v21), marital faithfulness (v27), divorce (31), personal honesty (v33), generosity (v38) and love for our enemies (v43). These are all real-life issues, not Sunday morning in church, but seven days a week in the world issues. Are we saltily flavoursome in our financial generosity or are we tasteless and tight-fisted? Are our relationships characterised by a lightsome smile or are they grey and full of shadows?

That is an awful lot of salt and light. Enough, in fact, to change the world, making it a tastier and brighter place.

Jesus
You truly were the light of the world
And the salt of the earth.
Help me become like you
That I might never lose my saltiness
Or hide my light.
And that the place where I live
Might be a better home.
Amen.

31. The Inner Walk with God

Matthew 6: 1 – 18

1 *"Beware of practicing your piety before others in order to be seen by them; for then you have no reward from your Father in heaven.*

2 *"So whenever you give alms, do not sound a trumpet before you, as the hypocrites do in the synagogues and in the streets, so that they may be praised by others. Truly I tell you, they have received their reward.* 3 *But when you give alms, do not let your left hand know what your right hand is doing,* 4 *so that your alms may be done in secret; and your Father who sees in secret will reward you.*

5 *"And whenever you pray, do not be like the hypocrites; for they love to stand and pray in the synagogues and at the street corners, so that they may be seen by others. Truly I tell you, they have received their reward.* 6 *But whenever you pray, go into your room and shut the door and pray to your Father who is in secret; and your Father who sees in secret will reward you.*

7 *"When you are praying, do not heap up empty phrases as the Gentiles do; for they think that*

they will be heard because of their many words. [8]
*Do not be like them, for your Father knows what
you need before you ask him.*

[9] *"Pray then in this way:*

*Our Father in heaven,
hallowed be your name.*
[10] *Your kingdom come.
Your will be done,
on earth as it is in heaven.*
[11] *Give us this day our daily bread.*
[12] *And forgive us our debts,
as we also have forgiven our debtors.*
[13] *And do not bring us to the time of trial,
but rescue us from the evil one.*

[14] *For if you forgive others their trespasses, your
heavenly Father will also forgive you;* [15] *but
if you do not forgive others, neither will your
Father forgive your trespasses.*

[16] *"And whenever you fast, do not look dismal,
like the hypocrites, for they disfigure their faces
so as to show others that they are fasting. Truly
I tell you, they have received their reward.* [17] *But
when you fast, put oil on your head and wash
your face,* [18] *so that your fasting may be seen not
by others but by your Father who is in secret; and
your Father who sees in secret will reward you."*

This is a long passage today, so you may need to read it
a couple of times to take it all in. It is about the three

inner points of personal spirituality, what we used to call acts of piety. It is also about the great rewards that flow from them.

- Almsgiving
- Prayer
- Fasting.

The three of them belong together forming a single reality, a three-legged stool, an equilateral triangle, a pyramid, a pure, strong and stable Trinitarian structure.

So firstly, a word of explanation about each of them and then a thought on how they work together.

'Almsgiving' is very difficult for us today because we are used to 'alms getting'. Most of us have been brought up on a constant lifestyle of 'must-have', 'I want', 'this is mine'. Here Jesus is talking about 'must-give', 'they need', 'this is their right'. Over the years, as I have followed Jesus, my own personal giving has grown from a rather pathetic 'how little can I get away with' to a more realistic 'how much should I give', and together with my wife (who is a much more generous person than me), it is becoming a 'how exciting to give to God's work and world'. We give to our church; to individuals we know who are in need; and to various charities that help the poor.

Daily personal times of prayer are an essential for anyone who wants to develop a healthy and joyful relationship with God. Here Jesus advises us to 'shut the door' on the world and turn off the radio so that we can be alone, deeply focused and ourselves with God. For some daily prayer is about long lists and requests. For others it is simply chatting, listening, and being aware of God. Most combine prayer with a bit of Bible reading and thinking of others who are in need. Regular personal time spent with God is like food and drink, sunshine and energy, refreshment and renewal to our inner personhood. The sooner you start developing it as part of your lifestyle, the better you will be. Prayer is like a telephone, it has a speaking bit and a listening bit. Some of us only ever use the speaking bit so we only have half a relationship and half a conversation.

What are the appetites in your life? Mine are all about food and drink, football and telly, sex, music and art. Fasting is not about denying any of these but about bringing them under control, going without something for a while so that we can fill that space with a growing love for and obedience to God. So don't just miss lunch twice a week, but fill your lunch break with a bit of Bible and prayer.

As I write this I am actually rather proud of myself (and yes I know it should be a secret but here goes). Some time ago my football team, Bradford City, were playing Aston Villa in the semi-final of the League Cup. We had never been in this semi-final before and we probably will never be there again in my lifetime. And, as with all of our games, I had a ticket. But there was also a meeting that I had been invited to. Not a very important, world-changing meeting by any means and I suspect that if I hadn't been there my presence would not have been missed. However, I think God wanted to be more important to me than Bradford City, so I gave my ticket away. I had a 'footie-fast'. Crazy, I know! (P.S. we won the match 3–1, I sort of both regret and am pleased that I was at the God-gathering.)

These three spiritual disciplines are like the three primary colours, out of which you can create a whole rainbow, they are like a three-lane motorway sweeping us forward and giving access to the presence of God. Of course there are problems with all three of these inner pathways or disciplines. In my case I am too busy to pray, too hard pressed to give and too stuck on fish and chips to fast. This in a nutshell is my three-fold roadblock rather than my three-lane motorway into a deep life-long relationship with God.

It is about developing a spiritual rather than a worldly appetite. How was Jesus able to be the man he was? How could he do the things he did and know the things he knew? And how could he keep on being Jesus day after day?

He could be and do and know because he had such a deep and real inner life in God. In sharing the secrets of almsgiving, of prayer and of fasting he was sharing his inner way of living. For a good fire you need three things, heat, fuel and oxygen. Maybe these three acts or pathways of piety were the three key elements in his inner fire. About each of them he says, do them privately (rather than for show) and your father will reward you.

Lord Jesus
May I follow your teaching and example
Help me to give something away today
Help me to pray for someone today
Help me to go without one thing today
And help me to do it all again in a few days' time.
Amen.

32. Stress Busting

Matthew 6: 24–34

24 "No one can serve two masters; for a slave will either hate the one and love the other, or be devoted to the one and despise the other. You cannot serve God and wealth.

25 "Therefore I tell you, do not worry about your life, what you will eat or what you will drink, or about your body, what you will wear. Is not life more than food, and the body more than clothing? 26 Look at the birds of the air; they neither sow nor reap nor gather into barns, and yet your heavenly Father feeds them. Are you not of more value than they? 27 And can any of you by worrying add a single hour to your span of life? 28 And why do you worry about clothing? Consider the lilies of the field, how they grow; they neither toil nor spin, 29 yet I tell you, even Solomon in all his glory was not clothed like one of these. 30 But if God so clothes the grass of the field, which is alive today and tomorrow is thrown into the oven, will he not much more clothe you—you of little faith? 31 Therefore do not worry, saying, 'What will we eat?' or 'What will we drink?' or 'What will we wear?' 32 For it

is the Gentiles who strive for all these things; and indeed your heavenly Father knows that you need all these things. [33] But strive first for the kingdom of God and his righteousness, and all these things will be given to you as well.

[34] *"So do not worry about tomorrow, for tomorrow will bring worries of its own. Today's trouble is enough for today."*

> 'Money makes the world go round' – Liza Minnelli in *Cabaret*
> 'Money, that's what I want' – The Beatles.
> 'Money, money, money in a rich man's world' – Abba.
> 'Living in a material world, and I am a material girl' – Madonna.
> 'Forget about the price tag' – Jesse J.

Of course everyone needs money. We need food and shelter, clothes and a roof and a certain amount of pleasure and luxury. Jesus understands our need for cash, but he also understands our love for it. It is this, our cash hunger, our money madness, our grubby, all consuming, love denying, and life absorbing gold lust that he sees as our ultimate life and peace despoiler.

So why did Jesus talk so much about money and wealth. He talked about it as a blockage to personal freedom, as something that changes our heart and causes us huge amounts of worry. Why? Because he brilliantly understands the world and you and me, and he wants something better for us. Most of us live and work as if money will make us happy; he turns this cash position upside down and gives us a glimpse of true happiness.

In this section of the Sermon on the Mount, Jesus is not primarily worried about money. He is worried about our worry which he seems to think is caused by our search for money and the things it brings. Now Jesus was never some sort of shallow hippy guru; 'forget about food and clothes and just live on 'flower power' type', but he was a 'let's keep it all in perspective and focus on the main issue' type of teacher. Vicars of course are supposed to be above grubby materialism. Well I am not. I am a vain creature with an appetite for expensive clothes. In particular I like smart shirts, brogue shoes and Levi 501s (I have never worn a pair of Asda jeans in my life). So I can vouch for the accuracy and truthfulness of Jesus' words. His down to earth practical advice is to strive not for the consumer goods of this world, but for the eternal goodness of the Kingdom. Then as we learn to trust in God all the other stuff will fall into place.

Today our big word for modern living is not trust, but stress. The very idea brings many of us out in a rash. All I have to do is hear the word 'stress' and I start stressing. For many of us daily stress has become normal, part of us, often we don't even know it's there. We stress about our kids, our home, our car, job, shopping, – we stress about our stress. It tells us always to be busy and never resting, to always go fast, never slow, to do two things at once, never one.

My wife and I are virtually polar opposites in all this. I am the stressful worrier, she is the peaceful truster. Actually life is never quite as black and white as this.

I have occasional bits of peaceful trusting in my 'stresser-mania' and from time to time she has occasional bits of panic in her 'trust-fest'. We sort of mutually impact and balance each other out.

It looks as if I have simply been put together in a different way from my wife. Whether it's down to childhood experiences or DNA, who knows, but it is the way I have turned out. But I don't want to stay for all my days as a stresser. I want to be and am trying to become a peaceful truster. So here I share with you five little tips, all taken from the Sermon on the Mount.

1. Build up the 'want to be' – 'hunger and thirst for righteousness' – the more you want it the more it will happen.
2. Give some away – 'whenever you give alms' – the more money you give away, the more relaxed you become about it.
3. Say your prayers – 'give us today our daily bread' – praying and trusting go together like 'salt and pepper', bacon and eggs'.
4. Look around you – 'see the lilies, how they grow' – God dresses the world better than we dress ourselves.
5. Pull away from a crazy world – 'for it is the Gentiles' – spend more time with the right sort of people.

> 'Lord you are more precious than silver,
> Lord you are more costly than gold,
> Lord you are more beautiful than diamonds,
> And nothing I desire compares with you.'
> Amen.

33. Big Decisions

Matthew 7: 24–29

> [24] *"Everyone then who hears these words of mine and acts on them will be like a wise man who built his house on rock.* [25] *The rain fell, the floods came, and the winds blew and beat on that house, but it did not fall, because it had been founded on rock.* [26] *And everyone who hears these words of mine and does not act on them will be like a foolish man who built his house on sand.* [27] *The rain fell, and the floods came, and the winds blew and beat against that house, and it fell – and great was its fall!"*
>
> [28] *Now when Jesus had finished saying these things, the crowds were astounded at his teaching,* [29] *for he taught them as one having authority, and not as their scribes.*

September 2001, Big Decision Time. I moved my house, my job, my friendships and family from the comfort zone of Bradford in Yorkshire (which incidentally included the best curry in England) to the completely unknown and slightly intimidating centre of Manchester. A great decision to take when you are a student, but not quite so great when you are a middle-aged vicar.

Every time I preach a sermon I give special thought to my ending. I don't want to just share a few nice spiritual thoughts and then leave them to die away. I want to proclaim Good News of how following Jesus can transform people's lives. Then I want to finish or draw to a climax by challenging my listeners to make decisions, to respond, to act on the word. I want people to change and become somehow different, somehow better, to move them on to a newer, richer place. I do this because this is what Jesus did with the Sermon on the Mount.

After all the guidance and teaching he finally invites them to make big decisions. Decisions that will have major lifestyle implications; that will mean significant changes; and that will run a long way into the future.

Three times he calls for a decision. Firstly he talks about deciding which master we will serve, God or wealth (6:24). Secondly, he invites us to decide which gate and pathway we will take on our journey through life (7:13). Thirdly, he conjures up a simple but straight-to-the-point image of a wise and foolish man.

The wise man builds his home, his daily life, his hopes and dreams on a solid rock. The foolish person builds on sand. Then, being a complete realist, Jesus talks not about *if* difficulties come but rather when they come.

> Poverty
> Cancer
> Drug addiction
> Car accident
> Divorce.

Sometimes the storms come once in a blue moon and sometimes they come one after the other, day after day.

Building our house on Jesus doesn't mean that we are suddenly immune from such things but rather that we are suddenly stronger and not alone in the face of them. It is the life built on obedience, i.e. not just liking but actually obeying him that stands strong.

Decisions come in different sizes. Many years ago I began to find Jesus, or perhaps I should say, he began to find me. Soon after that I made a huge decision, to serve God as my master, to follow the Jesus way and to build my life on the rock. Some people make one big decision, instantly leaping from sand to rock. Others make a series of gradual stepping stone like decisions shuffling from the one to the other. It is not so much about deciding to go to church or to read the Bible. It includes both of these but it is much more. It is a decision to rebuild our life, or to build it anew in a better place.

I love the Madness song 'Our House'. It captures ordinary life, family life, everyone trying to get on together life.

> Father wears his Sunday best
> Mother's tired she needs a rest
> The kids are playing up downstairs
> Sister's sighing in her sleep
> Brother's got a date to keep
> He can't hang around
>
> Our house, in the middle of our street
> Our house, in the middle of our ...

Our house it has a crowd
There's always something happening
And it's usually quite loud
Our mum she's so house-proud
Nothing ever slows her down
And a mess is not allowed.

If you want your house of life to stand up strong, build on the rock.

Lord God
Clarify my mind
That I might see the issues clearly.
Take away distractions
That I might make a strong decision.
Show me the plans... that I might understand.
Lead me to the rock of obedience
That I might build
Amen.

34. Crowds are Crumbly

Matthew 8: 18 – 22

> *18 Now when Jesus saw great crowds around him,
> he gave orders to go over to the other side.
> 19 A scribe then approached and said, Teacher,
> I will follow you wherever you go." 20 And Jesus
> said to him, "Foxes have holes, and birds of the
> air have nests; but the Son of Man has nowhere
> to lay his head." 21 Another of his disciples said
> to him, "Lord, first let me go and bury my father."
> 22 But Jesus said to him, "Follow me, and let the
> dead bury their own dead."*

Manchester United or Macclesfield – the biggest teams
have the biggest crowd. The slickest boy bands, the
greatest painters and the best churches, they all have the
biggest crowds, don't they?

Vicars, preachers, evangelists. We are a bit like politicians
in that we love crowds. Crowds of people listening to us,
responding to us and following our lead. I used to think
that Jesus was the ultimate crowd puller and worker.
I think the idea grew out of all those picture Bible
illustrations and was tattooed into my inner psyche by
my own relative failure to build and convert such crowds.
Crowds speak to us of success; they massage our ego

and establish our sense of importance in the religious pecking order.

How strange then that in the Jesus story crowds are often described quite negatively, seen as being shallow, lacking commitment and easily swayed. Small groups of highly motivated and wanting to learn disciples seem to be what Jesus is really all about if his Kingdom is to be established on Earth.

Straight after the Sermon on the Mount in Matthew 8: 1, we see great crowds 'following' Jesus. Are they following him wherever he goes, learning from him, adopting his teachings etc.? Or are they following him like children chasing after the ice-cream van? In the gospels there are nine big crowd scenes, the people are drawn, Jesus leads, everyone is happy, but in each case the crowd seem to fade away, like the audience after a great concert.

In Matthew 8: 20 Jesus seemed to be looking for a deeply committed, long-term following which involved putting him first.

In contrast to 'rent-a-crowd grand events', some of the best stories of Jesus' impact are about him meeting individuals such as a Roman Centurion (Matt. 8: 5), a possessed demoniac (8: 28) and a tax collector (Matt 9: 9).

Individuals start out as part of a crowd, but at some point they step out of the crowd and make their own personal journey to Jesus. The crowd is like a black hole pulling us in with its, 'think, talk and act like everyone else' gravity field.

L.S. Lowry is one of England's greatest and certainly the most well-known painter of crowds with his pale-faced match stick men and women. What is often unnoticed about his crowds is that hardly anyone touches anyone else; they have all got their own bit of human isolation. Lowry once said, 'all of my people are lonely people.' The perfect way to look at his paintings is whilst listening to *'Sgt Pepper's Lonely Hearts Club Band'*. The iconic Beatles album came out of the same place as Lowry's paintings.

Warm intimacy, deep trust, love and acceptance, these are the gifts of Jesus, but you have to step out of the crowd and come to him if you want to discover this treasure. Crowds look strong, powerful, impressive and world changing. But what really changes the world is not a lot of people with a bit of God inside them but a handful of people with a lot of God in their hearts.

Jesus is looking for people to step out of the crowd, to step out of their comfortable nest or burrow and out from all the ordinary people. Crowds come and go, one minute they are leaping, the next they are leaving. One minute this is the place, he is the one, this is the time and the next day they have found another place, a new celebrity and a better time. But individuals who are willing to step out of the crowd make their own difficult choices, who are swayed not so much by the masses but more by the man, these are the real world-changers. These are the followers of Jesus.

ROBIN GAMBLE

I don't suppose Genesis had Jesus in mind when they wrote this song, but it's great music and it works for me.

> Stay with me,
> My love I hope you'll always be
> Right here by my side if ever I need you
> Oh my love
>
> In your arms,
> I feel so safe and so secure
> Everyday is such a perfect day to spend
> Alone with you
>
> I will follow you will you follow me
> All the days and nights that we know will be
> I will stay with you will you stay with me
> Just one single tear in each passing year.

Lord Jesus
Help me to step out of the crowd of life.
To become a follower of the way, the truth and the life
And a deeply committed part
Of your band of disciples.
Amen.

35. Last of the Twelve

Luke 5: 27 – 32

> [27] *After this he went out and saw a tax collector named Levi, sitting at the tax booth; and he said to him, "Follow me." [28] And he got up, left everything, and followed him.*
>
> [29] *Then Levi gave a great banquet for him in his house; and there was a large crowd of tax collectors and others sitting at the table with them. [30] The Pharisees and their scribes were complaining to his disciples, saying, "Why do you eat and drink with tax collectors and sinners?" [31] Jesus answered, "Those who are well have no need of a physician, but those who are sick; [32] I have come to call not the righteous but sinners to repentance."*

Wandering around Galilee Jesus gained quite a following, not as many as he would have liked, and some were short lived in their following (more of this later). Nevertheless, he attracted a considerable number, probably a few hundred, of both men and women. It seems that most of these remained in their normal village lives, yet still following him. Some perhaps

143

followed him at certain times, there are hints of this in Luke 8: 1 and again in 10: 1. Central to the shifting, changing people movement there were 'The Twelve'. A bit like Robin Hood's Merry Men, these were hand-picked men who seem to have accompanied Jesus permanently on the road. The last of these twelve to be recruited was Levi.

Levi was a tax collector. That means he was basically working for the Romans and squeezing every last penny out of his fellow citizens. So he was despised but very rich. That is why he was able to throw parties, had a house big enough to hold them but could only get other tax collectors and 'sinners' to come as his guests. Levi was the lowest of the low, but one of the loaded of the loaded.

Jesus breaks all taboos, rejects all religious respectability and sees not the outer shell of the tax gatherer but the inner man of Levi. The story makes it look like this was the first encounter but I suspect they had already had previous chats, so that when Jesus offers the big invitation/challenge, 'follow me' Levi was ready.

Here we see a major human turning point. Levi leaves everything of his old life and then follows Jesus into the new. What does your human turning point look like? Have you reached it yet or are you still having preparatory conversations? Have you sensed Jesus reaching out to your inner you and saying, 'follow me'? Have you stood up, left, followed? Or are you just in the process of doing so?

Actually Levi didn't leave everything behind, he still, for a while at least, kept his friends. He invited them round for food and drink and to meet with Jesus. He was already acting like a disciple.

Some time ago, I spoke at a school presentation evening, a great opportunity to share the message with teenagers and parents, most of who wouldn't normally be seen dead in church. A few nights later I had arranged to meet one of the men from our church in the local pub. This wasn't any old pub, it was one of our locals 'with a bit of an image'. As always when I go in this particular pub in a dog collar there was a good deal of head turning and lively banter. Why, because the church has got a reputation for being a bit aloof, religious and distant. After a while a couple of fellas came in, they had been at the school prize-giving as fathers. Suddenly there was an immediate (though rather surprised) connection, there was warmth, relevance and the beginning of a relationship. The Pharisees, then as now, never quite got it. Jesus came to the ordinary people, he was a doctor coming to the needy, a saviour looking for the sinners.

Levi becomes the last of this inner group of followers. Now there are twelve, just like there were twelve tribes in the Old Testament people of God. Now there are twelve initial leaders, Apostles in the New Testament people of God.

Lord Jesus
As I follow you
Where the road leads
Help me to see
The distant horizon.
The place where I might be twelve months from
now
But also the next few steps along the path
Where I can be today
And tomorrow.
Amen.

36. The Central Team

Mark 3: 13–19

¹³ He went up the mountain and called to him those whom he wanted, and they came to him. ¹⁴ And he appointed twelve, whom he also named apostles, to be with him, and to be sent out to proclaim the message, ¹⁵ and to have authority to cast out demons. ¹⁶ So he appointed the twelve: Simon (to whom he gave the name Peter); ¹⁷ James son of Zebedee and John the brother of James (to whom he gave the name Boanerges, that is, Sons of Thunder); ¹⁸ and Andrew, and Philip, and Bartholomew, and Matthew, and Thomas, and James son of Alphaeus, and Thaddaeus, and Simon the Cananaean, ¹⁹ and Judas Iscariot, who betrayed him.

Jesus was quite keen on going up mountains. He did it for his great teachings; for the feeding of the 5,000; for his experience of transfiguration; and for his final sending out of the disciples after his resurrection. Perhaps it was the silence, or the isolation, or the big views but clearly mountain tops were a great place for him to pray and think and meet with God. And here a mountain top is a great place for him to have a very special meeting with the twelve.

I wonder how many people work for Manchester United? Trainers, players, learners, caterers, cleaners and car park attendants, there must be hundreds. They are all reds and they all have a part to play, but they are not all out there kicking the ball on a Saturday afternoon. This is a big moment for Jesus. So much so, that in Luke's account of this story, he spent the whole night in prayer (Lk 6: 12). He is setting up his key team. There will be lots of others involved in the movement; lots of other followers and disciples but these twelve are the core. They will be the first team squad to help him with his work in Galilee, they will follow him on his long march to Jerusalem. More than this however, they will be central to the ongoing mission after his resurrection and ascension. Then they will be called Apostles. They, more than anyone else, will take the Good News message and healing on into history and out to the world.

He is trusting them, depending on them, placing his life and work into their hands, even though one of them is a future traitor. So here are two big questions to think about:

- Why did Jesus entrust so much to so few? Were these few in particular not the right ones? Not quite up to it? What happened when they made mistakes or let him down? Were these few very special, exceptionally gifted or outstandingly talented or were they just very determined, obedient and humble followers of Jesus? And finally am I one of the few in my church, my group or my mission project?
- Is Jesus entrusting anything to me today? Right now, as I read these words, is he somehow

placing a trust in me, even depending, on me? Am I up to it? Am I good enough? Am I talented or faithful? Gifted or obedient? And how does it feel to be called by him?

These days when we look out for and appoint people to key positions of ministry and spiritual leadership we usually look for abilities, talents and gifts. In contrast Jesus seemed to look for faithfulness, followership, obedience and willingness to attempt things for him.

Today's church needs lots of Apostles. Today's church needs them because today's world is fast becoming a spiritual desert where people have lots of material things but precious little eternal joy. Apostles spend time with Jesus, proclaim the message and drive out demons. What would happen in our church today, in your church, if every clergy person, house group leader, youth worker, church warden or elder and many others too all saw themselves as Apostles?

Lord Jesus
As you go up the mountain
Help me to follow.
As you call
Help me to respond.
As you trust
Help me to be worthy.
As you give
Help me to take
That I might be the Apostle that you would have
me be.
Amen.

37. Amazing

Mark 6: 4–6

4 Jesus said to them, "A prophet is not without honour except in his own town, among his relatives and in his own home." 5 He could not do any miracles there, except lay his hands on a few sick people and heal them. 6 He was amazed at their lack of faith.

Luke 7: 2–9

2 There a centurion's servant, whom his master valued highly, was sick and about to die. 3 The centurion heard of Jesus and sent some elders of the Jews to him, asking him to come and heal his servant. 4 When they came to Jesus, they pleaded earnestly with him, "'This man deserves to have you do this, 5 because he loves our nation and has built our synagogue.'" 6 So Jesus went with them.

He was not far from the house when the centurion sent friends to say to him: "Lord, don't trouble yourself, for I do not deserve to have you come under my roof. 7 That is why I did not even consider myself worthy to come to you. But say the word, and my servant will be healed. [8] For I myself am a man under authority, with soldiers under me. I tell this one, 'Go,' and he goes; and that one, 'Come,' and he comes. I say to my servant, 'Do this,' and he does it."

[9] When Jesus heard this, he was amazed at him, and turning to the crowd following him, he said, "I tell you, I have not found such great faith even in Israel."

It takes quite a bit to be not just surprised, but amazed. Amazed, it is a 'Well, I didn't see that one coming!' or 'I would never have believed it!' or a 'That is completely outside my whole way of thinking!' experience. It is even harder to be amazed, to be truly gob smacked, if you are Jesus. A lot of people seem to think that Jesus had all the knowledge, power and insight of God built into his genes and flowing in his blood. In which case it would be impossible to be amazed. On the other hand if Jesus was the Son of God born to be a totally 'one of us' mortal man then amazement becomes a normal human experience. So if your version of Jesus is of a spiritual 'Superman' rather than a human 'Godly Man' then you need to adjust the picture.

There are two places in the Gospels where we read of Jesus being amazed. One is negative and the other a very positive attack of amazement.

His first 'amazing experience' was when he preached the Good News, healed the sick and brought release from possession in his home town of Nazareth. The people who knew him said "No Thanks" and he was amazed at their unbelief in him.

The second 'amazement story' is the big one. A Roman centurion i.e. a high-ranking officer, was willing to humiliate himself by asking a lowly village teacher and healer to heal his servant. Not only that but he doesn't think Jesus need come to his house to do it, just give the order. Jesus was 'amazed', 'blown away', 'made to think again', 'forced to widen his vision' by the man's belief in him. In a world of weariness, routine, greyness and 'things are ok' true amazement can be a beautiful, 'flash in the sky' and uplifting experience and encounter.

Here are a few of my own recent amazement stories.

> I travel around lots of different churches in my work. Many, in fact most, of them are great faith places. However I am sometimes disappointingly amazed when I find a place with little fire, passion and expectancy.

> My wife, Maureen, recently organised and ran a 'Start' group, a sort of little course for people who want to find out about God. I was amazed at her courage and how well it went.

> Two young twenty something men recently came for a meal. They are big night out boys with big gymed up muscles and tattooed bodies. In other words just the sort of people who do not normally come to church. I was

amazed at how hungry they were to find out about Jesus.

My son, Phillip, has a deep, servant like and very committed faith. It is rather hidden away with not a lot of surface froth and emotion. I was amazed when he went on a charismatic holiday convention. I was even more amazed when he phoned up half way through the week to talk to me about how the worship was uplifting and how the Holy Spirit had spoken to him.

Of course the key thing for us to ponder is 'What will amaze Jesus when he looks into our life today?'

Lord Jesus
Help me to see
To live and follow
To trust and accept
That you will be amazed
When you look at me.
Amen.

38. The Dead Rise

Luke 8: 40–42 and 48–56

40 Now when Jesus returned, the crowd welcomed him, for they were all waiting for him. 41 Just then there came a man named Jairus, a leader of the synagogue. He fell at Jesus' feet and begged him to come to his house, 42 for he had an only daughter, about twelve years old, who was dying.

49 While he was still speaking, someone came from the leader's house to say, "Your daughter is dead; do not trouble the teacher any longer." 50 When Jesus heard this, he replied, "Do not fear. Only believe, and she will be saved." 51 When he came to the house, he did not allow anyone to enter with him, except Peter, John, and James, and the child's father and mother. 52 They were all weeping and wailing for her; but he said, "Do not weep; for she is not dead but sleeping." 53 And they laughed at him, knowing that she was dead. 54 But he took her by the hand and called out, 'Child, get up!' 55 Her spirit returned, and she got up at once. Then he directed them to give her something to eat. 56 Her parents were astounded; but he ordered them to tell no one what had happened.

There are three stories in the gospels of Jesus raising the dead. In Luke 7 he interrupts the funeral procession of a boy who has died leaving a poor widowed mother behind. Jesus' heart 'went out to the mother', he touched the coffin and said, 'Young man get up.' In John 11 he is too late for the funeral. His good friend Lazarus is already buried when he arrives on the scene. Once again Jesus' feelings are deeply moved and he calls the dead man to come out of his tomb.

Of the three 'raising the dead' stories this one, concerning Jairus and his 12-year-old daughter is my favourite. I like the fact that Jairus is a ruler of the synagogue. It is good that some of the Jewish religious leaders had a very positive relationship with Jesus. I like the expression 'fell at his feet, pleading with him'. When was the last time I fell at Jesus' feet? I even like the human pathos and tragedy of a loving father losing his 12-year-old daughter.

To us death is the ultimate. Dark, cold, irreversible. It is the ultimate black hole, the inevitable ending, death is a pit, dying is a falling into the pit, being dead is a lying at the bottom of the pit. The Greeks called it Hades, the Jews referred to it as Sheol. We don't call it anything because we haven't really got the confidence or wisdom to talk about it anymore.

> 'Earth to earth
> Ashes to ashes
> Dust to dust'.

Here however, and again in the case of Lazarus, Jesus talks about it as sleeping. This is why we often put RIP (rest in peace) on gravestones. Death is not peaceful it is peace-empty, but a sleep followed by an awakening – that is peaceful.

Years ago I used to do a show called 'The Gospel according to Queen'. I used the song 'Who Wants to Live Forever' to talk about our death being transformed by Jesus' death.

> There's no time for us,
> There's no place for us,
> What is this thing that builds our dreams, yet slips away from us.
>
> Who wants to live forever,
> Who wants to live forever...?
> There's no chance for us,
> It's all decided for us,
> This world has only one sweet moment set aside for us.
>
> But touch my tears with your lips,
> Touch my world with your fingertips,
> And we can have forever,
> And we can love forever.   Queen.

So ask yourself the questions

> How much do you want to live?
> For a while or forever?
> For yourself or for Jesus?
> For now or forever?
> For self or for him?

For a good time or for a long time?
Who wants to live forever?

Lord Jesus
Open my eyes that I might see the light.
Open my heart
That I might feel the hope.
Open my mind
That I might find the faith.
And then touch my tears with your lips.
Amen.

39. The Big Battle

Mark 3: 20–27

> *20 and the crowd came together again, so that they could not even eat. 21 When his family heard it, they went out to restrain him, for people were saying, "He has gone out of his mind." 22 And the scribes who came down from Jerusalem said, "He has Beelzebul, and by the ruler of the demons he casts out demons." 23 And he called them to him, and spoke to them in parables, "How can Satan cast out Satan? 24 If a kingdom is divided against itself, that kingdom cannot stand. 25 And if a house is divided against itself, that house will not be able to stand. 26 And if Satan has risen up against himself and is divided, he cannot stand, but his end has come. 27 But no one can enter a strong man's house and plunder his property without first tying up the strong man; then indeed the house can be plundered.*

Jesus has been on a bit of a retreat, teaching the crowds, gathering disciples and assembling his core team of twelve. Now he is straight back into action.

It is action which completely confuses his family and confronts the religious leaders. 'Who does he think he is?', 'What is he doing?' and 'Where will it all lead to?'

Wherever Jesus is, evil personalised in the name of Satan or the Devil is never far away. He was there in the wilderness temptations, he will be there in Gethsemane at Jesus' arrest, ('but this is your hour, and the power of darkness' Luke 22: 53). Here we see Jesus in open conflict with him.

Jesus was 'casting out demons'. Now you can think of a demon as a sort of fallen angel serving Satan, as the actual touch of Satan himself or simply as a form of impersonal human destructiveness that has got a grip on a person's life. Addiction, obsession or possession, they are all dark and destructive. Jesus' mission is to cast out, to cleanse and to re-claim lives.

The scribes would have seen demons being cast out before, but they had not seen anyone do it like Jesus did it. They had not seen such power, such victory. Moreover, they are the ones from Jerusalem and the Temple. They are the accredited and recognised scribes. Jesus is very different and he is certainly not one of them so they can only assume, he must be with the other side, the dark side.

Jesus is not Darth Vader and makes it crystal clear; he is not Satan's ally but his absolute enemy. He is rising up against, breaking into the house of and setting free the captives of evil.

I once worked with a woman who had been
captive to drink... until Jesus set her free.
I once knew a man still under the shadow of
child abuse.
Two nurses living in a flat filled with frightening
happenings.
A young boy suffering with the psychological
impact of bullying.
A teenage girl self-harming.
A man who was demon possessed.

There was darkness then and there is darkness now.
Jesus liberated them then and he is still doing it.

So the big conflict, light versus darkness, healing versus
destructiveness, Jesus versus Satan, it begins. And in the
background another little battlefield is just opening up.
The scribes against Jesus, the religious power of
Jerusalem against a simple preacher man from Galilee.

I've never really liked the old Victorian hymn, 'Onward
Christian Soldiers'. Partly because it is just so long but
mainly because it's a bit militaristic. But I do think it has
got a point

> 'Onward Christian soldiers,
> Marching as to war,
> With the cross of Jesus
> Going on before.'

Lord Jesus
Help me to be a light in the darkness
A love in the hardness
A gift in the selfishness.
Help me to set people free
When they are bound
By evil.
Amen.

40. Parable of the Sower

Mark 4: 2–9,

2 He began to teach them many things in parables, and in his teaching he said to them: 3 "Listen! A sower went out to sow. 4 And as he sowed, some seed fell on the path, and the birds came and ate it up. 5 Other seed fell on rocky ground, where it did not have much soil, and it sprang up quickly, since it had no depth of soil. 6 And when the sun rose, it was scorched; and since it had no root, it withered away. 7 Other seed fell among thorns, and the thorns grew up and choked it, and it yielded no grain. 8 Other seed fell into good soil and brought forth grain, growing up and increasing and yielding thirty and sixty and a hundredfold." 9 And he said, "Let anyone with ears to hear listen!"

It does not look it but it is another big battle story. Except here the energy is not so much naked evil as shallow complacency, spiritual indifference and the often triviality of busy lives.

Jesus had the amazing knack of wandering around thinking about what he saw and then pulling amazing illustrations or stories out of it all. His Galilean world was a place of villages and fields. That's not the sort of pretty and prosperous countryside that we all love so much. His villages were filled with poverty; his fields were dry and stony. Farming then was part of a desperate struggle to survive. It is in this world that many of his parables were born.

Jesus wants to get across to the people that something new is happening, something is growing. It is the Kingdom. The growing is of God, but it is not simple and straightforward. There are reverses and failures, but the growing is happening. So he pulls out four, 'see that field over there,' type stories or parables.

- The Parable of the Sower (Mk. 4: 2)
- The Parable of the Growing Seed (Mk 4: 26)
- The Parable of the Mustard Seed (Mk 4: 30)
- The Parable of the Wheat and Weeds (Mt 13: 24)

I had been six months in my new parish as vicar. Good things were happening, new people were coming to church, but we had 11,000 people living in our parish and I wanted to get the word out to them. We produced a simple but attractive leaflet introducing ourselves, saying something of God's love and inviting people to come along. Every letterbox in the parish received a copy. I suspect that the vast majority of our leaflets hit the basket like snowflakes falling on warm pavements. Or, if you prefer, like seeds before hungry birds. I suspect that quite a few created a bit of interest, maybe even stirred a few good intentions. People however can be a bit spiritually shallow and anyway busy lives have a way of just crowding out the big issues.

So that is the story of the Sower and the Leaflets.

Not quite, first the lovely Joyce came along. She had been a Sunday school teacher many years earlier but had completely lost contact and the leaflet somehow found its way into her inner 'deep soil'. Then Kate and Jane – young and bubbly and interested. Then Gavin, Kate's husband and Matthew, Jane's partner, who first said he would never come to church, started coming a bit and eventually got baptised.

These days we are more inclined to use Facebook, Instagram and Twitter to scatter our seeds. I think there is a place for both social media and bits of paper. During the Coronavirus lockdown I saw one church with a big banner up simply saying 'We are praying for you'.

We often think Jesus was brilliantly successful at everything and we are not. Here Jesus is saying, 'most of my proclamations, acts of love, healings and feeding came to nothing. Some of my seed was just gobbled up by the birds of everyday living or fell on a shallow soil and couldn't stand the heat. Some started well but were simply squeezed out by what people thought of as more important issues.

But some bore real fruit, new lives, changed lives, eternal lives.'

Lord Jesus
Let the seed of Good News
Sink deep into my heart.

ROBIN GAMBLE

Let the seed of the Kingdom
Stir me to scatter seeds
To my friends and family

Lord Jesus
Help me to grow
Closer to you
And stronger for you
Amen.

41. The Wheat and the Tares

Matthew 13: 24–30

> ²⁴ He put before them another parable: 'The kingdom of heaven may be compared to someone who sowed good seed in his field; ²⁵ but while everybody was asleep, an enemy came and sowed weeds among the wheat, and then went away. ²⁶ So when the plants came up and bore grain, then the weeds appeared as well. ²⁷ And the slaves of the householder came and said to him, "Master, did you not sow good seed in your field? Where, then, did these weeds come from?" ²⁸ He answered, "An enemy has done this." The slaves said to him, "Then do you want us to go and gather them?" ²⁹ But he replied, "No; for in gathering the weeds you would uproot the wheat along with them. ³⁰ Let both of them grow together until the harvest; and at harvest time I will tell the reapers, Collect the weeds first and bind them in bundles to be burned, but gather the wheat into my barn."'

The last of the 'growth of the Kingdom' parables. The Kingdom is growing, nothing can fully stop it. It is organic, alive. 'All living things grow', the first of the great laws of science that we all learnt at school.

The law of life, applies to everything and everywhere in the universe. It applies to God's Kingdom with its strong DNA formed in Heaven. But the devil is back, doing his work and undoing the work of Jesus. I never like focusing too much on the devil and his doings. I have heard too much over the years that was too lurid, too negative and gave him too much influence. He is there however, in Jesus' teachings, in his world, and in ours. Jesus sows his good seed in the daytime, the devil at night. That tells us a lot.

The weeds can entangle, obstruct and spoil the growing Kingdom, but they cannot overcome it. The light has dawned and the darkness cannot fully put it out.

So without being too fearful, we can ask the question. If the Kingdom is growing in us and we are being drawn closer to, beginning to follow and trying to become like Jesus, where are the weeds? What is getting in the way? Who are the people that are obstructing and trying to strangle the good that is growing in us?

Because if Jesus is correct, and he certainly is in my case, then the night time planter will be hard at work.

And if we are trying to become like Jesus, scattering good seeds, growing good things in other people's lives. If we are 'Kingdom farmers' too, then where are the weeds in our work? If we are part of a church, group or movement that is trying to grow the Kingdom, make the world a better place, sharing the Good News with acts of love and words of life then where and what are the weeds?

These are not vague 'if this should happen' thoughts. I am convinced that in this story Jesus is reflecting on his own ministry, on the things that are happening around him and to him and the impact he is having. There was growth, but there were also weeds. It is a bit like the parable of the sower. We would love it all to go well and to grow. Jesus seems to be saying, 'this is how it has been in my mission and ministry, and this is how it will be in yours'.

> Some good, some bad
> Some growth, some dying
> Some success, some failure
> Some rejoicing, some disappointment.

Uncle Tom's Cabin is the ancestor of all great American slave literature. *Roots, Color Purple, Twelve Years a Slave* they all grew out of it. It was written by Harriet Beecher Stowe a dedicated follower of Jesus and opponent of slavery. In the novel she tells the story of 'Honest John Van Trompe'. Honest John refused to attend any church where the minister or pastor supported slavery. These were good Godly men leading good churches but there were too many weeds living amongst the wheat. Every church, group or Kingdom project that I've ever been involved with has always had someone or something spoiling the growth. In fact, in some cases I myself have been the someone.

Do not be defeated by the thin soil, the weeds and night-time spoiler. Keep growing, keep planting, keep tending the shoots.

Great children's literature knows all about the Devil and his attempts to spoil the garden of goodness.

He can be called Sauron, The White Witch, King Rat or Voldemort, but he or she is always the Devil.

> Lord help me
> To be deeply planted.
> To grow straight and strong.
> To be part of your Kingdom field.
> To bear fruit for you.
> Amen.

42. A Centurion's Servant

Matthew. 8: 5–13

⁵ When he entered Capernaum, a centurion came to him, appealing to him ⁶ and saying, "Lord, my servant is lying at home paralyzed, in terrible distress." ⁷ And he said to him, "I will come and cure him." ⁸ The centurion answered, "Lord, I am not worthy to have you come under my roof; but only speak the word, and my servant will be healed. ⁹ For I also am a man under authority, with soldiers under me; and I say to one, 'Go,' and he goes, and to another, 'Come,' and he comes, and to my slave, 'Do this,' and the slave does it." ¹⁰ When Jesus heard him, he was amazed and said to those who followed him, "Truly I tell you, in no one in Israel have I found such faith. ¹¹ I tell you, many will come from east and west and will eat with Abraham and Isaac and Jacob in the kingdom of heaven, ¹² while the heirs of the kingdom will be thrown into the outer darkness, where there will be weeping and gnashing of teeth." ¹³ And to the centurion Jesus said, "Go; let it be done for you according to your faith." And the servant was healed in that hour.

I know we have touched on this story once when we thought about what is 'truly amazing'. I want to revisit it again here to look at the important issue of Jesus' power and Roman power.

Some people think that in a fairly straightforward sort of way Jesus came for the poor and especially for the Jews and, of course, he did. Sometimes however, it is just when you think that you have got him sorted, that he suddenly does something completely different. Here he is doing a beautiful act of healing for an unJewish, very Gentile Roman, and not even a poor struggling one, but for a rich and powerful centurion.

Romans play an interesting part in the Jesus story. It was a Roman emperor who called for the registration which led to Jesus' birth in Bethlehem. Jesus advised the Jews to pay their taxes to Rome. It would be the Romans who would eventually fulfil Jesus prophecy of the destruction of the Temple (Luke 21: 5). A Roman governor, Pilate, would oversee his death, and a second centurion was present at the cross declaring 'Truly this man was God's son' (Matt. 27: 54).

So how does Roman power compare to Jesus' power and who is the truly powerful one in this story?

This first centurion however was clearly exceptional. The fact that he came to Jesus, a peasant preacher and asked for help meant that he risked humiliation. His looking up to Jesus and calling him 'Lord' would have been unheard of. His sense of unworthiness at the idea of Jesus coming into his house was a reversal of the usual Jew/Roman relationship. More than anything else, however, it was his understanding of true spiritual authority and power and his clear vision of who Jesus was and what he could do, that is rather breath-taking.

In my own ministry I have rarely come across such a humble, trusting and obedient person and that is amongst the Christians. The whole point about this story is that he is not a Christian; he is not a Jew; he is a Roman.

As soon as we put Jesus in a box or think we understand him we find him being and doing something outside the box. Jesus is supposed to be in the Jewish/Christian box. Suddenly he is in the 'aggressive Roman box'. He is supposed to have a caring relationship with those who care about him but in this story he cares deeply about someone who has never met him before. Rome and Jesus are supposed to be opposites but here they meet and become friends. Faith, friendship with Jesus and receiving his blessing is open to everyone and anyone. There is no box.

Because I am a vicar, and because I talk a lot about God and Jesus I often provoke the comment, 'I wish I had your faith' (if only they knew the truth) to which my reply is always, 'Well you can't have my faith, but you can have your own.' Anyone, everyone, sinner, failure, outsider, outcast, you can be like the Centurion.

So let it be for you according to your faith.

There is an ancient Christian hymn that is also a deep prayer/hunger/desire for all of us who would like to amaze Jesus.

> God be in my head
> And in my understanding.
> God be in mine eyes
> And in my looking.
> God be in my mouth
> And in my speaking.
> God be in my heart
> And in my thinking.
> God be at mine end
> And at my departing.
> Amen.

43. The Storm Calmer

Mark 4: 35–41

35 That day when evening came, he said to his disciples, "Let us go over to the other side." 36 Leaving the crowd behind, they took him along, just as he was, in the boat. There were also other boats with him. 37 A furious squall came up, and the waves broke over the boat, so that it was nearly swamped. 38 Jesus was in the stern, sleeping on a cushion. The disciples woke him and said to him, "Teacher, don't you care if we drown?"

39 He got up, rebuked the wind and said to the waves, "Quiet! Be still!" Then the wind died down and it was completely calm.

40 He said to his disciples, "Why are you so afraid? Do you still have no faith?"

41 They were terrified and asked each other, "Who is this? Even the wind and the waves obey him!"

Where would be the stormiest place in the world to live and sail? How about Albert Square, the home of *EastEnders*? There, love of money, fear, revenge, adultery, anger all washed down with plenty of booze make it a stormy little sea. How about inside my head or heart? It is an inland 'in-the-skull' sea where chronic insecurities, fear of impending failure, stress-filled relationships and a proven talent for saying the wrong thing at the wrong time all make for difficult sailing.

How about the Sea of Galilee? Blue, peaceful and sun kissed for most of the time, but with a reputation for sudden winds and rollers that can rock any boat.

Many people think that when they get involved with Jesus life will suddenly be peaceful, stress free and becomingly calm. After all, he is the 'King of Peace' and imparted his gift of peace to the disciples after his resurrection (John 20: 19). It is a complete misconception. There is no calmer than calm place. The Sea of Tranquillity exists on the face of the moon not the earth. A problem or difficulty in life is when something goes wrong inside the boat. A storm in life is when something goes wrong in the sea and the boat is tossed around like a tiny bit of flotsam. We have all had difficulties in our boats, things that we can solve or live with but a storm that is completely beyond our control that is something else.

This story is all about a real storm, in which people are really frightened. Before we get to the storm however, we are given the golden key: 'And when he got into the boat'. Before the gale gets up and before the waves get down he gets into the boat.

What a contrasting picture. The boat is in danger of being swamped and sinking. Jesus is asleep. The disciples are panicking; Jesus is resting.

The disciples are an interesting bunch. I do not just mean in their sailing across the lake I mean in their sailing towards and then onwards with Jesus. They still do not know fully who he is. They have seen him healing people and received great teaching at his feet. They have felt the pull of his personal call, but they haven't truly found it yet. Who is he? A rabbi? A great rabbi? Or perhaps more than that? Jesus hasn't told them, maybe he is still exploring 'who am I really Lord?' a little bit himself.

'So what sort of man is this, that even the wind and waves obey him'? Something is happening, it is utterly unique in human history. For the first and last time ever a human being has appeared who has command over the elements.

> We are sailing, we are sailing,
> Home again
> 'Cross the sea.
> We are sailing,
> Stormy water.
> To be near you,
> To be free.

We can sail through this life with its calm spells and storms alone. Or we can do it all with him sitting in our boat. What about your life today? Calm sea or storm

tossed? Sunshine or dark clouds? Jesus on the inside or
left behind on the quayside?

> Lord Jesus
> There is a storm brewing
> In and around my life.
> I know that you are in my boat
> But it feels like you are asleep.
> Help me to trust in you
> As you arise
> And steer me through the waves and weather.
> Amen.

44. Feeding the Five Thousand

Mark 6: 30–44

³⁰ *The apostles gathered around Jesus and reported to him all they had done and taught.* ³¹ *Then, because so many people were coming and going that they did not even have a chance to eat, he said to them, "Come with me by yourselves to a quiet place and get some rest."*

³² *So they went away by themselves in a boat to a solitary place.* ³³ *But many who saw them leaving recognized them and ran on foot from all the towns and got there ahead of them.* ³⁴ *When Jesus landed and saw a large crowd, he had compassion on them, because they were like sheep without a shepherd. So he began teaching them many things.*

³⁵ *By this time it was late in the day, so his disciples came to him. "This is a remote place," they said, "and it's already very late.* ³⁶ *Send the people away so that they can go to the surrounding countryside and villages and buy themselves something to eat."'*

³⁷ *But he answered, "You give them something to eat."*

They said to him, "That would take more than half a year's wages! Are we to go and spend that much on bread and give it to them to eat?"

[38] *"How many loaves do you have?" he asked. "Go and see."*

When they found out, they said, "Five – and two fish."

[39] *Then Jesus directed them to have all the people sit down in groups on the green grass.* [40] *So they sat down in groups of hundreds and fifties.* [41] *Taking the five loaves and the two fish and looking up to heaven, he gave thanks and broke the loaves. Then he gave them to his disciples to distribute to the people. He also divided the two fish among them all.* [42] *They all ate and were satisfied,* [43] *and the disciples picked up twelve basketfuls of broken pieces of bread and fish.* [44] *The number of the men who had eaten was five thousand.*

There are a few great miracle stories in the life of Jesus. Calming the storm, walking on water and the great feasts of the 5,000 and 4,000. Healing the sick and driving out demons is one thing but these sort of miracles take the whole 'Who is he and what could he achieve?' questions on to a higher place. There is one, even greater miracle still to come which will raise the bar even higher, and that is the resurrection.

> Is it worth the waiting for?
> If we live till eighty-four

All we ever get is gru...el.
Every day we say our prayer
Will they change the bill of fare?
Still we get the same old gru...el!
There's not a crust, nor a crumb can we find,
Can we beg, can we borrow or cadge?
But there is nothing to stop us from getting a thrill
When we all close our eyes and imag...ine

Food, glorious food.

Everybody loves this song from *'Oliver'*. My favourite bit is the fourth line.

Meals, along with all the friendship, hospitality, conversation and relationship building that go with them are very important in the Jesus story. In today's church we love meetings, usually with agendas, that is how we get things done, how we do our business. For Jesus, however, the business was people, the meeting was usually a sit down to eat and drink and the agenda 'So how can God help you with your life'. Jesus liked meetings where there was a real meeting (people meeting people and people meeting God).

A few years ago I designed a series of evangelistic weekends based around what I thought of as the 'four great Jesus feasts':

- The Levi Party – a gathering in his own home, at which his friends could meet Jesus.
- The Last Supper – bread and wine becoming his body and blood and open to everyone.

- The Resurrection Breakfast – a Sunday morning service which literally incorporated breakfast and an opportunity to experience the 'alive again' Jesus.
- The Feeding of the 5,000 – on the weekend this would usually take the form of a great day out or barbeque etc., at which a special treat was brought forward as a sort of inspirational gift to all.

In those days when I talked about the feeding of the 5,000 I dwelt on the crowd who were drawn to Jesus looking for teaching, for his special touch. Then I would talk about Jesus being 'the bread of life' and meeting our hunger for life.

In recent years however, looking at my own ministry and that of other people in our church, many of whom are new Christians, I have flicked over to John's story of the feeding. There is a boy here who has five barley loaves and two fish, John 6:19. He is a generous boy or perhaps it is meeting Jesus that brings out the generosity in him. Mixing with Jesus' followers over many years I have always found that there are some generous followers, some very un-generous ones and then there are people like me. I am by nature not that generous but as I spend time with Jesus he increases my willingness and joyfulness in giving. I am convinced that today Jesus still needs people like that young boy to give up their own meal so that others may be fed.

Frankly I find it easy to become resentful at how much time, love, prayer and money I give to the church or others. Then I get excited when I think of myself as a small boy offering Jesus my bit of food for him to use in his big feeding.

Lord Jesus
I offer my bread
To you the Bread of Life.
I offer my fish
To the great Fisher of Men.
May you bless my offered gift
That others might be blessed.
Amen.

45. Walking on the Water

Mark 6: 45–51

45 Immediately Jesus made his disciples get into the boat and go on ahead of him to Bethsaida, while he dismissed the crowd. 46 After leaving them, he went up on a mountainside to pray.

47 Later that night, the boat was in the middle of the lake, and he was alone on land. 48 He saw the disciples straining at the oars, because the wind was against them. Shortly before dawn he went out to them, walking on the lake. He was about to pass by them, 49 but when they saw him walking on the lake, they thought he was a ghost. They cried out, 50 because they all saw him and were terrified.

Immediately he spoke to them and said, "Take courage! It is I. Don't be afraid." 51 Then he climbed into the boat with them, and the wind died down. They were completely amazed,

'One small step for man,
One giant leap for mankind.'

These are the words spoken on that epic day when Neil Armstrong stepped on to the surface of the moon. Perhaps we should see Jesus stepping onto the surface of the lake as a similar sort of small step/giant leap moment. The great thing about Neil Armstrong was that in his humility he saw himself as a representative of humankind. It was thought at the time that there would be lots more 'small steps' onto the moon's surface, that there would be more 'small steps' on to other planets and that the benefit for humankind would be great. In fact, there have been only a tiny handful of moonwalkers, no one has yet reached any other planet and the benefits for the rest of us are questionable to say the least.

The big difference between Armstrong's moonwalk and Jesus' water walk is that Jesus is not doing this as a representative of humankind. Neither has he needed lots of other people to make it possible. It was all his own achievement and he is representing not so much humanity as something very different, deeper, more mysterious to the point that the disciples thought he was a ghost and were rather fearful of him.

The thing about Jesus is that there is more than one thing. My favourite side of him is his humanity. I love the fact that he is made out of ordinary human flesh, had a normal human childhood shared with brothers and sisters, shares in human temptations, hungers and struggles. All this points to the idea that he fully understands me. The other thing about Jesus, the other worldly, mysterious, impossible to understand, slightly scary stuff is what I don't relate to that well. Yet this is the side, or the aspect, of Jesus that we see in this story. Jesus comes from another place, is a creature of eternity, the living word and the son of God and every now and again he shows us that.

We all love sea stories. From Jonah to Robinson Crusoe, from Moby Dick to Hornblower. In all these epic tales there is always an extra, unknowable and threatening character and that is the sea itself. My favourite bit of the story is when 'he saw'. The disciples are out on the lake, Jesus needs to be alone and he is up the mountain at night. Despite the distance and the darkness, 'he saw'. He has gone up the mountain prayerfully to be with God the Father but he is still aware of his disciples. This is so important to me because I keep straining at the oars and because I often find myself thinking that he is stuck up a mountain back in Heaven and having a great time with his Father. My cry in these moments is, 'Where are you Jesus when I need you?'

And yet, and yet he sees me, he leaves the mountain and he walks on the water towards me. At the moment I am straining at two oars. One is my job, struggling to help churches grow and individuals come to faith is an exciting but often disappointing and lonely task. My second oar is my family, or to be precise, my daughter. My daughter is called Zoe, which means life, but actually because of her multiple disabilities she has a very small life.

I am straining, i.e. I am struggling, finding it hard work, rather resenting and yet trying to keep going. He sees me, walks on the water to me and says 'Take courage! It is I. Don't be afraid' and then he gets into my boat, in a way that no-one else ever gets into it.

So what are you straining at today?

And can you see him seeing you?

> Lord Jesus
> I am straining at the oars,
> Life is hard work
> I am spiritually tired
> And my arms ache.
> Can you see me?
> Walk towards me
> And climb into my boat.
> Amen.

46. Son of Man

Mark 8: 31–33

31 Then he began to teach them that the Son of Man must undergo great suffering, and be rejected by the elders, the chief priests, and the scribes, and be killed, and after three days rise again. 32 He said all this quite openly. And Peter took him aside and began to rebuke him. 33 But turning and looking at his disciples, he rebuked Peter and said, "Get behind me, Satan! For you are setting your mind not on divine things but on human things."

> Lord
> Messiah
> Son of God
> Word
> Christ
> Saviour.

They are all titles, names, labels for the most impossible to label man who ever lived. Jesus was a bit like a diamond, many sided, each title is focussed on one of its faces or sides. Jesus' own favourite way of naming or describing himself however was the title 'Son of Man'.

ROBIN GAMBLE

Names that we choose for ourselves, as opposed to the ones chosen by our parents, have a particular significance because they describe how we feel about ourselves. So when Jesus keeps referring to himself as Son of Man he is giving us a big clue into his own self-identity.

Theologians have picked out masses of possible meanings for the 'Son of Man' name. Basically there are two big Old Testament ideas behind it. The first one comes from Daniel 7: 13 where the 'Son of Man' comes 'riding on the clouds' as a sort of cosmic, messianic saviour. His Kingdom will be established as a thing of glory that will last for ever. This is a spectacular vision of a glorious, one and only one, super-hero.

> *13 I saw in the night visions, and, behold, one like the Son of man came with the clouds of heaven, and came to the Ancient of days, and they brought him near before him.*

The second 'big idea' is the exact opposite and comes from Psalm 8: 4.

> *4'What are human being that you are mindful of them,*
> *The Son of Man that you care for them.*

Here 'Son of Man' refers to the whole of humanity, ordinary 'Joe Public', 'Mr Average'.

So when Jesus calls himself 'Son of Man' he seems to be saying:

- I am the long-awaited saviour.
- I am one of you, just another human, fleshy, homo sapiens.

The two ideas seem to contradict each other. How can he be utterly unique and at the same time completely typical? How can he be riding on the clouds of Heaven whilst walking on the dust of the earth?

Somehow Jesus of Nazareth, Son of Man combined the glory of divinity with the body odour of humanity. The one who came to save us was at the same time 'one of us'. The people's saviour.

Today's cinema goers are very familiar with the idea of cosmic superheroes. We love Superman with his superhero powers and Batman with his superhero technology. Jesus the Son of Man was more of a super-sacrifice than a superhero. He was an ordinary man, his only power or gadgetry was in his self-offering; his great love for the poor and needy; his super be-friending of the rejected and his super awareness of the needs of children and women.

How can one person be both 'superman' and 'ordinary man' all at the same time? The answer is Jesus.

> Son of Man
> Everyman
> Ordinary man
> God's man
> Spirit man

Sacrifice man
Just like you and me man.
Behold the Man.

'The Son of Man came to seek out and to save the lost'
(Luke 19: 10).

Jesus
Son of Man
May you see me
And understand me
In your humanity
And also see me
And understand
What I can be
In your love for me.
Amen.

47. The Kingdom

Luke 11: 1–4

¹He was praying in a certain place, and after he had finished, one of his disciples said to him, "Lord, teach us to pray, as John taught his disciples." ² He said to them, "When you pray, say:

Father, hallowed be your name.
Your kingdom come.
³ Give us each day our daily bread.
⁴ And forgive us our sins,
for we ourselves forgive everyone indebted to us.
And do not bring us to the time of trial."

Most great orators or public speakers have a 'big phrase'. They are memorable 'pictures in words' that capture everything they are about. So Churchill kept talking about 'Victory', Margaret Thatcher banged on about 'No turning back' and Martin Luther King had 'A dream'.

Jesus' big picture phrase was the Kingdom. It could be either 'Kingdom of God' or 'Kingdom of Heaven', but it was always 'Kingdom'. He used it in his parables about wheat and fields to talk about the impact of his mission; he used it when looking forward to his resurrection and second coming; he used it to describe the impact of his healings and exorcisms; and here he uses the Kingdom idea as the place to begin in our prayers.

Everyone listening to all of Jesus' kingdom talk would have clicked with it straightaway, because they all knew about kings. Everybody had a king. The king demanded constant obedience, took everyone's money in huge tax demands and ruled over the whole town, village, and valley – the whole domain of a person's life. The king was often hard, unforgiving, cruel, greedy and demanding.

The king that Jesus talked about was the exact opposite of all of this. His was a king who was very forgiving; who healed and set people free, 'as I cast out demons, then the Kingdom of God has come to you' (Luke 11: 20); who invited his followers to sit down and eat and drink with him, 'at my table in my Kingdom' (Luke 22: 30). This is why Christians are always singing or worshipping the King –

> 'Reign in Me'
> 'The Splendour of the King'
> 'The King of Love My Shepherd'.

Perhaps the biggest difference of all is that while the kings of this earth impose or force their power and rule onto us, the divine King invites us to accept his rule.

Now I quite like the idea of God being my helper, my guide, my saviour. But I like to be my own king. I like to rule over my money, my lifestyle, my family, my time.

I like to be in charge of my life because it is all mine. So to make God my king, to hand it over to him, let him make the decisions and me obey him... 'Dodgy'.

When I pray 'Your Kingdom come' I am praying for something to happen in the world, I am praying for something to develop amongst all his people in the church but more than anything I am praying that he might be King of my life.

Why don't you stop right now and think of the next few days of your life stretching out in front of you. Work, faith, money, relaxation, friendships, they are all there, and then to pray

> **Dear Lord Jesus**
> **Your Kingdom come**
> **My life become your place**
> **Come into what I am doing**
> **Become my King.**
> **And let me be your servant.**
> **Amen.**

48. A Suffering Woman

Mark 5: 24–34

²⁴ *And a large crowd followed him and pressed in on him.* ²⁵ *Now there was a woman who had been suffering from haemorrhages for twelve years.* ²⁶ *She had endured much under many physicians, and had spent all that she had; and she was no better, but rather grew worse.* ²⁷ *She had heard about Jesus, and came up behind him in the crowd and touched his cloak,* ²⁸ *for she said, "If I but touch his clothes, I will be made well."* ²⁹ *Immediately her haemorrhage stopped; and she felt in her body that she was healed of her disease.* ³⁰ *Immediately aware that power had gone forth from him, Jesus turned about in the crowd and said, "Who touched my clothes?"* ³¹ *And his disciples said to him, "You see the crowd pressing in on you; how can you say, 'Who touched me?'"* ³² *He looked all round to see who had done it.* ³³ *But the woman, knowing what had happened to her, came in fear and trembling, fell down before him, and told him the whole truth.* ³⁴ *He said to her, "Daughter, your faith has made you well; go in peace, and be healed of your disease."*

In Jesus' world women were second class citizens. In Jesus' Jewish religion the women who bled were unclean third-class citizens. For a young rabbi trying to establish a position in the public eye this scenario has got flashing warning lights all over it. Jesus, however, was never too worried about his own position and reputation. His concern was for others, their plight and situation.

Throughout his ministry we see Jesus caring for, mixing with, touching and being touched by women. He was breathtakingly enlightened and inclusive. 'Ahead of his time' hardly does justice to his embracing, respecting and accepting of women. We live in an age when women right across the world are calling out for leading men in politics, business, education and the professions to show the sort of attitudes that Jesus displayed 2,000 years ago. The feminist movement should make him their Patron Saint.

Back to the story and to the plight of a desperate woman. She is at the end of her struggles; she has trusted in doctors, spent all her money. She has nowhere else to go and no-one else to go to. She is a desperate searcher, needing to find something. Like so many desperate people she is hidden in the world. She pushes herself to the front and silently reaches out a nervous hand. She had heard about Jesus, more than that she had some sort of faith in him.

Some years ago I led a series of 'Mission Weekends', where I would turn up at a church with a small team.

There would be a series of meetings, big and small, and one or two special services at which we would present the contemporary reality of Jesus and invite people to follow him. It soon became clear that the most successful of these gatherings was always the women's night. Loud music, big fun, great food and drink, lots of conversation and laughter. Women are always better than men at throwing a party! During the evening I would interview a couple of Christian women about the place of Jesus in their lives. Then I would give a short punchy talk about the 'men in your life', husbands, sons, brothers, fathers. These were usually men that the women loved and valued but by whom they had often felt let down. I would then invite them to make Jesus the main man in their life, the one man who would never let them down.

I used to finish with pictures of women and men and Jesus, all to the great Roberta Flack song, 'I Heard He Sang a Good Song'.

> I heard he had a good song,
> I heard he had a style
> And so I came to see him
> To listen for a while
> And there he was this young boy
> A stranger to my eyes.
> Strumming my pain with his fingers
> Singing my life with his words.
> Killing me softly with his song.

There were often tears, prayers and ministry to follow.

This just happens to be a story about women reaching out to Jesus. Whether you are male or female why don't you make him the main man in your life?

> Lord Jesus
> I am reaching out
> Reading your story
> Hearing your song
> Feeling your fingers
> I want to find you
>   to follow you
>   to become like you
> Amen.

49. An Adulterous Woman

John 8: 3–11

3 The scribes and the Pharisees brought a woman who had been caught in adultery; and making her stand before all of them, 4 they said to him, "Teacher, this woman was caught in the very act of committing adultery. 5 Now in the law Moses commanded us to stone such women. Now what do you say?" 6 They said this to test him, so that they might have some charge to bring against him. Jesus bent down and wrote with his finger on the ground. 7 When they kept on questioning him, he straightened up and said to them, "Let anyone among you who is without sin be the first to throw a stone at her." 8 And once again he bent down and wrote on the ground. 9 When they heard it, they went away, one by one, beginning with the elders; and Jesus was left alone with the woman standing before him. 10 Jesus straightened up and said to her, "Woman, where are they? Has no one condemned you?" 11 She said, "No one, sir." And Jesus said, "Neither do I condemn you. Go your way, and from now on do not sin again."

Adultery is a bad thing, a sign of lives gone wrong. Sometimes it represents a genuine search for love in a loveless marriage, for real fire in a grate that has stood cold for years. Often it is a selfish desire for extra pleasure. It causes deep and lasting pain and can completely wreck a life. It always leaves someone, be they a wife, husband or child, filled with deep regrets. If this woman is adulterous then there is pain, breaking of trust and guilt all over the place.

Yet there is something far worse than adultery here. Bullying a vulnerable person, and they always are vulnerable, is a terrible thing. I used to be a bully and I still look back with shame at the brutal pain I caused. This is a story of powerful men colluding with religion to bully and use a vulnerable woman. She seems to be nothing to them, a sinner, someone who has to be punished. Why is it that this dark cocktail of powerful men and religion has produced such a hard time for women over so many years? Even today we are still struggling with it.

The Christine Keeler story, as told in the movie *'Scandal'* and then rehashed in a TV series is about a couple of young, attractive and very sexy women. They get involved with a bunch of rich, powerful and older establishment men. When the dirty washing starts to come out the men draw close together, the establishment supports them and guess who gets sent to prison?

Jesus, of course, ignores all the usual conventions and expectations. Frankly I find this story breathtaking in the way Jesus takes everyone by surprise. He is far more than an 'outside the box thinker', he is an 'outside the box liver and carer'. He is not fearful of the power of the Pharisees and he doesn't seem to be too shocked by the woman's adultery either. He sees the woman not so much as a sinner, more as a sinned against. He utters three wisdom and compassion loaded statements:

> 'Let anyone who is without sin…'
> 'Neither do I condemn you'
> 'Do not sin again'.

The final one, lest we forget, takes us back to where we started. She was an adulterous woman; she was caught in the act. Jesus wants her to start again and to sin no more. This story has gone down as one of the great short stories of world literature.

> Wisdom and perception
> Compassion and understanding
> Fearlessness and truth
> Softness and strength
> Freedom and forgiveness.

No wonder I came searching for Jesus all those years ago. No wonder I made myself follow him. No wonder I am trying today to be like him. Where else could I find someone like him?

Where have you got to in your search for the deep reality of Jesus?

Lord Jesus
Who am I judging today?
Who am I pointing fingers at?
Who am I looking down on?
May you touch my heart
With empathy, understanding and sensitivity.
Amen.

50. Wonderful Women

Luke 8: 1–3

^{1} Soon afterwards he went on through cities and villages, proclaiming and bringing the good news of the kingdom of God. The twelve were with him, ^{2} as well as some women who had been cured of evil spirits and infirmities: Mary, called Magdalene, from whom seven demons had gone out, ^{3} and Joanna, the wife of Herod's steward Chuza, and Susanna, and many others, who provided for them out of their resources.

I have been an ordained clergyman in the Church of England for over 40 years. For most of that long time almost all my bosses, all the people wielding the power, making the key decisions and setting the agenda have been men. (Thank God that at last things are changing). Everywhere I have worked however, I have always felt that most of the servants, the givers, the deep and sympathetic understanders have been women. This short little passage was invisible to me for many years, when I finally discovered it, it was a revelation.

In a Jewish, village based, conservative culture of 2000 years ago the men were always the most important, the decision-makers, the most prominent. In this story of

Jesus and his followers the women look to be a lot more involved and integrated than I had ever been led to expect. Theirs was an ancient world with strong male and female boundaries. Jesus' band of men and women followers was fully pushing at these boundaries and establishing a new way of operating.

Women played a key role in the life of Jesus. Here they are part of his 'Merry Men' and providing out of their resources. Women were the last people at the cross and the first at the resurrection.

These women were from a range of backgrounds. Some appear to be quite rich and influential; others have come out of hopeless lostness and possession. The common unity factor is Jesus. They are drawn to him, they have been touched by him, now they want to follow and provide for him. They are sharing in his mission. These are women who have received the life changing impact of Jesus, but they are not content to just receive and hold on to that impact. They want it to flow through them and out to others. They are healed healers, missioned missionaries, receivers who became givers.

Gladys Aylward was a lesser-known missionary in the 1930s. As a working class woman she had little education. So when God called her to go to China the missionary society rejected her because of her lack of learning. Refusing to be 'put down' she worked as a servant and saved up the money to travel out to China by herself. Once there she managed to establish herself in a remote mountain city. The locals first treated her as a 'foreign devil' but her constancy of loving care for them changed their hearts towards her. She spent over twenty years on the mission field, leading people to Christ, caring for women and children. She never had official approval simply the call of Jesus.

I once knew a woman like this. She was an ordinary sort of church member in an ordinary sort of church in an ordinary sort of North of England town. One day she went off to university. There she met a band of young passionate Christians. They had all had powerful experiences of Jesus and they passed it on to her. Soon she was part of the travelling band. When she came home for holidays she was different, sort of 'Jesus alive'. She gave time, money and passion as she shared her 'Jesus aliveness' with others. Each year she would go with other students on great travelling missions. Sharing, meeting, communicating, moving on. After university she got a job teaching in a college and once she was settled in she invited some of her students to form a small Christian group.

I was so impressed by this woman and the change I had seen in her. She was on a mission with Jesus, part of the team. In fact I was so impressed I joined the team, embraced the mission and much later married the woman.

> Lord Jesus
> Your mission has touched my life.
> Set me free, led me forward.
> May I be part of your mission band
> Men and women together
> Bringing new life to the world.
> Amen.

51. Disciples on Mission

Matthew 10: 5–14

> *⁵ These twelve Jesus sent out with the following instructions: "Go nowhere among the Gentiles, and enter no town of the Samaritans, ⁶ but go rather to the lost sheep of the house of Israel. ⁷ As you go, proclaim the good news, 'The kingdom of heaven has come near.' ⁸ Cure the sick, raise the dead, cleanse the lepers, cast out demons. You received without payment; give without payment. ⁹ Take no gold, or silver, or copper in your belts, ¹⁰ no bag for your journey, or two tunics, or sandals, or a staff; for labourers deserve their food. ¹¹ Whatever town or village you enter, find out who in it is worthy, and stay there until you leave. ¹² As you enter the house, greet it. ¹³ If the house is worthy, let your peace come upon it; but if it is not worthy, let your peace return to you. ¹⁴ If anyone will not welcome you or listen to your words, shake off the dust from your feet as you leave that house or town."*

If you have got the impression so far that Jesus was continually on the move, village to town, town to city, teaching and proclaiming, healing and driving out demons, then you have got the right impression. Jesus was a sent man. Sent from Heaven to Earth, from God to lost people. He was a missionary man and his mission was to seek and to save the lost (Luke 19: 10).

When we think of Jesus and Christianity today we tend to link it straightaway with the idea of church. Whether we think of church as a building, people, a series of services and meetings or all three we still envisage something which is stationary, standing still. The church is there in a certain place, it might do a little bit of moving around occasionally but then it is back to the routine, back to the building, back to the same bunch of people. Worship and prayer, buildings and finance, meetings and fellowship. Our shared experience during the Covid 19 pandemic has loosened up and made more flexible our experience of church but still everything seems to be more pressing than sharing the good news.

The problem here is that we are often putting the cart before the horse. For Jesus the key thing was the driving, powerful and fully alive missionary movement. The churches or little village-based communities of believers came along after the mission. We have got it the wrong way around, as one great theologian once said we have got 'a church that has a mission, we should have a mission that has got a church'.

Jesus is on a mission, sent from God to rescue his lost children. Jesus gathers a handful of disciples. Disciples are learners and followers. If they are going to follow the great missionary Jesus they will have to become missionaries themselves. Jesus is setting up a movement not an institution. If they are going to be his disciples they will have to keep moving.

Here the disciples are not so much students as apprentices. A good apprentice does three things. First, they watch the craftsman do the job. Second, they learn to help the craftsman. Third, they do the job themselves with the craftsman watching.

As the Father sent the Son, so the Son sends his followers to all the towns and villages, so that none are missed. Even more challenging when they reach a village they are to go to each individual house. Now here is a question, in fact a series of questions: -

- What would happen to this country if the Christians could re-capture this sense of missionary movement?
- What would happen to your church if it went on a mission to its local neighbourhood?
- What would happen to you if you became a missionary follower?

I recently contacted a young man I knew some time ago. We met for a coffee and when I invited him to a Christian enquirers group I was amazed that he straightaway said yes. In contrast I have spent years patiently trying to be a mission person to a member of my family. It has not really happened yet but I am still in there.

The Jesus missionaries proclaim the good news, cure the sick and cast out demons. So here is the final and biggest question; thinking of your family, your work colleagues and friends, which of these do you think Jesus might be sending you to as his personal missionary?

> Lord Jesus
> You were sent by your father to our world,
> May you send me to my world.
> Show me who to go to,
> Encourage me as I go.
> Equip me to minister to them when I arrive,
> That your mission might be my mission.
> Amen.

52. Teaching the Disciples

Matthew 13: 36 – 50

³⁶ *Then he left the crowds and went into the house. And his disciples approached him, saying, "Explain to us the parable of the weeds of the field."* ³⁷ *He answered, "The one who sows the good seed is the Son of Man;* ³⁸ *the field is the world, and the good seed are the children of the kingdom; the weeds are the children of the evil one,* ³⁹ *and the enemy who sowed them is the devil; the harvest is the end of the age, and the reapers are angels.* ⁴⁰ *Just as the weeds are collected and burned up with fire, so will it be at the end of the age.* ⁴¹ *The Son of Man will send his angels, and they will collect out of his kingdom all causes of sin and all evildoers,* ⁴² *and they will throw them into the furnace of fire, where there will be weeping and gnashing of teeth.* ⁴³ *Then the righteous will shine like the sun in the kingdom of their Father. Let anyone with ears listen!*

⁴⁴ *"The kingdom of heaven is like treasure hidden in a field, which someone found and hid; then in his joy he goes and sells all that he has and buys that field.*

 ⁴⁵ *"Again, the kingdom of heaven is like a merchant in search of fine pearls;* ⁴⁶ *on finding one pearl of great value, he went and sold all that he had and bought it.*

⁴⁷ *"Again, the kingdom of heaven is like a net that was thrown into the sea and caught fish of every kind;* ⁴⁸ *when it was full, they drew it ashore, sat down, and put the good into baskets but threw out the bad.* ⁴⁹ *So it will be at the end of the age. The angels will come out and separate the evil from the righteous* ⁵⁰ *and throw them into the furnace of fire, where there will be weeping and gnashing of teeth."*

When we read of Jesus' teaching ministry in the Galilee we are often struck by the pictures of him teaching the crowds. They leave a lasting impression, especially when produced in colourful children's Bibles. Just as important, in fact possibly more important is the hidden away picture of him taking a handful of disciples and giving them in-depth explanation and analysis. To be a disciple is to be a learner, a student. Jesus was a Rabbi or teacher and he loved to run these in-depth teaching seminars for those who were closest to him.

In today's story Jesus has left the crowds, withdrawn into the privacy of his house and his chosen few are hungry to learn more. He offers them an in-depth explanation of the parable the weeds which had been about the planting and growing of the Kingdom. Then he follows this up with three more discovery parables of the Kingdom. The central thought of which is that in the midst of a full life the treasure, the pearl and the very special fish of the Kingdom are the most valuable parts.

It is a story of a leader with much to teach and of followers who are hungry to learn. A few years ago I gathered together a bunch of recent newcomers to our church and invited them to attend a Christian enquirers or first steps course called 'START'. Most of the group were youngish parents keen to find something for their children and then keen to find something for themselves.

Two or three years down the line and the group are still together and they have invited a few more to join them. Now they meet once a fortnight in different houses to study the Bible, share experiences and to encourage each other. They have moved on from being enquirers to serious learners. They are becoming disciples.

We have already seen Jesus sending his disciples out to continue his mission. That was a sort of learning by doing it, a sort of apprenticeship version of learning. Here we see Jesus treating the disciples more as students, they are learning by discussing, listening and careful thinking.

Our group are doing it the other way round. They began in a small 'student type' of group. Increasingly they are now learning by doing. Attempting to share their faith with friends and family, helping with children's groups, doing odd pieces of work in church, picking up bits of leadership responsibility and learning to pray.

So far we have focussed on the disciples, how they learn from, follow and 'become like' Jesus. However there is also something to be learned here about leadership, by looking at Jesus. Lots of leaders today seem to operate with the model of 'Command and Control'. The underlying principle of which is 'I am in charge, I tell you what to do'. There is a bit of this in Jesus but not very much. His model is more like 'Encourage and Enable'. Finding people, building them up and launching them into ministry.

Disciples are learners that is what the word means. The key to learning is hunger. Jesus' disciples were hungry to learn, 'his disciples approached him, saying "Explain to us"'. If you are hungry to learn, to become like him, then he is even hungrier to teach. So beef up your appetite.

> Lord Jesus
> Give me that hunger to learn.
> Help me to find a few others that I can learn with.
> Lead me into trusting relationships as we learn together.
> Lord Jesus
> May you be our Master and our teacher.
> Amen.

53. The Big Turning Point

Matthew 16: 13–23

13 Now when Jesus came into the district of Caesarea Philippi, he asked his disciples, "Who do people say that the Son of Man is?" 14 And they said, "Some say John the Baptist, but others Elijah, and still others Jeremiah or one of the prophets." 15 He said to them, "But who do you say that I am?" 16 Simon Peter answered, "You are the Messiah, the Son of the living God." 17 And Jesus answered him, "Blessed are you, Simon son of Jonah! For flesh and blood has not revealed this to you, but my Father in heaven. 18 And I tell you, you are Peter, and on this rock I will build my church, and the gates of Hades will not prevail against it. 19 I will give you the keys of the kingdom of heaven, and whatever you bind on earth will be bound in heaven, and whatever you loose on earth will be loosed in heaven." 20 Then he sternly ordered the disciples not to tell anyone that he was the Messiah.

21 From that time on, Jesus began to show his disciples that he must go to Jerusalem and undergo great suffering at the hands of the elders and chief priests and scribes, and be killed, and *on the third day be raised. ²² And Peter took him aside and began to rebuke him, saying, "God forbid it, Lord! This must never happen to you." ²³ But he turned and said to Peter, "Get behind me, Satan! You are a stumbling-block to me; for you are setting your mind not on divine things but on human things."*

This is one of the big 'change in the direction' moments in the ministry of Jesus. Together with the Transfiguration which comes in the next chapter we have two stories which are all about the disciples seeing and recognising who Jesus was. The two stories belong together like salt and pepper and together they form a huge double cairn, a great big swerving bend in Jesus' pathway. From here he changes direction. 'The Galilean Spring time', with its healings and joyful crowds, is over; the journey to Jerusalem and to the cross outside the city walls is now beginning.

First however, we have to discover what actually happened in both of these critical incidents. This story is all about the disciples, led by Peter, fully recognising and declaring their recognition of who Jesus really is. They had begun by seeing him as the best rabbi or teacher in town. In the course of the year or so that they had been following him around they must have increasingly realised that he was far more than a rabbi. They had serious twinges of disclosure with incidents such as him walking on the water and the feeding of the five thousand. Sometimes the utterings of demons and of odd people along the way had stretched their thinking. In all this time Jesus had never actually taught them much about who he was, he seems to have been waiting for them to 'get it' for themselves. Now on a gentle retreat in the hidden away beautiful location of Caesarea Philippi he suddenly puts them on the spot and asks them right out in the open the big question. The spiritual game of blind man's bluff is over now, it is time for recognition, declaration and for the nailing of colours to masts.

In saying, 'you are the Messiah, the Son of God' Peter is not just making a comment about Jesus, he is also saying something about himself. In effect he is offering his worship and obedience. In declaring Jesus to be the Messiah he is signing himself up to be the first of the Messiah's Men.

From a distance it looks as if the disciples, led by Peter, have suddenly passed their driving test. The 'L' plates are off and it's full speed ahead. A church will be built, Peter is the rock, and hey presto here are the keys to Heaven.

But it is full speed ahead to Jerusalem, the suffering and to the chief priests. No more Galilee, no more crowds, no more great feastings and rejoicings.

Once again Peter speaks up. Now the same voice which had made such a declaration has become the voice of a tempting devil. It is not that Peter is such a devilishly bad person but that the words he utters in a 'trying to be helpful' sort of way are just the sort of words that Jesus didn't need to hear at this key time. This is the second of the three great temptations that Jesus faced during his mission. The first was in the wilderness and the third will be in Gethsemane. On this, the occasion of the second great temptation, it is almost as if Peter is the dummy and the devil is the ventriloquist.

As with Jesus so with us, we are about half-way through on our 100-day journey. Perhaps this is a key moment for you. A moment of recognition of who Jesus really is. Or of publicly declaring what you think about him. Maybe it is time for a change of direction or tempo as you seek to follow and become like him. Right now could be the perfect time for you to think about the question – 'Who do I say that Jesus is?' and 'What am I going to do about it?'

Lord Jesus
I am half way on my journey
Help me to find who you really are.
To follow in your footsteps
And to become like you
Every day
Amen.

54. The Big Mountain

Matthew 17: 1–13

^{1}*Six days later, Jesus took with him Peter and James and his brother John and led them up a high mountain, by themselves.* ^{2} *And he was transfigured before them, and his face shone like the sun, and his clothes became dazzling white.* ^{3} *Suddenly there appeared to them Moses and Elijah, talking with him.* ^{4} *Then Peter said to Jesus, "Lord, it is good for us to be here; if you wish, I will make three dwellings here, one for you, one for Moses, and one for Elijah."* ^{5} *While he was still speaking, suddenly a bright cloud overshadowed them, and from the cloud a voice said, "This is my Son, the Beloved; with him I am well pleased; listen to him!"* ^{6} *When the disciples heard this, they fell to the ground and were overcome by fear.* ^{7} *But Jesus came and touched them, saying, "Get up and do not be afraid."* ^{8} *And when they looked up, they saw no one except Jesus himself alone.*

^{9} *As they were coming down the mountain, Jesus ordered them, "Tell no one about the vision until after the Son of Man has been raised from the dead."* ^{10} *And the disciples asked him, "Why, then, do the scribes say that Elijah must come first?" [11] He replied, "Elijah is indeed coming and will restore all things; [12] but I tell you that Elijah has already come, and they did not recognize him, but they did to him whatever they pleased. So also the Son of Man is about to suffer at their hands." [13] Then the disciples understood that he was speaking to them about John the Baptist.*

Everyone needs a mountain top experience from time to time. This was Jesus'.

A few years ago I found myself on the way to Mount Horeb in Israel, the scene of today's story. As the coach pulled into the car park I was terrified at the sight of the tacky, little ski-lift that lay ahead. As someone who is frightened of heights, it was something to be dreaded not anticipated. But I was determined to make the ride, partly because I was leading the party, secondly because I wanted to get to the top of the Mount of Transfiguration.

Swaying around on my wobbly little seat with a couple of hundred feet of fresh air below me was every bit as terrifying as I had anticipated. I suppose at this stage you are expecting me to say that despite all my fears it was worth it when I got to the top. Well, the truth is it wasn't. Once I was up there I spent all my time wondering how I was going to get down. I didn't have a mountain top experience on Mount Horeb, but Jesus did. In fact, not just Jesus but Peter, James and John, his 'inner three' were all pulled into it too. It appears to be a deeply mystical, out of body and beyond the bounds of possibility experience. But then given that Jesus was the divine word, the one and only Son of God and the most special human being (Son of Man) that ever walked this planet I think that the odd supernatural experience is allowable.

> Jesus shines like the sun
> He glows, his face radiant
> Moses and Elijah
> The two great spiritual heavyweights of the Old Testament
> They are there to offer support
> The three disciples
> Jaws dropping, are all wondering and not understanding
> And then the voice
> The voice which links it all back to the baptism
> The voice of God
> And then on the way down
> The voice of Jesus
> Looking ahead to the resurrection.

The whole thing points from Earth to Heaven. Jesus and the disciples have climbed above the normal, the everyday, the routine, the usual. They have looked into the distance, the distant past and the distant future. That is largely why people climb mountains, to see into the distance. To see beyond the normal, to look down and see the everyday routine as so many ants scrambling about in the dust. To see beauty, mystery, light and shade.

Here on the mountain top, they see, get excited and begin to feel things they have never felt before.

Now here's the thing about mountain top experiences. You don't have to go up a mountain to have one. It can come to you whilst you wander around the park, whilst losing yourself in a great hymn or sitting in your favourite armchair and reading the Bible at the beginning of the day. You do need to find a bit of escape, a bit of silence and space, your mind does need to soar above the everyday routine. And then you are ready to dream the dream and get excited.

'The Who' get it right:

> Listening to you, I get the music
> Gazing at you, I get the heat.
> Following you, I climb the mountain
> I get excitement at your feet.
> Right behind you, I see the millions
> On you, I see the glory.
> From you, I get opinions
> From you, I get the story.

Lord God
Heavenly Father
Help me to be silent
To listen
To gaze
To wonder
To hear
And then take me
Up the mountain
Amen.

55. An Epileptic Boy

Matthew 17: 14–21

> [14] *When they came to the crowd, a man came to him, knelt before him,* [15] *and said, "Lord, have mercy on my son, for he is an epileptic and he suffers terribly; he often falls into the fire and often into the water.* [16] *And I brought him to your disciples, but they could not cure him."* [17] *Jesus answered, "You faithless and perverse generation, how much longer must I be with you? How much longer must I put up with you? Bring him here to me."* [18] *And Jesus rebuked the demon, and it came out of him, and the boy was cured instantly.* [19] *Then the disciples came to Jesus privately and said, "Why could we not cast it out?"* [20] *He said to them, "Because of your little faith. For truly I tell you, if you have faith the size of a mustard seed, you will say to this mountain, 'Move from here to there,' and it will move; and nothing will be impossible for you."*

The disciples were Jesus' students, his learners, his apprentices. This is a 'trying to do it like he did it story'. A sort of 'we had a go, but didn't get it quite right' narrative. What an encouragement for people like me who are still trying to be Jesus' apprentices but who are still not getting it right.

Jesus was a proclaimer of the 'Good News', a healer and a driver out of demons. Not content with his own three-fold ministry he tried to teach and equip his disciples to repeat it. Often they went with him, watching, remembering, and no doubt discussing it all afterwards. On some occasions Jesus sent them out on missions as an extension of his own. First he sent out the 12 and then the 72. They copied and learnt from him. But they didn't do it as well or as effectively as him and why should they have? Sometimes the student surpasses the teacher, occasionally an apprentice will paint better than the master, but not often and certainly not when the teacher, master craftsman is the utterly unique Jesus.

In this story Jesus is returning from the Mount of the Transfiguration with his three chosen closest followers, Peter, James and John. He discovers that the rest of his disciples have been approached by a desperate father to heal his epileptic son. The poor old disciples have tried and failed in front of a large crowd. We have all been there. I have been there too many times to remember, prayed for healing while others watched, called for people to step out in faith in front of a watching church, and realised halfway through that this was not going to work.

Many times I have listened to preachers going on about John 14: 12, 'very truly I tell you, the one who believes in me will also do the works that I do and, in fact, will do greater works than these'. Always I have felt impelled to do these greater works and yet have never really believed that I could or would.

So I love this story, of these vulnerable and naïve disciples trying and failing before the watching and judging crowd. I feel I am in good company.

Does this then mean that we can just give up and abandon the whole thing as an impossible idea? Not at all, I go on learning and trying to follow the master, but perhaps with a more realistic expectation. The key to the disciples' failure is their lack of faith, or of their only having little faith. The disciples then and the disciples now, that is you and me, need to have greater faith. Greater faith in God and probably greater faith in ourselves too.

Now before finishing on a rather negative note here are two positive ideas. Firstly, just about every time I pray for someone to get better, or lay hands on someone they always seem to like it. There is almost always a sense of peace, thankfulness and some sort of blessing. Secondly, the more I attempt this sort of ministry the more happens. Conversely the more I collapse internally and avoid it, the less I see happen. Today or maybe tomorrow, or perhaps both, you are going to meet someone who needs positive prayer. You will probably hear two voices. Voice number one will say, 'Go on, jump in and offer to pray for them.' Voice number two, which is often the 'in control' voice will say something like, 'You can't say that, they may feel uncomfortable, it might not work.'

Which voice are you going to listen to?

> Lord Jesus
> You were the greatest of leaders
> Help me to learn from you
> To become like you
> And to step out in faith.
> Amen.

56. Three Times He Tells Them

Mark 10: 32–34

32 They were on the road, going up to Jerusalem, and Jesus was walking ahead of them; they were amazed, and those who followed were afraid. He took the twelve aside again and began to tell them what was to happen to him, 33 saying, "See, we are going up to Jerusalem, and the Son of Man will be handed over to the chief priests and the scribes, and they will condemn him to death; then they will hand him over to the Gentiles; 34 they will mock him, and spit upon him, and flog him, and kill him; and after three days he will rise again."

On three occasions, right in the middle of the Jesus story we find him telling his disciples that he will be betrayed, die and rise again on the third day. He told them at Caesarea Philippi. He will tell them finally as they travel up to Jerusalem and here as they gather themselves for a final time of preparation before the journey.

Together these three predictions form a central core and a turning point in the whole story. They are a crossroads with one signpost reaching back to a time of celebration and joy in Galilee and another one pointing toward suffering and sacrifice in Jerusalem. The disciples just don't get it, and until they understand his death they will never fully understand him. There is a desolate pathos hanging over these three passages, not just in his impending doom but in the loneliness with which he approaches it.

If you want to understand the shape and the story of Jesus' ministry you have to understand the weightiness and the place of these three predictions. Together they form the big change of direction, impetus and mood.

I have sat for hours watching and re-watching endless *Harry Potter* films, and even reading a couple of the books. I never really 'got it'. I was always outside the constantly expanding Harry Potter bubble. I sat and watched because the rest of my family loved it.

I did however get a bit of it. The Dark Lord (can't remember his name, but do remember that he had no nose) hated Harry, largely because of his father. Harry gained lots of followers, but none of them really understood him. Harry was always a young vulnerable and lonely boy with a massive sense of destiny, of being drawn forward to a climactic 'winner takes all' moment. There was going to be an almighty show down. As with so many fictional heroes; Superman and Batman, Robin Hood and King Arthur, Aslan and Frodo; the idea of lonely goodness drawn into a final battle goes back all the way to Jesus.

'On the third day' – What a power filled phrase. Hope, sunrise, new beginning, victory and ultimately laughter, are all to be found in this 'On the third day'. We often find ourselves being squashed or frightened on the first or second day. Everyone needs a 'third day' hope in their life:

Facing financial ruin	– early on the first day
Marriage falling apart	– around about lunchtime on the first day
Diagnosed with cancer	– on the first day that might be the last day
Losing your house	– on the day after the first day
Gradually declining into Alzheimer's	– this could be a lot of days
Losing your faith	– at the end of the second day
Being bullied at home or work	– most days

And then everything began to change on the third day.

Three times he told the disciples and perhaps because we forget and doubt and disregard and lose it, he needs to tell us three times.

That he is Jesus, that we are following him and trying to become like him.

That no matter what life is throwing at us, no matter how big the darkness – 'on the third day he will be raised'.

> **Lord God**
> **Help me on my first day,**
> **When the pain first hits me**
> **Be with me throughout the second day,**
> **When I am at my lowest**
> **And raise me to new life on the third day**
> **That I might live again.**
> **Amen.**

57. Making Disciples

Luke 9: 57 – 62

> *57 As they were going along the road, someone said to him, "I will follow you wherever you go." 58 And Jesus said to him, "Foxes have holes, and birds of the air have nests; but the Son of Man has nowhere to lay his head." 59 To another he said, "Follow me." But he said, "Lord, first let me go and bury my father." 60 But Jesus said to him, "Let the dead bury their own dead; but as for you, go and proclaim the kingdom of God." 61 Another said, "I will follow you, Lord; but let me first say farewell to those at my home." 62 Jesus said to him, "No one who puts a hand to the plough and looks back is fit for the kingdom of God."*

This is all about roads and following. Jesus was in the business of making disciples. Today we vicars and evangelists are often struggling to create converts and church attenders. Of course a disciple is a convert and a good one will be a church attender but there is much more to it than this.

Converts think Jesus is a good guy and his ideas are true. Disciples think Jesus is the most important person they have ever met, and that his ideas are life transforming. They don't just agree with him in their mind, they set out to follow him with all of their lives. So for the next three days we shall be looking at three discipleship issues bubbling up out of the Jesus story. But first I thought I would share what I think of as the discipleship formula: -

$$D = L \times F \times HS \longrightarrow W.C$$

Where D = disciple
      L = learner
      F = follower
      HS = Holy Spirit
And WC = world changer
(So here is something for you to ponder – disciples become world changers)

The phrase 'Follow me' is a key one for Jesus and often reminds me of the childhood game 'Follow my Leader'. Here there are two people saying to Jesus 'I will follow you' whilst to a third Jesus actually takes the initiative in saying 'follow me'.

Now here are three key elements in all this 'following' way of life:

Following Jesus means making choices. 'Yes' to Jesus means 'No' to other options. Too many people say yes without ever saying any nos. The result is they are always a bit half-hearted, always holding too many cards, never quite focussed. Why, because they have never made a clear and definite choice.

If you are not following Jesus, who are you following? Are you following the crowd like a sheep? Perhaps you are listening to all the crazy opinions and rival philosophies that we find in the media. Or maybe you are following your own materialistic self-centred self? The biggest choice in *my* life is, 'Will I follow Jesus Christ or Robin Gamble?'

Followers keep close to Jesus. At the time in his life when Jesus gave out all this 'following teaching' he was literally on the road. He was a travelling man. Anyone who held back or delayed or did a few other things was going to lose contact, because Jesus, the Son of Man, was on the big Kingdom March. Sometimes you have got to 'keep up to keep close'. So, yes this makes discipleship a tough business, but I would never give it up for the world. One, we are on a road that actually leads somewhere. Two, we are following the greatest leader that the world has ever seen. Three, I keep meeting lots of other people travelling alongside me on the road.

Alfred Wainwright was one of the most respected road followers of our time. Most of his roads led him through the Lake District and the North of England generally. Thousands have read his books and followed his paths – roads. Here is a big piece of advice that he offers to all road following disciples.

"One should always have a definite objective, in a walk as in life – it is so much more satisfying to reach a target by personal effort than to wander aimlessly. An objective is an ambition, and life without ambition is... aimless wandering."

Heavenly Father
I have discovered
Or been discovered by Jesus, your son.
Help me now to become his follower
To say some 'Nos'
And a big Yes.
To place my feet upon the road
And to follow him.
Amen.

58. Cracks Appear

Matthew 20:20–28

²⁰ Then the mother of Zebedee's sons came to Jesus with her sons and, kneeling down, asked a favour of him.

²¹ "What is it you want?" he asked.

She said, "Grant that one of these two sons of mine may sit at your right and the other at your left in your kingdom."

²² "You don't know what you are asking," Jesus said to them. "Can you drink the cup I am going to drink?"

"We can," they answered.

²³ Jesus said to them, "You will indeed drink from my cup, but to sit at my right or left is not for me to grant. These places belong to those for whom they have been prepared by my Father."

²⁴ When the ten heard about this, they were indignant with the two brothers. ²⁵ Jesus called them together and said, "You know that the rulers of the Gentiles lord it over them, and their high officials exercise authority over them. ²⁶ Not

> *so with you. Instead, whoever wants to become great among you must be your servant, [27] and whoever wants to be first must be your slave – [28] just as the Son of Man did not come to be served, but to serve, and to give his life as a ransom for many."*

Jesus chose twelve disciples. These were to be his main men. He prayed over them and gave them extra teaching and training. These were the ones he invested himself in and on whom he was to depend. At the end of his time on earth he entrusted his whole mission to them. Twelve special men, the great ones, the faithful ones. One for each of the Old Testament tribes so forming the New Israel. So special in fact that today we see them in our stained-glass windows and remember their names.

In actual fact one of them betrayed Jesus, another one denied him three times whilst a third lost all faith in him. And here are two of his inner core of three completely eaten up by ego and power lust, and not only that but they are hiding it behind their mother's skirt. James and John are supposed to be the Sons of Thunder!

I work as part of a large team. We cover just about every aspect of church life from the wellbeing of our schools to the care of our buildings to the support for overseas mission. Somewhere in the middle of all this I am embedded doing my church growth and evangelism stuff. We are a good team made up of good people. Though we have different tasks we share a common vision, 'to change the world' in God's name.

So why do I feel the need to be that much more important, successful and influential than the others? Why can't I be happy to be simply part of the team? Is it due to my insecurities or my ego or a deadly cocktail of both? Why am I not content to simply sit at the table rather than feeling the need to sit 'at his right or left'?

Most human organisations, clubs, families, offices and empires are basically set up as power pyramids. Jesus turns the whole thing on its head. 'The first must be last, the top must go to the bottom, the king must become a servant'.

Every now and again it is actually helpful to realise what a bunch of malfunctioning misfits the disciples were. It makes me feel that there is room for me. If they can be disciples then I can be a disciple as well. Sometimes I read all the stuff about commitment, giving things up, forgetting about self, loving the whole world, not turning back, oh and forgiving all the people who do awful things to you, and think, 'I'm just not that good'. So to discover that there is a great tradition in the Bible of people who were 'just not that good', but who were still 'good enough' for Jesus reassures, encourages and makes me feel ok.

> Yes I have betrayed you,
> And I keep denying you before my friends,
> Ego and vanity both live in me
> And as for faith,
> Well I sometimes think I lost it a long time ago.
> My love is often loveless,

My commitment lacks commitment
And the road is unwalked
Yet still you call me
> believe in me
> trust in me.
Are you just naïve, over simple
Or just not very good at the disciple business
Or is it that you are Jesus?

Lord Jesus
I will never be the perfect disciple
I may never be a very good disciple
But help me, as I follow you
To be the best disciple I can be
Amen.

59. Jesus Spoils the Party

Luke 11: 37–44

> *37 While he was speaking, a Pharisee invited him to dine with him; so he went in and took his place at the table. 38 The Pharisee was amazed to see that he did not first wash before dinner. 39 Then the Lord said to him, "Now you Pharisees clean the outside of the cup and of the dish, but inside you are full of greed and wickedness. 40 You fools! Did not the one who made the outside make the inside also? 41 So give for alms those things that are within; and see, everything will be clean for you.*
>
> *42 "But woe to you Pharisees! For you tithe mint and rue and herbs of all kinds, and neglect justice and the love of God; it is these you ought to have practised, without neglecting the others. 43 Woe to you Pharisees! For you love to have the seat of honour in the synagogues and to be greeted with respect in the market-places. 44 Woe to you! For you are like unmarked graves, and people walk over them without realizing it."*

I have to confess that I am not a great one for inviting people round for meals. As a young couple my wife

Maureen and I were always enthusiastic socialisers. These days, as I get older, I am much more of a hermit. Nevertheless, we do recognise the human/spiritual importance of hospitality and sitting, either with friends or sometimes with complete strangers, around the meal table. There are thirteen separate stories in the gospels of Jesus eating and drinking with other people. At these tables significant conversations were held, people opened up, laughter, tears and deep feelings were shared.

> Partying with the sinners
> Water into wine
> Feeding 5,000
> Becoming the Bread of Life
> Grazing in the cornfields
> Tea with Zacchaeus
> Banqueting with the Pharisees
> Dinner at Lazarus's house
> A last supper
> Breakfast on the beach.

At this meal however, the table becomes a place of conflict and distancing, rather than of warmth and meeting. When I ask people into my house for Sunday lunch, a quick bite to eat, a leisurely coffee or a Saturday night curry, I expect them to behave in a certain way. I expect them to respect my home and family. Most of all, I expect them to respect me. I don't expect them to start arguing with me and I certainly do not appreciate it if they start making deeply judgemental and insulting remarks about me.

So what is it about the normally patient, tolerant and putting up with people Jesus that he suddenly becomes the dinner guest from the 'angry people society'? This is the same man who can sit down with a party full of publicans and sinners and become their friend. Yet here with a seemingly good and highly regarded religious leader, the sparks fly, the gloves are off, the words cut deep.

It began back in Galilee and has gradually gathered momentum. The Jesus versus Pharisees and scribes, lawyers and priests conflict is the key drama to the Jesus story. Here he is getting closer to Jerusalem and the drama is getting deeper and more wounding. There will be no turning back or making of an armistice after this. Soon it will simply explode into open warfare.

> Lord Jesus
> Where is the table you want me to sit at?
> Who are the people you want me to invite to my table?
> What is the conversation
> You want us to have?
> May you lead me and show me.
> Amen.

60. Beelzebub

Luke 11: 14–23

[14] *Now he was casting out a demon that was mute; when the demon had gone out, the one who had been mute spoke, and the crowds were amazed.* [15] *But some of them said, "He casts out demons by Beelzebul, the ruler of the demons."* [16] *Others, to test him, kept demanding from him a sign from heaven.* [17] *But he knew what they were thinking and said to them, "Every kingdom divided against itself becomes a desert, and house falls on house.* [18] *If Satan also is divided against himself, how will his kingdom stand? — for you say that I cast out the demons by Beelzebul.* [19] *Now if I cast out the demons by Beelzebul, by whom do your exorcists cast them out? Therefore they will be your judges.* [20] *But if it is by the finger of God that I cast out the demons, then the kingdom of God has come to you.* [21] *When a strong man, fully armed, guards his castle, his property is safe.* [22] *But when one stronger than he attacks him and overpowers him, he takes away his armour in which he trusted and divides his plunder.* [23] *Whoever is not with me is against me, and whoever does not gather with me scatters."*

He is on the road to Jerusalem. The clouds are gathering, enemies are circling, there is going to be some sort of climactic showdown. You can almost hear the driving, drumming music in the background as kingdoms are in collision.

With Beelzebub and demons, exorcists and Satan, Kingdom and castles, this story reads like an excerpt from 'The Lord of the Rings'. Jesus is on a military type campaign breaking in to an evil fortress and setting captives free.

I've never actually penetrated a castle, got past the armed guards and looked through the bars of a dark prison to see chained up prisoners. I did however once know a man who was utterly in the grip of a gambling addiction. He was a good, hard-working Christian man. He provided for his family and was a committed member of his church. But he was chained to gambling, especially to the machines (aptly called one armed bandits, because that is exactly what they are). His addiction almost destroyed him, his marriage, his relationship to his children and his faith.

I once knew a woman possessed by lust and a young man haunted by inner anger, which wasn't all that 'inner'. And as for drink and drugs, well suddenly we are into something of plague proportions.

Who is there to set these people free? Whether you see Beelzebub and the demons as real, actual characters or as metaphors for human weaknesses and problems, what is abundantly clear is that thousands, hundreds of thousands, millions of people in our own country are held in some sort of human captivity.

There are lots of varied agencies, charities, health workers and therapies etc. that can all help in a range of ways. Many of them were actually first set up by followers of Jesus who were part of the anti-Beelzebub struggle. To my mind however we will always need something beyond the efforts of human helpers because the ultimate enemy is stronger than human flesh and blood.

Light overcomes darkness, form and shape and gives order to chaos, goodness defeats badness and Jesus sets people free from Beelzebub.

Every one of us has got some sort of captivity issue. Some are bigger and more severe than others. Perhaps you have a persistent gossip problem or maybe a deeply hidden pornography struggle. Maybe you are filled with hatred or just with hurting. Who is going to set us free? Then there are the people we work with, are married to or have given birth to. Who is going to set them free?

For some fortunate souls the freedom comes quickly and immediately with a single act of prayer. For some of us, it is taking a lifetime to get us out of the prison.

Freddie Mercury famously sang 'I want to break free' but I think Charles Wesley put it better.

Long my imprisoned spirit lay,
Fast bound in sin and nature's night;
Thine eye diffused a quickening ray –
I woke, the dungeon flamed with light;
My chains fell off, my heart was free,
I rose, went forth, and followed Thee.
My chains fell off, my heart was free,
I rose, went forth, and followed Thee.

Lord Jesus
Where are the demons in my life?
Where are the chains biting into me?
How long have I been in prison?
How I long
To see my prison door opened
And my chains to fall off
May you be my liberator.
Amen.

61. King of Kings

Matthew 2:1–2

¹ After Jesus was born in Bethlehem in Judea, during the time of King Herod, Magi from the east came to Jerusalem ² and asked, "Where is the one who has been born king of the Jews? We saw his star when it rose and have come to worship him."

Matthew 13: 31–32

³¹ He told them another parable: "The kingdom of heaven is like a mustard seed, which a man took and planted in his field. ³² Though it is the smallest of all seeds, yet when it grows, it is the largest of garden plants and becomes a tree, so that the birds come and perch in its branches."

Jesus loved to talk about the Kingdom. Sometimes he called it the Kingdom of Heaven and sometimes the Kingdom of God. Jesus used different pictures or parables to talk about the Kingdom. On one occasion the Kingdom was breaking into the great fortress of dark evil and setting free the captives. Another time the Kingdom was like a great banquet to which everyone, rich and poor were invited. Here the Kingdom is a tiny seed which, when planted, grows and grows. A Kingdom is a place ruled over by a King but Jesus doesn't talk about a place but about the human heart or a bunch of human hearts. In the middle of my heart or mind there is an imaginary throne and every day I have to decide who is going to sit on the throne. Will it be me with my own ego or will it be God with his divine will? I sometimes visualise the throne as the big, powerful captain's chair in *Star Trek*. The one who sits in that seat decides where the ship is going and gives out orders to the whole crew. If the King is a caring King, if the captain knows well what he is doing then the Kingdom, the ship will flourish. To have our heavenly father sitting on our throne or in our captain's seat is the best way to flourish and navigate our whole life.

There are some big questions for us here.

- Who is King of my life today?
- Is God really on the throne or my own passions and desires?
- Is the Kingdom of God growing in my life or standing still?
- Finding Jesus means we see the Kingdom.
  Following Jesus means we invite him into our life. Becoming like Jesus happens when we put God on the throne.
  So of these three stages where are you at?
- What do we really mean when we say, 'Thy Kingdom Come'?
  The growing mustard seed Kingdom is not just about our individual lives. If we are part of a

church or Jesus' community then our church should be growing. It should be growing spiritually as together we all become more like Jesus. It should be growing missionally as we reach out to the local community. It should be growing numerically as more birds of the air come and rest in our branches.

The ever popular *'Lion King'* captures something of the King and the Kingdom. When the great and good King Mufasa is killed his dark hearted brother Scar takes over and life is suddenly much harder for everyone. In the background however Simba the good King's son is waiting and preparing. At first he is a tiny mustard seed like cub but he grows and finally drives out Scar and becomes the Lion King.

Lord God
You are the great and powerful King
You are also our loving father.
May you become King of my life
Leading me and showing me how to live.
And may your Kingdom grow every day in my life.
Amen.

62. Jesus and the Holy Spirit

John 7: 37–39

> [37] *On the last and greatest day of the festival, Jesus stood and said in a loud voice, "Let anyone who is thirsty come to me and drink.* [38] *Whoever believes in me, as Scripture has said, rivers of living water will flow from within them."* [39] *By this he meant the Spirit, whom those who believed in him were later to receive. Up to that time the Spirit had not been given since Jesus had not yet been glorified.*

I remember visiting my poor old dad in hospital. He had just had a small internal operation. The operation had been a success but he had a sign attached to his bed reading 'Nil by mouth'. After a day or so he was allowed a tiny container of water. It was made worse by the fact that this was all happening in high summer and the ward was sweltering. My poor old dad, I don't think I have ever seen anyone as thirsty. Except today I see lots of spiritual thirstiness. We are just so flat, so grey, so ok, so emptily human. We need the water of life, the spiritual water of light and eternity flowing in us. The inner life-transforming and soul-filling water of life is the Holy Spirit, the Spirit of God – the very inner essence of God poured out on his people.

Without this Holy Spirit then I, Robin Gamble, am just an ordinary person trying to be a Christian or follower of Jesus, and doing it all in my own strength. If on the other hand I can somehow receive, be filled by a drink of God's Holy Spirit then I am no longer an ordinary person doing it in my own human way. Suddenly I am human plus spiritual, Robin Gamble plus Holy Spirit following Jesus by using his strength and resources as well as my own.

I need the empowering, the refreshment and the reward of the Holy Spirit and I need it in three areas of my life.

Firstly, I need it to help me help my family. I have a wife that needs to be loved, even when I don't feel like loving her. I have a son who needs to be listened to and befriended, even when I don't feel like befriending him. I have a daughter with extra needs. She needs me to forget about myself and care for her, even when I don't feel like caring for her.

Secondly, I need the Holy Spirit to give me power in my life's mission. For me helping other people to find Jesus is my way of following him but I can't do this in my own strength.

Lastly, though maybe it should be firstly, I need the Spirit so that I can be me. My human spirit or nature is basically insecure, negative, full of doubt and even self-pity. Left to my own resources I have a rather depressive personality and it is getting harder the older I get. I need the Holy Spirit to pump up my balloon, to pour the water of life into my grey and dusty mouth, to make flowers grow in the desert regions of my soul.

This coming gift of the Spirit was so important that Jesus 'stood and said in a loud voice'. He was inspired, urgent, emphatic, he really wanted everyone to get it. All this and more I need. Not as a one-off mega conversion experience. I don't need a great big holy flood and then gradual drying out. I need a tap. Not a rusty, old, neglected tap, but one that I can turn on every day. Why? Because every day is precious, and I need to be watered, filled, renewed at the beginning of every one.

> Lord Jesus
> I live in a desert
> Help me every day
> To be still
> To be thirsty
> To be open
> Open to receive
> Open to drink
> Amen.

63. The Crowd and the Cross

Mark 8: 34

> *34 Then he called the crowd to him along with his disciples and said: "Whoever wants to be my disciple must deny themselves and take up their cross and follow me."*

If you flick through the pages of any children's Bible or story of Jesus books you will keep seeing lovely colourful pictures of happy, smiling and often arm-raising and jumping up and down people. They are the crowd or crowds. Watch any big action hero or war film and there are always lots of extras, usually in uniform or period dress. The 'crowd' are the extras in the Jesus story, all in their beards and headscarves, sandals and striped robes.

As with film extras, we usually ignore the crowd in the gospel story treating them basically as part of the human background scenery to the main star characters. But who were they, what sort of parts do they play and how did Jesus treat them? Were the crowd just an unknowable bunch of walk on extras to him or did he have an eye for them as distinctive and important individuals?

The first appearance of a real crowd in the gospels comes at the end of a busy day for Jesus. In Mark 1: 32

the 'whole city' were gathered at his door as many were cured and others were set free from demon possession. The crowd or crowds however that I want to focus on are the Galilean northerners, not the more sophisticated, metropolitan Jerusalemites.

The Galilean crowds keep coming at every opportunity. We see them at the lakeside, jumping into boats to follow him, and gathering in their thousands on the hillsides for teaching and healing. First they are coming from local villages and later from distant towns and regions.

My favourite crowd painter is L.S. Lowry, I have already mentioned him but he deserves a second look. His crowds are made up of ordinary 'working and finding life to be a struggle northerners', just like Jesus'. Lowry paints them in large numbers and usually fairly dull colours. Quite a few of them are often struggling with children, prams and unwell bodies. And because he separates them all so that they are hardly ever touching each other there is a sort of atmosphere of aloneness and going nowhere-ness in his crowds. I often feel that people should look at Lowry paintings whilst listening to the Beatles 'Eleanor Rigby' or 'Nowhere Man' in the background.

Jesus' crowds were all looking for something more out of life and were drawn to him as the one who could provide it. For his part Jesus was deeply moved by them –

> 'He had compassion for the crowd'
> 'Come to me all you that are weary'
> 'The fields are ripe for harvesting'.

He seems to have had a two-pronged approach to the crowd. His first prong was to affirm, teach, heal and dish out food to them all; a sort of universal blessing for the 'unblessed'. Prong number two takes crowd members to a deeper level. We use the term 'following the crowd' almost as a term of abuse. It indicates lack of individuality, weakness, a failure to be our true selves. The crowd tells us what to wear, watch on the telly, eat and drink and even where to go on holiday. Jesus sets people free from following the crowd and calls on them to step out and follow him.

The first fishermen disciples, the unlikely tax collector, women that had been set free from possessive devils and oppressive men, a rich man in Jericho and a blind man on his way up to Jerusalem. In each case Jesus sees them not as numbers in a crowd but as individuals with names and faces.

I am surrounded by a crowd, family members, friends old and new, acquaintances, Facebook people and work colleagues. The list goes on, the crowd gets bigger. So what would it mean to offer some sort of over-all warmth or love to them all? Whilst inviting the odd individual to step out of the crowd so that I can pray for them, have a conversation and build a relationship.

In fact my church too is surrounded by crowds. People coming for weddings and funerals, occasional attenders, parents who want their children christened and entering our school, those who come to our fund-raising events and special festival services. Like Jesus we want to offer something good to them all, but how about going one

step further and calling people to come out of the crowd
and become part of his community.

> All the lonely people
> Where do they all come from?
> All the lonely people
> Where do they all belong?
>
> 'Eleanor Rigby' by The Beatles.

Lord Jesus
Help me to step out of the crowd
To be my true self.
Follow my chosen path
And think my own thoughts.
Help me to hear your voice
And to respond.
Amen.

64. The Parable of the Good Samaritan

Luke 10: 25–37

25 On one occasion an expert in the law stood up to test Jesus. "Teacher," he asked, "what must I do to inherit eternal life?"

26 "What is written in the Law?" he replied. "How do you read it?"

27 He answered, "'Love the Lord your God with all your heart and with all your soul and with all your strength and with all your mind'; and, 'Love your neighbour as yourself.'"

28 "You have answered correctly," Jesus replied. "Do this and you will live."

29 But he wanted to justify himself, so he asked Jesus, "And who is my neighbour?"

30 In reply Jesus said: "A man was going down from Jerusalem to Jericho, when he was attacked by robbers. They stripped him of his clothes, beat him and went away, leaving him half dead. 31 A priest happened to be going down the same road, and when he saw the man, he passed by on the other side. 32 So too, a Levite, when he came to the place and saw him, passed by on the other

side. ³³ But a Samaritan, as he travelled, came
where the man was; and when he saw him, he
took pity on him. ³⁴ He went to him and bandaged
his wounds, pouring on oil and wine. Then he
put the man on his own donkey, brought him to
an inn and took care of him. ³⁵ The next day he
took out two denarii and gave them to the
innkeeper. 'Look after him,' he said, 'and when
I return, I will reimburse you for any extra
expense you may have.'

³⁶ "Which of these three do you think was a
neighbour to the man who fell into the hands
of robbers?"

³⁷ The expert in the law replied, "The one who
had mercy on him."

Jesus told him, "Go and do likewise."

It took me years to get my inbred racism sorted out, or
perhaps I should say, to let Jesus get it sorted out. I grew
up in a northern, working-class culture in the late fifties
and sixties. So it wasn't so much that I had a bit of racism
in my system, more that racism was a part of me.
I come from Yorkshire, where we didn't just look
down on people from other countries, we had an arrogant
sense of superiority even to people who lived in other
counties, especially if they were from Lancashire or
'down South'.

My racist attitudes were matched by my sexist ones,
by my working-class prejudices and my cultural
snobbishness. In the parable of the Good Samaritan
it is not so much that Jesus campaigns against prejudices

but rather that he transcends all our modern moralities and political correctness with a story of ridiculously generous love.

Morality is about a new sense of accepted rules, political correctness is born out of a new social and cultural awareness but love comes out of a completely new sort of heart.

In Jesus' day the Samaritans were sort of 'renegade, mixed up, not proper Jews'. They were patronised, looked down upon and even despised by the quite proper and pure Jews of Jerusalem. So for Jesus to tell a story where the spiritual leaders of the pure people are put in the shade by a Samaritan was both crazy and controversial. The story begins with a discussion about 'the law', Jesus takes it all up to a much higher level. This is a story of compassion and caring, of giving and remembering. It is the ultimate story of love, which is why it has become one of the most cherished and well-known stories in the world. It is a story of ordinary morality (rule keeping) overshadowed, of social norms and correctness overwhelmed.

I remember the first time my wife suggested that we gave, what for us at the time was a large amount of money, to some needy friends. I was of course used to giving the usual small or modest amounts to God's work or the needy. But this suggested gift was of another order. She shamed me into it. In a small way we were being 'Good Samaritans' in a more generous way than we, or I, had ever been before. At first I resented the money we gave but very soon I became very pleased with what we had done and it opened a door in my heart that I hope is still open. It was a work of Jesus.

I can't remember the first time Jesus started challenging me about my prejudices and dark attitudes. It started many years ago. He has had to work hard on me over a lengthy period and it is still ongoing. He wants me to realise that 'Samaritans', whoever they may be, are just as special and wonderful in God's eyes as I am myself.

Why don't we spend all of today being a 'Good Samaritan' and then if it feels good, we can do it again tomorrow.

> The road is long, with many of winding turns
> That lead us to (who knows) where, who
> knows where?
> But I'm strong, strong enough to carry
> him-yeah
> He ain't heavy – he's my brother
>
> So long we go, his welfare is my concern
> No burden is he to bear, we'll get there
> But I know he would not encumber me
> He ain't heavy – he's my brother.   The Hollies

Lord Jesus
Burn out my racial prejudice
Expose my sexism
Eradicate my snobbishness and sense of
superiority
Help me to see, to accept
And to love
In a new way.
Amen.

65. Good Shepherd

John 10: 1–11

[1] "Very truly I tell you Pharisees, anyone who does not enter the sheep pen by the gate, but climbs in by some other way, is a thief and a robber. [2] The one who enters by the gate is the shepherd of the sheep. [3] The gatekeeper opens the gate for him, and the sheep listen to his voice. He calls his own sheep by name and leads them out. [4] When he has brought out all his own, he goes on ahead of them, and his sheep follow him because they know his voice. [5] But they will never follow a stranger; in fact, they will run away from him because they do not recognize a stranger's voice." [6] Jesus used this figure of speech, but the Pharisees did not understand what he was telling them.

[7] Therefore Jesus said again, "Very truly I tell you, I am the gate for the sheep. [8] All who have come before me are thieves and robbers, but the sheep have not listened to them. [9] I am the gate; whoever enters through me will be saved.[a] They will come in and go out, and find pasture. [10] The thief comes only to steal and kill and destroy; I have come that they may have life, and have it to the full.

11 "I am the good shepherd. The good shepherd lays down his life for the sheep.

In a world of over-heated music stars, egotistical footballers and know-all pundits, Jesus makes just about the most 'everybody look at me' claim ever. In fact he does it seven times in John's Gospel.

- I am the bread of life
- I am the light of the world
- I am the gate of the sheep
- I am the good shepherd
- I am the resurrection and the life
- I am the way, the truth and the life
- I am the true vine.

In these 'I ams' he is not self-promoting but self-offering. He is simply saying, 'I am what you need'.

'I am the Good Shepherd' – 'Not in our modern world of factory farming you aren't'. Today's shepherd gets as many sheep as he or she can, gets them as fat as they can and gets them to market as soon as they can. In our world sheep are not so much individual creatures with a God given right to live and wander, so much as factory units producing meat and wool that will be turned into cash.

When Jesus talks about sheep and a shepherd two pictures come into my mind. The first one comes from my wanderings in the Yorkshire Dales. Here I am approaching a lovely green ridge and suddenly about a hundred or so ridiculously healthy-looking sheep, all fat and woolly come wandering over the ridge towards me. Then a moment later appears the shepherd on his quadbike with a couple of dogs, he is driving the sheep. My second picture originates from my first visit to the Holy Land. Here, in a dry and rocky valley, a tall gaunt man is striding out and a straggly bunch of different shapes and sizes of sheep come following him. The shepherd knows where there is a flowing stream and a bit of decent grass, he is leading the sheep.

So think of yourself as a sheep, and of you and your family and friends and your church as a flock of sheep. All sheep need a shepherd. Do you want a good shepherd or a less caring, greedy and hard one? This passage from John's Gospel picks out five features of Jesus the Good Shepherd:

- He enters our lives properly through the front door. He does not climb or force his way in.
- He knows his sheep by name. Each one of us is a special individual to him.
- He understands our individual lives and the world we live in, and so he leads us.
- We follow him, because we have learned the sound of his voice and we have come to trust him.
- Not only does Jesus enter our life through the gate, but he then becomes a greater gateway so that we can enter the life of God and salvation.

Then Jesus takes the whole thing to a different level. Ultimately all sheep die to produce the food, blood, wool etc. to keep the shepherd alive. But in this shepherd's tale the shepherd dies so that the sheep can live.

Two thoughts on sheep and shepherds. Firstly, there are lots of clever, persuasive and gifted people telling us all the time what to think, in whom to believe in, how to live our lives and on what to spend our money. They are politicians, TV experts, pundits, people who write for papers and magazines, parents, friends and teachers. They are all shepherds, but which ones are 'Good Shepherds'?

Secondly, Jesus the Good Shepherd wants us to have life 'in abundance'. I am a bit of a depressive with masses of insecurities. I work too hard at too many projects, trying to please too many people. So what does 'abundant life' mean for me?

My daughter, Zoe, has major learning difficulties and will never be able to live a 'normal' independent life. What is 'abundance' for her and who is the shepherd that can lead her there?

My wife, Maureen, spends much of her energies looking after me and Zoe and a host of others. In between times she has her own hopes and joys to find. Where is her 'abundance'?

I sometimes think of my son, Phillip, as the one truly normal person in our family. He has lots of gifts, freedom, popularity and some affluence. But he has needs too and things he is still searching for. What does a Phillip-type 'abundant life' look like?

The answer to all our abundant life issues, and to yours too, is 'I am the Good Shepherd'.

Lord Jesus
You are the Good Shepherd
I am one of your many sheep
Yet you know my name
And I am beginning to know your voice.
Help me as I follow you
Into an abundant life.
Amen.

66. The Pearl of Great Price

Matthew: 13: 44 – 46

> [44] *"The kingdom of heaven is like treasure hidden in a field. When a man found it, he hid it again, and then in his joy went and sold all he had and bought that field.*
>
> [45] *"Again, the kingdom of heaven is like a merchant looking for fine pearls.* [46] *When he found one of great value, he went away and sold everything he had and bought it."*

A couple of parables all about treasure, money, wealth, but not about that sort of treasure. In fact, we have already heard what Jesus said about it in Matthew chapter 6, verses 19–21

> [19] *"Do not store up for yourselves treasures on earth, where moths and vermin destroy, and where thieves break in and steal.* [20] *But store up for yourselves treasures in heaven, where moths and vermin do not destroy, and where thieves do not break in and steal.* [21] *For where your treasure is, there your heart will be also."*

Some time ago I read a tragic story of a young couple who won seven million pounds on the lottery and lost their ticket. I don't know whether they ever got their hands on the money but at the time they were pretty heartbroken – and who wouldn't be!?!

One year I was preaching on Easter Sunday morning in a little church in Manchester. After the service I found myself in the car park and discovered that the next-door building was a casino. What a contrast! How many people had spent the Saturday night trying to hit the jackpot? How many had been in church that Sunday morning re-living the resurrection and celebrating the jackpot?

Now let's be honest, if we had to choose between knowing Jesus and winning £5,000,000 who knows what we would do. But bear in mind that winning the money is just a dream, whilst knowing Jesus is a reality. Money can only last as long as we last, but eternal life makes us last a lot longer. And at the end of the day most of us need some sort of peace, joy and power in our heart not our pocket.

So let's get real, for most of us the money is just not going to happen but Jesus is there, right by us, right now.

The story of the Pearl of Great Price is about hitting the jackpot. There are three things to think about in the story:

- Finding the pearl
- Enjoying the pearl
- Not losing the pearl

If you are still trying to find the pearl of the Kingdom of God then you are still trying to find Jesus.

Some time ago I went to visit a young couple, Dennis and Lucy. They had been coming to our church for a while. At first I felt they were a bit disinterested and were basically coming for the kid's sake. Then I invited them to a gathering where a friend of mine was talking about the 'great pearl' in his life and they were interested. They were getting closer all the time. The point is, Jesus is the ultimate treasure so keep on searching.

Secondly, if the pearl is such a treasure then enjoy it. Too many Christians are too grey, too miserable, too non-joyful. Here in the story is a man who searches for fine pearls and suddenly he stumbles across the best he has ever seen. I think knowing Jesus is the best deal in the world. If I can't be positive, joyful and feel good about knowing him, then what can I feel good about?

For some who find Jesus it sort of cools down into a 'yes I go to church, yes I believe and yes it is fine'. What was a great pearl has settled down into a sort of okay minor bauble? As with every relationship we can lose the love, pause on the passion and basically let the fire slowly fade-away. Jesus is not a pearl but *the* pearl. Don't lose it, keep the relationship alive, hungry and fresh.

I'm a great fan of Charles Dickens' novels. In almost all of them however, there seems to be a line. Above the line people have quite a lot of money. They are usually quite happy and content. Below the line it is quite the opposite, little money and lots of misery. *David Copperfield, Great Expectations, Oliver Twist,* they all seem to be ruled by money or the lack of it.

Now I do realise that real poverty does make life very hard, especially in a rich country like ours. It is difficult to feel good when you and your children are hungry and cold. Yet even here in the midst of poverty there is still a great treasure or pearl waiting to be found.

Jesus the Treasure
I stumbled across you in a field,
I found you in a market of busyness,
I heard you in a crowd of voices.
May you now become the great treasure in my life.
Amen

67. The Prodigal Son

Luke 15: 11–32

^{11} *Jesus continued: "There was a man who had two sons.* ^{12} *The younger one said to his father, 'Father, give me my share of the estate.' So he divided his property between them.*

^{13} *"Not long after that, the younger son got together all he had, set off for a distant country and there squandered his wealth in wild living.* ^{14} *After he had spent everything, there was a severe famine in that whole country, and he began to be in need.* ^{15} *So he went and hired himself out to a citizen of that country, who sent him to his fields to feed pigs.* ^{16} *He longed to fill his stomach with the pods that the pigs were eating, but no one gave him anything.*

^{17} *"When he came to his senses, he said, 'How many of my father's hired servants have food to spare, and here I am starving to death!* ^{18} *I will set out and go back to my father and say to him: Father, I have sinned against heaven and against you.* ^{19} *I am no longer worthy to be called your son; make me like one of your hired servants.'* ^{20} *So he got up and went to his father.*

"'But while he was still a long way off, his father saw him and was filled with compassion for him; he ran to his son, threw his arms around him and kissed him.

21 "The son said to him, 'Father, I have sinned against heaven and against you. I am no longer worthy to be called your son.'

22 "But the father said to his servants, 'Quick! Bring the best robe and put it on him. Put a ring on his finger and sandals on his feet. 23 Bring the fattened calf and kill it. Let's have a feast and celebrate. 24 For this son of mine was dead and is alive again; he was lost and is found.' So they began to celebrate.

25 "Meanwhile, the older son was in the field. When he came near the house, he heard music and dancing. 26 So he called one of the servants and asked him what was going on. 27 'Your brother has come,' he replied, 'and your father has killed the fattened calf because he has him back safe and sound.'

28 "The older brother became angry and refused to go in. So his father went out and pleaded with him. 29 But he answered his father, 'Look! All these years I've been slaving for you and never disobeyed your orders. Yet you never gave me even a young goat so I could celebrate with my friends. 30 But when this son of yours who has squandered your property with prostitutes comes home, you kill the fattened calf for him!'

³¹ "'My son,' the father said, 'you are always with me, and everything I have is yours. ³² But we had to celebrate and be glad, because this brother of yours was dead and is alive again; he was lost and is found.'"

This should be a story about serious religious honour, faithfulness and obedience and about how the older brother is the only one who gets it.

Fortunately for all of us Jesus sees it differently. For him the story is all about the lost son. And that, of course, is what most of us are, lost sons and daughters. We might not be spending a fortune in a weekend, living on champagne followed by pigswill but we are lost.

To my mind no-one has ever captured this sense of lost-ness better than Bob Dylan (the Psalmist of the 20ᵗʰ century).

> 'How does it feel?
> To be on your own,
> With no direction home
> A complete unknown,
> Like a rolling stone.'

So what of the soft-brained and deluded father? He is God the Father, except he is not soft-brained but soft-hearted and not deluded but determined. Determined to welcome back his lost children, to celebrate, forgive and party.

Many years ago I was made a priest in the Church of England. As such I was given a charge 'to go out into the wilderness' and find the Father's lost children.

I think all of us who have ourselves enjoyed the 'welcome back into' should then take part in the 'going out again to find'.

It is probably the most famous and the best loved short story in the whole world. Although I personally have never liked it. I think it's sentimental, naïve and just way too soft and idealistic. If it was down to me (which thankfully it isn't) I would do it in a much more hard-faced but realistic way.

So this is the Robin Gamble version of the Prodigal Son:

- The youngest son was a spoilt little brat and who spoiled him? The father of course. So being the completely self-centred, greedy, decadent, 'couldn't give a damn about anyone else', 'me obsessive' that he was takes the money, walks out on the family and lives for the now. If he ever had a favourite song it was probably Queen singing 'I want it all, and I want it now!'
- The father is just a big sugar fairy with too much money and too little sense. He spoilt the youngest son as a kid and now he is spoiling him as a man. He makes it all just way too easy.
- The oldest brother is the only one with any sort of backbone at all. He is careful, hard-working, respectful of his father and the family tradition. He stood by quietly the first time around but not anymore. He has had enough of his useless younger brother and of his totally indulgent ageing father and so he takes over, tells a few home truths and seriously kicks a few butts.

Thinking about myself in real life however, I have a very strong feeling that I could never measure up to the high standards of the older brother. In contrast and desperate gratitude I could look up to the overwhelmingly generous forgiveness and 'begin again' love of the father.

Heavenly Father
Is it really true?
That I can come back to you
That I can be forgiven
That I can begin again?
Thank you because you tell me in this story
That the answer is always yes.
Amen.

68. Parable of the Talents

Luke 19: 11–26

¹¹ *While they were listening to this, he went on to tell them a parable, because he was near Jerusalem and the people thought that the kingdom of God was going to appear at once.* ¹² *He said: "A man of noble birth went to a distant country to have himself appointed king and then to return.* ¹³ *So he called ten of his servants and gave them ten minas. 'Put this money to work,' he said, 'until I come back.'*

¹⁴ *"But his subjects hated him and sent a delegation after him to say, 'We don't want this man to be our king.'*

¹⁵ *"He was made king, however, and returned home. Then he sent for the servants to whom he had given the money, in order to find out what they had gained with it.*

¹⁶ *"The first one came and said, 'Sir, your mina has earned ten more.'*

¹⁷ *"'Well done, my good servant!' his master replied. 'Because you have been trustworthy in a very small matter, take charge of ten cities.'*

¹⁸ *"The second came and said, 'Sir, your mina has earned five more.'*

¹⁹ *"His master answered, 'You take charge of five cities.'*

²⁰ *"Then another servant came and said, 'Sir, here is your mina; I have kept it laid away in a piece of cloth.* ²¹ *I was afraid of you, because you are a hard man. You take out what you did not put in and reap what you did not sow.'*

²² *"His master replied, 'I will judge you by your own words, you wicked servant! You knew, did you, that I am a hard man, taking out what I did not put in, and reaping what I did not sow?* ²³ *Why then didn't you put my money on deposit, so that when I came back, I could have collected it with interest?'*

²⁴ *"Then he said to those standing by, 'Take his mina away from him and give it to the one who has ten minas.'*

²⁵ *"'Sir,' they said, 'he already has ten!'*

²⁶ *"He replied, 'I tell you that to everyone who has, more will be given, but as for the one who has nothing, even what they have will be taken away."*

As a teenager I was a football obsessive, watching it, reading about it in magazines, playing and fantasising about it. Of course, I was nothing like my superheroes, in fact, I was nothing like the best players in my school or even my class. I was a four talent footballer, a bit better at rugby – perhaps six talents, but I was always surrounded by others with eight, nine or ten talents. I was also surrounded by one, two and three talent players but that's another picture.

The point is I never compared myself to the lesser talents and thought, 'Oh, I'm ok at this game'. I always looked at the biggest and the best and thought, 'They are really good but I'm pretty rubbish'.

When I started following Jesus it was exactly the same. I was in a big Christian youth group. I was good with the God talk but not so good at the walk. There were always others who were nicer, kinder, more prayerful and less screwed up than me. The same thing happened when I became a young vicar, an older vicar and even now when I am a pretty ancient vicar. There are always others who are wiser, more peaceful, less angry and more Godly. I seem to be permanently living as a four to six talent person surrounded by superstars.

Actually this story is not about giving us marks. Jesus is not a judge in 'Strictly Come Christian', holding up a notice board and commenting on our footwork. He is an encourager, not a 'pointer-outer'. That is to say whether we are very talented or have lesser things to offer he welcomes all of us as fellow Kingdom builders.

It is about every one of us offering, giving, trying, doing and never burying. How much of our precious lives have we buried whilst lying on a sofa, watching rubbish telly, or endlessly flickering away on our phones? How many hours have been frittered away? How much action put into the non-action bin and creative, wonderful, truth-seeking thinking been put to sleep while we meandered aimlessly through so much YouTube nonsense? So stop burying and start living, doing and thinking.

In his '12 Rules for Life' Jordan Peterson, the ultimate Godfather of all self-improvement gurus, warns us never to compare ourselves to others, we will always come off badly. Instead compare yourself to yourself as you were twelve months ago. Even if you are a one talent person see how your one talent has become better, deeper, richer and more golden. Be encouraged rather than discouraged, built up rather than brought down and taken forward rather than taken to task.

So can you work out one clear talent that God has given you?

> Lord God,
> Help me to be the person you have made me,
> To use the talent you have given me,
> To reflect the light you have shone on me,
> And to live the life you have opened for me.
> Amen.

69. The Two Sisters

Luke 10: 38–42

> ³⁸ *As Jesus and the disciples continued on their way to Jerusalem, they came to a certain village where a woman named Martha welcomed him into her home.* ³⁹ *Her sister, Mary, sat at the Lord's feet, listening to what he taught.* ⁴⁰ *But Martha was distracted by the big dinner she was preparing. She came to Jesus and said, "Lord, doesn't it seem unfair to you that my sister just sits here while I do all the work? Tell her to come and help me."*
>
> ⁴¹ *But the Lord said to her, "My dear Martha, you are worried and upset over all these details!* ⁴² *There is only one thing worth being concerned about. Mary has discovered it, and it will not be taken away from her."*

Now this may come as an unusual thought to you but Jesus might have been the first and almost certainly he was the greatest 'women's libber' of all time.

Jesus lived in a world that was run by the men and for the men. Women were used and abused, expected to fill secondary and often menial roles, were rarely listened to and never fully respected. So how revolutionary and 2,000 years ahead of their time were Jesus' attitudes and actions towards women. He treated them as full and important people, listened to their conversation, was incredibly aware of their needs and desperate situations, was completely non-judgmental and was even willing to depend on them in the carrying out of his mission.

There are lots of great stories of Jesus and women, this is one of my favourites. The very fact that Jesus is clearly so relaxed and non-superior in their presence is breathtaking. It reads more like a story out of the 20th, rather than the 1st century. Mary and Martha are two sisters who live with their brother Lazarus. In a world where virtually everyone got married this is an odd little family. We shall come across them again when Jesus attends what should be Lazarus' funeral and ruins the occasion by raising him from the dead.

Both Mary and Martha are welcoming and at-home with Jesus, but it is usual to differentiate between the two on the basis that Martha is 'practical' and in the kitchen, whilst Mary is 'spiritual' and at the feet of Jesus. There is a real truth in this dividing of the sisters, it is a part of the story and we can easily see where the emphasis lies.

As a Northern working-class man, it has taken me many years to fully appreciate and then to start living out the attitudes and lifestyle of Jesus. I grew up in Yorkshire where being a male chauvinist pig is basically an art form. I have had to wade through layers of prejudice and think long and deeply about how

I have often used my mother, my older sister and even my dear wife, Maureen and allowed her to occupy a servant role. So how was Jesus able to be so incredibly clear-sighted and understanding? How did he find the courage to be so different from other men? And what did women feel like when they encountered him – how special and precious did he make them feel? No wonder Mary Magdalene in *'Jesus Christ Superstar'* sings 'I don't know how to love him'.

When I read the Mary and Martha story I see two women completing two essential tasks between them. They are tasks or life-options that we should all be good at but which, in my experience, men are usually not. The first task is all about caring for people, making them feel welcome, providing great hospitality and comfort. This is the basic stuff that makes human relationships feel so good. The second task or activity is more about spirituality than domesticity. I visit lots of churches, religious events, conferences, jamborees and courses etc. and at every point I see lots of women and a few men who are really good at it, who are prayerful, understanding, spiritually receptive and comfortable simply sitting at the feet of Jesus.

It is high time that we men started learning from all the Marys and Marthas that we know, perhaps that we are married to and start catching up.

A final thought and a final question.

It is so easy to lose ourselves in domesticity, in jobs that need to be done and an unending stream of busyness.

In fact, it is so easy that many of us just become lost in this world of doing and never make time or space for simply sitting at Jesus' feet, gazing up into his eyes and listening to his voice.

Have you got enough time and space in your life to sit at the Lord's feet?

> Lord
> I welcome you into my life this day
> Can I settle you
> And help you to feel comfortable?
> May I now sit at your feet
> And listen?
> Amen.

70. He Set Her Free

Luke 13: 10–17

¹⁰ *One Sabbath day as Jesus was teaching in a synagogue, ¹¹ he saw a woman who had been crippled by an evil spirit. She had been bent double for eighteen years and was unable to stand up straight. ¹² When Jesus saw her, he called her over and said, "Dear woman, you are healed of your sickness!" ¹³ Then he touched her, and instantly she could stand straight. How she praised God!*

¹⁴ *But the leader in charge of the synagogue was indignant that Jesus had healed her on the Sabbath day. "There are six days of the week for working," he said to the crowd. "Come on those days to be healed, not on the Sabbath."*

¹⁵ *But the Lord replied, "You hypocrites! Each of you works on the Sabbath day! Don't you untie your ox or your donkey from its stall on the Sabbath and lead it out for water? ¹⁶ This dear woman, a daughter of Abraham, has been held in bondage by Satan for eighteen years. Isn't it right that she be released, even on the Sabbath?"*

¹⁷ *This shamed his enemies, but all the people rejoiced at the wonderful things he did.*

Another story about Jesus and women, and why not? It's a story that is not told enough. All women, and men as well, need to get a big picture, blue sky image of Jesus' amazing love for women.

A crippled woman is helped to walk by Jesus. We take the story for granted, 'well of course Jesus helped this woman', but that's not how things worked out in Jesus' day. Women were expected to put up with afflictions and men were expected to concentrate on other men. So for Jesus to be aware of and committed to such a woman is revolutionary, it has taken the Western World two thousand years to catch up with him.

- His own mother at the cross
- A prostitute caught in the act
- A sick woman robbed by the doctors
- A lonely woman who had had five husbands
- A mother whose son had died.

He understood and reached out to touch them all. Maybe he was the one man who has understood and given more to women than any other man.

Some time ago I was doing a women's night as part of a mission. The home women had booked a smart hotel, organised great food, designed a great women's quiz, brought in a DJ and wanted me to speak about Jesus in a woman's life. I first interviewed a couple of women. Then I talked about how I thought the key women in my life gave me more than I gave them. I spoke about Jesus as the 'exceptional man' who gave so much more to women gradually moving my words into a Power

Point of Jesus pictures with music. Hearts were opened and tears flowed and there was laughter too as women who were givers discovered or re-discovered the man who gave them so much.

Maureen Gamble has had three main men in her life. Her Dad was Sam, her son is Phillip and I am Robin, her husband. All three of us have realised what a special woman she is and we have loved her as a daughter, a mother and a wife. But I have always been aware of her love for each of us being more generous, more positive and more 'full of grace' than ours for her.

There is of course, one truly great and special man in Maureen's life. He sees her, calls her over and touches her. He is called Jesus. He is the one man who fully understands and is always, always fully there for her.

> Looking out on the morning rain
> I used to feel so uninspired
> And when I knew I had to face another day
> Lord, it made me feel so tired
> Before the day I met you, life was so unkind
> But you're the key to my peace of mind
>
> 'Cause you make me feel
> You make me feel
> You make me feel like
> A natural woman (woman).
>
> When my soul was in the lost and found
> You came along to claim it
> I didn't know just what was wrong with me

'Til your kiss helped me name it
Now I'm no longer doubtful, of what I'm living
for
And if I make you happy I don't need to do
more

'Cause you make me feel
You make me feel
You make me feel like
A natural woman (woman).   Aretha Franklin

How does knowing Jesus make you feel at the beginning
of every day?

Lord,
At the beginning of the day
Remind me to look to you.
Tell me again about who I am
And who you are.
Help me to live it as a special day
And remind me at the end of the day
To look to you again.
Amen

71. Ten Lepers

Luke 17: 11–19

¹¹ *Now on his way to Jerusalem, Jesus travelled along the border between Samaria and Galilee.* ¹² *As he was going into a village, ten men who had leprosy met him. They stood at a distance* ¹³ *and called out in a loud voice, "Jesus, Master, have pity on us!"*

¹⁴ *When he saw them, he said, "Go, show yourselves to the priests." And as they went, they were cleansed.*

¹⁵ *One of them, when he saw he was healed, came back, praising God in a loud voice.* ¹⁶ *He threw himself at Jesus' feet and thanked him – and he was a Samaritan.*

¹⁷ *Jesus asked, "Were not all ten cleansed? Where are the other nine?* ¹⁸ *Has no one returned to give praise to God except this foreigner?"* ¹⁹ *Then he said to him, "Rise and go; your faith has made you well."*

They were the uncurables. With a disease so contagious that they had to be separated from everyone else. Living, or existing, outside their home towns and villages with an illness eating away at their outer body parts. They were seen as the living dead. They were the lepers.

Leprosy still exists, but not in the way it did in Jesus' days, and not in my town. Despite this I have met plenty of modern-day lepers. Here are ten of them: -

- A father hated by his children
- A paedophile rejected by everybody
- An unfaithful wife rejected by her husband
- A heavy smoker living with lung cancer
- An alcoholic drinking more every day not less
- A drug addict who stole every day from his family
- A loving and much-loved man slipping into dementia
- A young man fading away from AIDS, having already lost the love of his life
- A middle-aged angry white man full of racism and bad language
- A lonely woman, living alone, and who smells badly

It is a list of the people we don't want to be, of the ones we don't want our children to become. They are the people we avoid, and who everyone else avoids too. We don't want them living next door, marrying into our family. We don't even want them in our church even though we realise how much they need to be in a church somewhere.

In the story the ten lepers, it reminds me of the children's song 'Ten Green Bottles' – and if one green bottle should accidentally fall. These lepers are going to fall one by one until eventually there will be no green bottles. In a last desperate appeal they call out to Jesus.

Perhaps because he is on his way to his own anticipated death in Jerusalem, he is particularly aware of them. Or perhaps it is just the ordinary, everyday, reaching out to the outcast, love of Jesus.

All ten lepers are healed, only one comes back to say thank you. Where are the others? What are they thinking? Do they ever say thank you for anything? Do they ever stop and think about the goodness of God? Or the close cleansing presence of Jesus? I am one of these naturally me-centred people to whom saying thank you does not come easily. I have had to learn how to realise, stop, turn back and say, 'thank you'. What I have learned is that to be thankful is not just a respectful, courteous and right thing to do. It is actually the very best, the juiciest thing, the thing that makes me feel good.

Time for another song

> Thank you for free and full salvation
> Thank you for grace to hold it fast
> Thank you, O Lord I want to thank you
> That I'm free to thank!
> Thank you, O Lord I want to thank you
> That I'm free to thank.

Lord Jesus
Thank you for your healing touch.
For your touch on my body
In my mind
And deep into my soul.
May you continue to reach out and touch me
And may I continue to say Thank You.
Amen.

72. Jesus and Zacchaeus

Luke 19: 1–10

¹ *Jesus entered Jericho and was passing through.* ² *A man was there by the name of Zacchaeus; he was a chief tax collector and was wealthy.* ³ *He wanted to see who Jesus was, but because he was short he could not see over the crowd.* ⁴ *So he ran ahead and climbed a sycamore-fig tree to see him, since Jesus was coming that way.*

⁵ *When Jesus reached the spot, he looked up and said to him, "Zacchaeus, come down immediately. I must stay at your house today."* ⁶ *So he came down at once and welcomed him gladly.*

⁷ *All the people saw this and began to mutter, "He has gone to be the guest of a sinner."*

⁸ *But Zacchaeus stood up and said to the Lord, "Look, Lord! Here and now I give half of my possessions to the poor, and if I have cheated anybody out of anything, I will pay back four times the amount."*

⁹ *Jesus said to him, "Today salvation has come to this house, because this man, too, is a son of Abraham.* ¹⁰ *For the Son of Man came to seek and to save the lost."*

Say hello to Zacchaeus, the Danny DeVito of the Gospels. Big house, plenty of money, other rich friends and despised by the people. Why, because he is the exact opposite of Robin Hood. Zacchaeus is a tax collector which means he squeezes the money out of the people, gives some of it to the Romans, but keeps a big cut for himself.

On the day that Jesus comes to Jericho, Zacchaeus is at the back of the queue. He struggles to peer over shoulders and so climbs a tree. This is a classic 'Children's Bible' picture, crowds of people all in bright colours, Jesus teaching and healing, everyone happy. All preachers, leaders and evangelists love crowds, we love being listened to by lots of people. We all have a bit of a rock star complex. But not Jesus.

> He is more into people than popularity
> More righteousness than reputation
> More concerned with others than his own ego.

When it comes to numerical growth his favourite number is one.

So Jesus looks above the heads of the crowd and spots a single lone individual. Then he does what no populist preacher/celebrity ever does. He walks away from the multitude and pours himself into one ignored, disliked and back of the queue person called Zacchaeus.

Jesus, Saviour of the whole world and yet at the same time Saviour of one lost isolated Zacchaeus. This is just one of the many rich things that makes me want to be like Jesus.

His special love for individuals, his willingness to spend time with and to listen to the one person sitting in the corner. Why is this so special to me, because I am not part of the crowd, a number. I am me, unique, one-off.

> I am not a number,
> Not part of a crowd,
> And the other people like me,
> They're all quite different.
> I have my own issues, problems,
> And things that I wish I had never done.
> I have also got my hopes, my dreams
> And some stuff that I am proud of.
> I don't just want to sit in a big hall and listen to Jesus
> I want him to walk over, smile and talk to me.

The ever-present spirituality of U2 gets close to it.

> One love
> One life
> One life
> You got to do what you should
> One life
> With each other
> Sisters and my brothers
> One life
> But we're not the same
> We get to carry each other, carry each other.

But it is not just about Jesus and his one-on-one love for me. It is also about how I become like him and operate in his name. When I first became a Christian, I wanted to tell lots of people. When I became involved with youth work, the desire to speak to lots of young people grew.

It grew even more when I became a vicar and positively mushroomed in my early days of evangelism.

Quite a few years passed before I fully realised that Jesus loved to touch people one at a time, and that he wanted me to do the same.

A big question then for me and for you, 'Who is the one key individual who I already know and who may be interested in my faith, my relationship to Jesus and who may well want to find out more?'

Lord Jesus,
Where, or rather, who is the Zacchaeus in my life?
Slow me down, that I might remember him
Help me to recall her voice, his face.
Help me to notice him, to visit her.
Amen.

73. Jesus and Children

Mark 10: 13–16

13 People were bringing little children to Jesus for him to place his hands on them, but the disciples rebuked them. 14 When Jesus saw this, he was indignant. He said to them, "Let the little children come to me, and do not hinder them, for the kingdom of God belongs to such as these. 15 Truly I tell you, anyone who will not receive the kingdom of God like a little child will never enter it." 16 And he took the children in his arms, placed his hands on them and blessed them.

What a picture – 'he took them in his arms'. When you take a child in your arms you are lifting them up, saying they are special, protecting them, taking responsibility for them, pressing them to your heart and blessing them.

Many years ago there was a common essay title for students of New Testament theology, 'Was Jesus a revolutionary?' In those days many of us were wearing our Che Guevara T-shirts and thinking of Marxist or Marxist-type revolutionaries. The answer then was no, but today it is yes. If we look at the way Jesus cared for the poor and lepers and his incredible interest in and respect for women and children we see a revolutionary.

His was not a political revolution but a reaching out, loving one. Children in his day were on the edge, not really listened to and thought about, so the disciples are typical in their disregard of them. Jesus on the other hand thinks they are special, vulnerable and important.

We today are completely different. As parents and grandparents, aunts and uncles we are positively obsessed by our children. We are indulgent to a fault and often completely sentimental in how we think about them. They are at the centre of everything, shielded from infections, abuse and from all manner of dangerous play activities such as climbing trees, riding their bikes on proper roads and wandering off into woods and parks. We spend small fortunes on them at Christmas, birthdays and holiday times and devote a chunk of our lives to driving them around from school to clubs to shopping centres.

I wonder however if there is one vital area of living and growing where children are perhaps more deprived than ever before. We provide for their material, physical and educational development but what about their spiritual growth?

Luke's picture of Jesus as a young boy gives us a great model of a child growing healthily in a rounded way. Jesus 'grew strong, filled with wisdom and the favour of God was upon him' (2: 40). Jesus the child grew in body, mind and spirit. We are all desperate to see our children grow up strong and healthy. We want them to do well at school and pass their exams with massive 'A' star approval. But what are we doing to develop them spiritually, how are we nourishing their souls, their own individual spark of divinity which rests inside them?

The very physical act of Jesus taking children in his arms meant that he clutched them to his heart. He laid his hand on them and blessed them. If we are following Jesus there is a big series of footsteps here for us to walk in. They are about helping the children in our church, in our friendship circle and in our own family. Building relationships with these children, having conversations with them, praying for them and encouraging them to join in with a children's Christian group. So here are a couple of questions for you to think about:

- Who is the child in your life that you can help to draw closer to Jesus?
- Where is the child in you that you that still needs to be taken up in his arms?

Dear Lord Jesus
What about my children,
My grandchildren,
Nephews and nieces,
The children of my friends and neighbours?
How they need to be lifted up in your arms
And held to your heart
Perhaps they need a bit of help from me
To make it happen.
Amen

74. Jesus in the Midst

Matthew 18:20

[20] For where two or three gather in my name, there am I with them.'

Jesus was clearly looking beyond the immediate moment of his teaching his disciples. He was looking beyond his crucifixion, resurrection and ascension to a time when he would have returned to Heaven and his followers would feel themselves without him. Today we are still in that 'without him time' and the promise is still with us that when we gather in his name he is in the middle of the circle. This simple gathering together we call church.

'Jesus, Yes, the Church, No.' so said the mighty, Mick Jagger. Well Mick, 'Rock Star, Yes, Theologian, No.' The church is not some great English institution like the House of Lords, public schools and county cricket. It is the most amazing, broken, world changing and yet messed up bunch of people the world has ever known. In its simplest sense the church is simply a few Jesus followers, the sort that he himself classified as brothers and sisters, getting together in his name.

Two or three thousand at a Christian festival, two or three hundred in a wonderful open act of worship or maybe just two or three having honest prayer and conversation. There he is in the midst of them.

This is why Jesus kept building his followers into communities. Peter, James and John, the 'twelve', the supporting women in Luke 8, his followers and his family mentioned together in Acts 1, the women at the cross. These are not, however, standing still and meeting every week for the 'same old, same old'. They are movements. Moving forward, gathering in others, moving the world.

In my own experience, there are a handful of things that I do with other Christians that often turn into truly transcendent experiences of joy, wordless warmth and excitement. Sometimes it happens when we are singing a beautiful and uplifting song of worship; at other times it might happen as a few of us read the Bible together and suddenly there is a shared 'dropping of the penny'. The moment sometimes comes when I join with a few brothers and sisters in an act of mission and evangelism or simply when I am down the pub and having a drink with a few Christian buddies.

During the coronavirus pandemic of 2020 it seemed as if churches were going to have to close down and Christians would lose all sense of togetherness. Almost immediately, however, people started phoning each other up to check up on each other's needs. Services went online. Daily prayers started attracting large numbers. Prayer and study groups began meeting on Zoom and there was a new discovery of Jesus being 'in the midst of them'. If you are becoming a bit isolated as a follower or just not spending enough time with the right people then why don't you get back to being a living and positive part of his family/church/movement. It is both a very warm human experience and a deeply spiritual one when we join in a two or three, a twenty or thirty or even a two hundred or three hundred and discover him in the midst. There is something very special in being part of a group. It is there in 'The Hobbit' with Bilbo and the dwarves travelling together, it is there in the Western Epic of 'The Magnificent Seven' and in the Second World War story, 'The Band of Brothers'. It is even to be found in Enid Blyton with the 'Famous Five' and the 'Secret Seven'.

This sort of belonging calls on others to be loyal to us and on us to be loyal to them.

The big question is 'who are your two or three and how committed to them are you?

> Lord Jesus
> If I am to truly follow you
> Then I need to follow you with some others.
> I need them
> And they need me.
> May we follow you together
> And may you be in our midst?
> Amen.

75. Lazarus

John 11: 30-51

³⁰ Now Jesus had not yet entered the village, but was still at the place where Martha had met him. ³¹ When the Jews who had been with Mary in the house, comforting her, noticed how quickly she got up and went out, they followed her, supposing she was going to the tomb to mourn there.

³² When Mary reached the place where Jesus was and saw him, she fell at his feet and said, "Lord, if you had been here, my brother would not have died."

³³ When Jesus saw her weeping, and the Jews who had come along with her also weeping, he was deeply moved in spirit and troubled. ³⁴ "Where have you laid him?" he asked.

"Come and see, Lord," they replied.

³⁵ Jesus wept.

³⁶ Then the Jews said, "See how he loved him!"

³⁷ But some of them said, "Could not he who opened the eyes of the blind man have kept this man from dying?"

³⁸ *Jesus, once more deeply moved, came to the tomb. It was a cave with a stone laid across the entrance.* ³⁹ *"Take away the stone," he said.*

"But, Lord," said Martha, the sister of the dead man, "by this time there is a bad odour, for he has been there four days."

⁴⁰ *Then Jesus said, "Did I not tell you that if you believe, you will see the glory of God?"*

⁴¹ *So they took away the stone. Then Jesus looked up and said, "Father, I thank you that you have heard me.* ⁴² *I knew that you always hear me, but I said this for the benefit of the people standing here, that they may believe that you sent me."*

⁴³ *When he had said this, Jesus called in a loud voice, "Lazarus, come out!"* ⁴⁴ *The dead man came out, his hands and feet wrapped with strips of linen, and a cloth around his face.*

Jesus said to them, "Take off the grave clothes and let him go."

⁴⁵ *Therefore many of the Jews who had come to visit Mary, and had seen what Jesus did, believed in him.* ⁴⁶ *But some of them went to the Pharisees and told them what Jesus had done.* ⁴⁷ *Then the chief priests and the Pharisees called a meeting of the Sanhedrin.*

"What are we accomplishing?" they asked. "Here is this man performing many signs. ⁴⁸ *If we let him go on like this, everyone will believe in him, and then the Romans will come and take away both our temple and our nation."*

⁴⁹ Then one of them, named Caiaphas, who was high priest that year, spoke up, "You know nothing at all! ⁵⁰ You do not realize that it is better for you that one man die for the people than that the whole nation perish."

⁵¹ He did not say this on his own, but as high priest that year he prophesied that Jesus would die for the Jewish nation,

Mary, Martha and Lazarus, two sisters and a brother, what a strange little household they were. No marriages (unless husbands and wife had died) and no children. They are portrayed in the gospels not so much as disciples or followers of Jesus but as very special friends. No wonder then that Jesus wept at the tomb of a very good friend and how reassuring to see that Jesus had all the emotional sadness of grief that we experience. And how tragically ironic that in raising a man to life he condemns himself to death.

If I was Aladdin and Jesus was my genie of the lamp what three things would I wish for?

First, restoration and healing for my daughter, Zoe.

Second, something very special for my wonderful wife, such as a much better husband (she deserves it!)

And third, life after death, resurrection, a beginning again after the cemetery. Lazarus gets wish number three.

When Jesus says 'Lazarus, come out',
　Come out of the tomb
out of the pit
　　　the darkness.
　Come out of the black hole that is about
　to swallow you forever.
　Come into the light
　　　into the land of new beginnings
　　　where life is deeper, brighter, bigger.
Come out of the death
And into the life

So is Lazarus the single luckiest person in the whole world or is he a pathfinder, a beacon, an image of everything Jesus wants to do for every one of us?

Many years ago I was sitting or lazing on the sofa watching a film. It's my day off and the end of a very busy week. The film is called *'Highlander'* and half way through a Queen song kicks in ……..

'Who wants to live forever?'

I am immediately pulled back to full wakefulness, partly by the dramatic melody but more by the repetitive asking of the question. Straightaway I am thinking of lots of people who need to be confronted by the question whilst also silently shrieking my own answer. I do, I want to live forever, I've always wanted to live forever.

There's no time for us
There's no place for us
What is this thing that builds our dreams
Yet slips away from us?

Who wants to live forever?
Who wants to live forever?

There's no chance for us
It's all decided for us
This world has only one
Sweet moment set aside for us.

Who wants to live forever?
Who wants to live forever?
Who?

Who dares to love forever
Oh, when love must die?

But touch my tears with your lips
Touch my world with your fingertips.

And we can have forever
And we can love forever
Forever is our today.

Who wants to live forever?
Who wants to live forever?
Forever is our today.

Who waits forever anyway?

Sometime after this I actually got to meet the truly lovely and gentle Brian May. He told me how he had written this song when he heard about Freddie Mercury's impending death. I think we have all got an impending death. It takes us all and steals from us all.

Lazarus was not the luckiest, he was the first of many. The word for it is not lucky but blessed. Blessed with resurrection, blessed with a second chance, blessed with eternity.

Caiaphas, the High Priest, didn't realise what a great and prophetic statement he was making. 'It is better for you to have one man die for the people than to have the whole nation destroyed.'

> **Lord Jesus**
> **Help me to hear you calling me by name,**
> **To hear you calling me out of the tomb**
> **And back to light and life**
> **Help me to respond to you**
> **And to live again.**
> **Amen.**

76. On the Road to Jerusalem

Luke 13: 22,

²² Then Jesus went through the towns and villages, teaching as he made his way to Jerusalem.

Luke 14: 25,

²⁵ Large crowds were travelling with Jesus, and turning to them he said:

Luke 18: 31–33,

³¹ Jesus took the Twelve aside and told them, "We are going up to Jerusalem, and everything that is written by the prophets about the Son of Man will be fulfilled. ³² He will be delivered over to the Gentiles. They will mock him, insult him and spit on him; ³³ they will flog him and kill him. On the third day he will rise again."

Jesus is on the road to Jerusalem. He is travelling there with his disciples but others join them in a sort of travelling pilgrimage convoy. Perhaps the crowd are there because they are simply caught up in the moment. The disciples are there because they are following and learning from Jesus. Jesus is there because it is his destiny, his purpose, the reason why he came.

His travelling on the road has something of the 'Follow the Yellow Brick Road' feel from the *'Wizard of Oz'*. The difference is he is not travelling to the Emerald City but to the 'Holy City'. Except when he gets there he will discover that rather than being the 'Holy City' it is:

> the 'Empty City'
> the 'Rebellious City'
> the 'We are in control City'
> and as in the Wizard of Oz it will all be a bit of a sham.

Or as the great Bob Dylan might sing

> How does it feel
> How does it feel
> To be on your own
> With no direction home
> Like a complete unknown
> Just like a rolling stone?

Jesus would have preferred to be going to Jerusalem to gather its people to him like a bird with its chicks under its wings. That was never going to happen. Instead there is an ominous gathering of grey clouds. He is on the road to

> A climactic show down
> An ultimate collision

A last battle
A Jerusalem finale
    Or perhaps just to hand himself in.

It is a bit like Frodo and Sam on their way to the mountain top darkness of Mordor in 'Lord of the Rings'. The difference here is that it is not the ring but the ring bearer who must be destroyed and there will be no rescuing eagles at the end of Jesus's road.

If we are following Jesus then we must be on a road too. Where is your purposeful road taking you to? Or are you aimlessly drifting? Or perhaps you are sitting on a roadside bench and you have been on it longer than you realise? Or maybe you are stuck at a crossroads or repeatedly going round a roundabout and uncertain which exit to take?

Of course the big difference between us and Jesus is that he was on the road to the Old Jerusalem. We are travelling to the New one, to a place of light, healing and eternity. You can read about it in Revelation chapter twenty.

The American poet, Robert Frost, talks about walking through a 'yellow wood'. Suddenly the road forks. Will he follow the main and well-worn pathway or will he go on the grassier one, 'the one less travelled'. The poem reminds us of Jesus talking about the two roads, the broad 'full of people' road and the 'more demanding' less used uphill track. In both cases the 'road less travelled' is the best one to follow. Life as a journey is a very common metaphor. Of course, thinking and reading about the journey is one thing but actively following Jesus, striding out on the road is another matter.

> Get your feet on the path
> Keep going
> Meet other people on the way
> Enjoy the occasional picnic
> Live the adventure.

Question, which line in this little piece best applies to where you are on the journey?

Lord Jesus
As you travelled, help me to travel
To walk in your footsteps
To live the adventure
And to arrive at the New Jerusalem.
Amen

77. The Blind See

John 9: 1–10

> [1] *As he went along, he saw a man blind from birth.*
> [2] *His disciples asked him, "Rabbi, who sinned, this man or his parents, that he was born blind?"*
>
> [3] *"Neither this man nor his parents sinned," said Jesus, "but this happened so that the works of God might be displayed in him. [4] As long as it is day, we must do the works of him who sent me. Night is coming, when no one can work. [5] While I am in the world, I am the light of the world."*
>
> [6] *After saying this, he spit on the ground, made some mud with the saliva, and put it on the man's eyes. [7] "Go," he told him, "wash in the Pool of Siloam" (this word means "Sent"). So the man went and washed, and came home seeing.*
>
> [8] *His neighbours and those who had formerly seen him begging asked, "Isn't this the same man who used to sit and beg?" [9] Some claimed that he was.*
>
> *Others said, "No, he only looks like him."*
>
> *But he himself insisted, "I am the man."*
>
> [10] *"How then were your eyes opened?" they asked*

Blindness was a much bigger problem in Jesus' time than it is today. Poor living conditions, lack of sanitation and masses of venomous insects made it a common illness which usually resulted in people becoming beggars. Of all the healing miracles there are three of blind people having their sight restored that stand out. The man of Bethsaida who when first touched by Jesus saw people looking like trees and then on the second touch saw them as people. Bartimaus was a blind beggar in Jericho, when Jesus healed him he became one of his followers on the way. Here, in this third story, we meet a man blind from birth.

The Jews believed that such a condition was a judgement on sin but Jesus dispels this idea.

The restoration of the man's sight is then seen as a pointer to Jesus being 'the Light of the World' and beyond that of how we need to have our spiritual eyes opened.

As one born and brought up in the city of Bradford I, like most of my peers, was blinded by racism. This rejection of 'the other' may have been in my DNA, in my 'nature'. It was certainly in my 'nurture'. There were just so many voices, opinions, ignorant views and terms of abuse in common use to reinforce and bolster this spiritual blindness that it was almost unavoidable. It took Jesus years and years to open my racist eyes, to gradually bathe away the prejudice and enable me to see.

Spiritual blindness can be found in lots of 'isms'. None more so than atheism; atheists are people who do not believe in the existence of God. I have met quite a few atheists over the years. Occasionally, though quite rarely, I meet one who has carefully thought through the issues of belief, faith and God and has decided that they just cannot accept them. In most cases, however, it seems like they have simply closed their eyes to the possibilities and made their minds up. Christians are often accused of taking a blind leap of belief. The American novelist John Updike spoke of the 'blind leap of unbelief' being much wider. Atheism can be a prejudice, a blind faith. When Boris Pasternack, the author of Doctor Zhivago, was asked by his atheist friends why he had stopped attending their meetings he replied that he had 'lost his faith'. He had opened his eyes and discovered God.

> The eye that doesn't see,
> The mind that cannot open,
> The truth that is hidden
> And the beauty obscured.
>
> The voice that is not heard,
> The music unloved,
> And the life unlived.
>
> How we need Jesus,
> To open our eyes.

In each of the three big 'healing of the blind man' stories that I mentioned earlier, there is a very strong sense of Jesus standing right in front of the blind man, focusing on him as an individual and reaching out to his blindness. As you read this he is looking into your face and eyes and reaching out to touch you.

So today's question is simple, 'Where is your blind spot?'

Lord Jesus
There are things I just cannot see
Words I cannot hear.
I am blind and deaf
In ways I cannot grasp.
Reach out and touch me
And give me a true vision.
Amen

78. The Night Before

John 12: 1–11

¹ *Six days before the Passover, Jesus came to Bethany, where Lazarus lived, whom Jesus had raised from the dead.* ² *Here a dinner was given in Jesus' honour. Martha served, while Lazarus was among those reclining at the table with him.* ³ *Then Mary took about a pint of pure nard, an expensive perfume; she poured it on Jesus' feet and wiped his feet with her hair. And the house was filled with the fragrance of the perfume.*

⁴ *But one of his disciples, Judas Iscariot, who was later to betray him, objected,* ⁵ *"Why wasn't this perfume sold and the money given to the poor? It was worth a year's wages."* ⁶ *He did not say this because he cared about the poor but because he was a thief; as keeper of the money bag, he used to help himself to what was put into it.*

⁷ *"Leave her alone," Jesus replied. "It was intended that she should save this perfume for the day of my burial.* ⁸ *You will always have the poor among you, but you will not always have me."*

⁹ *Meanwhile a large crowd of Jews found out that Jesus was there and came, not only because of*

him but also to see Lazarus, whom he had raised from the dead. ¹⁰ So the chief priests made plans to kill Lazarus as well, ¹¹ for on account of him many of the Jews were going over to Jesus and believing in him.

When I was a boy I used to get very excited about the Cup Final and I would often try to imagine what it was like in the team hotel on the night before the match. Were they nervous or excited? Quiet or rowdy? Confident or pessimistic? And the most important question of all, were they looking forward to the biggest match of their lives or were they fearful and frightened by it?

In our Jesus story, we are with Jesus and his disciples the night before it all kicks off. Tomorrow he will march into Jerusalem, this will be the great climax, the big battle, the final countdown and this final peaceful Saturday night with friends is the night before his Cup Final. So is he looking forward to it or is he dreading it?

Jesus is staying in a 'safe house', the home of the odd little triplet of Lazarus and his two sisters Mary and Martha. Odd because it seems that none of them were married, very unusual in Jewish culture. Here we see Lazarus as the host, Martha as the hospitality provider and Mary as the worshipper. This is the scene of a previous great event when Jesus had raised Lazarus from the dead. The memories of that, the anticipation of the great feast of the Passover and Jesus' own feelings about what lay ahead were all floating heavily in the atmosphere as they sat around the table.

It is one of the most beautiful pictures of an individual offering a personal act of worship that we read about in Jesus' story. Mary comes before Jesus, anoints his feet with costly perfume and then dries them with her hair. The room is silent in awe and wonderment, the air is filled with fragrance. Only the grumblings of Judas's disturbed spirit breaks the mood.

There is a threefold act of devoted worship here. One, she kneels before Jesus; two, she offers an expensive gift and three, she dries his feet with her hair. This is devotion, worship and generosity. Together they form a three cord promise of love. I think it is this moment or this spirit of the devoted Mary which Andrew Lloyd Webber captures in his great *'Jesus Christ Superstar'* song.

> I don't know how to love him
> What to do, how to move him
> I've been changed, yes really changed
> In these past few days, when I've seen myself
> I seem like someone else

There is a time to stride out and follow Jesus, to be an activist, a committed disciple. To walk in his footsteps along his road with courage and commitment in our heart. There is another time to sink onto our knees, to worship him, dry his feet and look deeply into his eyes. Activists like me often squeeze out these silent acts of worship, adoration and contemplation with our constant 'doing'. 'Busyness' fills the space that is reserved for 'beingness'.

When was the last time you fell on your knees in silence and in space before Jesus?

> Lord Jesus
> Help me to slow down.
> To stop,
> To breathe deep
> And to fall on my knees.
> To worship you in silence and stillness,
> To be at your feet.
> Amen.

79. Palm Sunday

Mark 11: 1–10

¹ *As they approached Jerusalem and came to Bethphage and Bethany at the Mount of Olives, Jesus sent two of his disciples,* ² *saying to them, "Go to the village ahead of you, and just as you enter it, you will find a colt tied there, which no one has ever ridden. Untie it and bring it here.* ³ *If anyone asks you, 'Why are you doing this?' say, 'The Lord needs it and will send it back here shortly.'"*

⁴ *They went and found a colt outside in the street, tied at a doorway. As they untied it,* ⁵ *some people standing there asked, "What are you doing, untying that colt?"* ⁶ *They answered as Jesus had told them to, and the people let them go.* ⁷ *When they brought the colt to Jesus and threw their cloaks over it, he sat on it.* ⁸ *Many people spread their cloaks on the road, while others spread branches they had cut in the fields.* ⁹ *Those who went ahead and those who followed shouted,*

"Hosanna!"

"Blessed is he who comes in the name of the Lord!"

¹⁰ *"Blessed is the coming kingdom of our father David!"*

"Hosanna in the highest heaven!"

Every year the pilgrim crowds poured into Jerusalem to celebrate the Passover. This year it was different because Jesus was one of them. The crowds would have known about his great healings and teachings and so the big questions hanging in the air were, 'Is this the year?' and 'Was he the one?'

Like a boxer climbing into the ring,
A bride arriving at the church door,
A rock star walking onto the stage,
Or the accused entering the law court,
Like a rat entering the trap,
Or a blind man about to fall into the pit.

Except,
He is not blind,
He is not the pathetic victim,
He can see what is happening,
Yet still he enters,
Because he is the Lamb of God.

So he comes to Jerusalem,
Expectation and anticipation,
Laughter and worship,
Entrance, end-game and eternity.

They are waiting for him,
The Pharisees and Priests,
The rich and the Romans,
The cynics and the 'seen it all befores'.
Blessed is he
Who comes in the name of the Lord.

The crowd are loud and joyful, Jesus is calm and collected riding not on a conqueror's stallion but on a humble peacemaker's donkey. The disciples are somewhere between the two. They are waving branches and singing hosannas but they are also feeling something of the gathering heaviness on Jesus' shoulders.

Welcome to Palm Sunday

Some years ago, I was running 'The Christian Pub' in the middle of Bradford. The staff were all Christians with wonderful servant attitudes and the beer was the best for miles around. One Sunday I found myself half terrified standing in front of the bar with a basket full of palm crosses and telling everyone that it was Palm Sunday, that if they hadn't seen one for years they still remembered what a palm cross was and they were free to take one. Sunday lunchtime was a big drinking time for us, these were pub goers not church goers and I felt vulnerable and open to derision as I made my stand. I was amazed and speechless to discover half an hour later that the basket was empty.

What is it about this strange little symbolic cross that still has the power to remind and touch the human heart?

Here then is something for you to ponder, as you conjure up the picture of Jesus on the donkey and look deeply into his face, ask yourself the question, 'Where am I in the crowd?' Am I hanging back on the edge? Somewhere in the undecided middle? Or am I close up amongst the disciples, following and supporting Jesus?

Lord Jesus
As I read of and think about this decisive day
Help me to make some decisions,
To decide what I think about you.
Where I am in the following crowd
What I want to do as your supporter.
Help me to see, to remember and to become a disciple.
Amen

80. Deep Cleansing the Temple

> ^{15} *On reaching Jerusalem, Jesus entered the temple courts and began driving out those who were buying and selling there. He overturned the tables of the money changers and the benches of those selling doves,* ^{16} *and would not allow anyone to carry merchandise through the temple courts.* ^{17} *And as he taught them, he said, "Is it not written: 'My house will be called a house of prayer for all nations'? But you have made it 'a den of robbers.'"*
>
> ^{18} *The chief priests and the teachers of the law heard this and began looking for a way to kill him, for they feared him, because the whole crowd was amazed at his teaching.*
>
> ^{19} *When evening came, Jesus and his disciples went out of the city.*

It is the Monday of Holy Week. Jesus had entered Jerusalem on Palm Sunday, come to the Temple for a look around at everything then returned to spend the night at his 'safe house' in Bethany.

We call it the cleansing of the temple, you could just as easily call it the scouring of the pot or the hacking back and weeding of the overgrown garden. This is real *'Game of Thrones'* stuff. You can almost hear the theme tune as he climbs up the entrance steps. This was the Father's throne, the priests made it theirs and Jesus is now reclaiming it.

The Temple was a massive place, one of the wonders of the ancient world. It dominated the whole city of Jerusalem and was the centre of the Jewish faith. Honest and devout pilgrims came from all over the world to gaze on its awesome presence, to breathe its air and to prayerfully kneel on its stones. Underneath this surface of religious piety, however, there was another Temple reality. At its heart the Temple was about power, domination and money. At the top of the heap, as in all great national and historic institutions, were the rich and powerful, the priests. They ran the whole show, controlled the Sanhedrin or ruling council and played up to the Romans who were happy to keep them in power. At the bottom were the spiritually obedient and generous faithful pilgrims, many of whom were poor and vulnerable. They lived on the edge and came to the centre to be ripped off. Jesus had once said that it was not the outside but the inside that made a thing unclean. Here he is entering and cleansing the very heart of Jerusalem.

I am often confused and left bewildered by all those who claim religion and politics shouldn't mix. Here we see the two woven together in the righteous and prophetic rebellion of Jesus. Tables are overturned, spivs and scoundrels are driven out and words are spoken.

'This should be a house of prayer

You have made it a den of thieves.'

The writing is on the wall, the bell has been rung and the first shot fired. Jesus has thrown down the gauntlet, the priests and scribes pick it up and run with it. They are afraid of Jesus and of his spell binding impact on all the people. The great game over the ultimate spiritual throne has begun.

What to do then with this story? Well, I like to think of my everyday life, my thinking mind, my passionate heart as a Temple. As a place where God could live. I want him to be dominant in the *Game of Thrones* which goes on every day in my life between my own selfish ego and my full of grace heavenly Father. Now is a good time then to think about my own attitudes towards all sorts of things such as money, sex, race, saving the environment and caring for my family and friends.

How clean is my Temple?

> **Lord Jesus**
> **May my body be a temple**
> **My mind a sanctuary**
> **My heart an altar**
> **May my temple be your home**
> **Turn over my tables**
> **Call me again to prayer**
> **And make my inner being a sacred place.**
> **Amen.**

81. On the Big Stage

Luke 19: 47–48

47 Every day he was teaching at the temple. But the chief priests, the teachers of the law and the leaders among the people were trying to kill him. 48 Yet they could not find any way to do it, because all the people hung on his words.

Tuesday morning in the final week of Jesus' life, what we today call Holy Week. He began on Palm Sunday by entering the powerhouse of Israel, the city of Jerusalem. On the Monday he stormed into and cleansed its central fortress, the Holy Temple. Then he makes it his own place. He has much to say, much to share and teach and he does it in the Temple. In a flash the place where animals were ritually slaughtered and offered to God becomes the place where liberating teachings are spoken out and offered to the ordinary people. The place which was the central power base of the priests has become the preaching platform for Jesus. There is a lovely quote of Maya Angelou, "When you learn, teach, when you get, give." This is exactly what he is doing, the Word is full of words. Over three days Monday, Tuesday and Wednesday he turned the Temple into a theatre, a House of Commons, a great lecture hall and an all-day concert venue.

At the beginning of 2020 thousands of people were reading the novel *'Ordinary People'*. It was top of the best sellers' lists for months and was turned into a runaway success of a TV series. Judging by my reading and watching, it seems the life of the 'ordinary people' in our country today is fuelled by sport, telly, masses of alcohol and lots of sex and angst. Love, long lasting relationships, deep inner thinking and spirituality, sense of journey and the discovering of God and joy seem to be completely out of the window. I expect it was pretty much the same for the 'ordinary people' of Jesus' day (though without the telly).

Yet here in the Temple theatre with the great teacher before them they found meaning, wisdom and words they had never heard before. The 'ordinary people' become special people.

> The ordinary people 'heard him gladly'.
> 'With delight'
> He spoke with an authority
> Not like their usual scribes and teachers
> Never had anyone spoken like this.
> They were spellbound
> Even many of the authorities believed in him.

Still today, Jesus' words have a special power. They are not offered to help us to live religiously but to help us to live. They are filled with light, promise, hope and deep wisdom. They are balanced, truthful and lead people through this world and into the next.

When was the last time you read the words of Jesus?

When was the last time you took just one of his parables and allowed it to slowly sink in and change you?

Following Mary, when was the last time you pondered his words? There was a time in my life when I decided to read a little bit of the gospel story every day. (I don't actually do it every day.) This was one of the biggest game changers cum 'step up', cum 'living a much richer daily existence' of my life.

This then is the challenge, to spend some time every day listening to him. This will transform you from being an 'ordinary' person to someone who is special, unusual and joyful with a greater sense of peace than 'normal' people. It will give you a centre, make you a journeyer; you will have an added dimension to your whole life.

I rather like painting pictures of Jesus. This scene of his teaching in the Temple I am doing on a broad canvas so I can get the backs of lots of heads in. I am painting the heads in a full rainbow range of colours. Why? Because the words of Jesus speak to the full spread of 'ordinary people'.

> Lord Jesus
> As you speak help me to listen
> To hear what you are saying to me.
> Guidance and advice
> Encouragement and reproof
> Help me to hear it all.
> Amen.

82. Parable of the Vineyard

Mark 12: 1–12

^{1} *Jesus then began to speak to them in parables:
"A man planted a vineyard. He put a wall around
it, dug a pit for the winepress and built a
watchtower. Then he rented the vineyard to some
farmers and moved to another place.* ^{2} *At harvest
time he sent a servant to the tenants to collect
from them some of the fruit of the vineyard.* ^{3} *But
they seized him, beat him and sent him away
empty-handed.* ^{4} *Then he sent another servant to
them; they struck this man on the head and
treated him shamefully.* ^{5} *He sent still another,
and that one they killed. He sent many others;
some of them they beat, others they killed.*

^{6} *"He had one left to send, a son, whom he loved.
He sent him last of all, saying, 'They will respect
my son.'*

^{7} *"But the tenants said to one another, 'This is the
heir. Come, let's kill him, and the inheritance will
be ours.'* ^{8} *So they took him and killed him, and
threw him out of the vineyard.*

^{9} *"What then will the owner of the vineyard do?
He will come and kill those tenants and give the*

vineyard to others. [10] Haven't you read this passage of Scripture:

"'The stone the builders rejected has become the cornerstone;

[11] the Lord has done this, and it is marvellous in our eyes'?"

[12] Then the chief priests, the teachers of the law and the elders looked for a way to arrest him because they knew he had spoken the parable against them. But they were afraid of the crowd; so they left him and went away.

This is the first of Jesus' big teachings in his festival of teaching in the last week of his life. It is a big parable and it is a destiny story. It is all about who he is, what he is doing and where he is going.

If you follow the young Luke Skywalker in the original *Star Wars* trilogy you see him discovering, wrestling with and finally fulfilling a strong sense of destiny. It all begins with his birth and a spiritual awakening brought to him by Obi-Wan Kenobi.

This awakening is a calling but he is free to either reject or follow his destiny. The same story of a destiny accepted and followed is present in *Harry Potter*, *Lord of the Rings* and *Superman* etc. In all these stories the word destiny is tied to the word destination. The destination of all these heroes is victory in the face of overwhelming odds. For Jesus the destination, the climax of his destiny is the cross.

In Jesus' parable the vineyard represents Israel, God's special people. The vineyard is looked after by the priests and leaders of the people. As the vineyard planter and owner God will provide peace and prosperity but would like a little bit of thankfulness, prayer and spiritually true living in response. God sent the Old Testament prophets to collect from the tenants but they were rejected and sometimes killed. Now he is sending his own beloved son. Once Jesus had told the story there was no turning back. The priests, scribes and leaders got the point, you can almost hear the big penny dropping. Jesus has just moved a few more steps on his destiny road.

As a follower of Jesus I spend a lot of time thinking about what I expect from him. Guidance, help with my struggles, inner peace and comfort are all on what is a long list. I like living in God's vineyard. I do not spend nearly as much time thinking about what he would like to see growing on my individual vine. I want to enjoy his fruit, I need to give more thought to him enjoying mine.

This then is my destiny road. Firstly to live out good things which I offer to the Father. Secondly to go with Jesus into the vineyard of this world and to try and open peoples' eyes and spirits to God. To gather in the fruits of his creation.

> **Lord God**
> **Thank you that I am living in a vineyard**
> **Not in a wild place.**
> **Thank you for the soil, the rain and the sunshine.**

Help me to grow rich fruit
And to give back to you
Something of what you have given to me.
May this be my destiny.
Amen.

83. The Head on the Coin

Mark 12:13–17

> [13] *Later they sent some of the Pharisees and Herodians to Jesus to catch him in his words.* [14] *They came to him and said, "Teacher, we know that you are a man of integrity. You aren't swayed by others, because you pay no attention to who they are; but you teach the way of God in accordance with the truth. Is it right to pay the imperial tax to Caesar or not?* [15] *Should we pay or shouldn't we?"*
>
> *But Jesus knew their hypocrisy. "Why are you trying to trap me?" he asked. "Bring me a denarius and let me look at it."* [16] *They brought the coin, and he asked them, "Whose image is this? And whose inscription?"*
>
> *"Caesar's," they replied.*
>
> [17] *Then Jesus said to them, "Give back to Caesar what is Caesar's and to God what is God's."*
>
> *And they were amazed at him.*

It's not so much about taxes, more about power and its power cousin – subservience.

Actually it is a bit about taxes so let's get this out of the way first. The idea of everyone paying an acceptable tax amount to a form of government be it the emperor or the Temple which provides strong walls and roads, peace and protection, justice and provision for the poor is a really good thing. I enjoy paying tax, it makes me feel like a proper citizen both contributing and benefitting. All tax dodgers, whether they are big international companies or local plumbers are robbing the state, robbing me and robbing needy people. Clearly in this story Jesus has no problem with the idea of paying taxes, in fact he seems to think it is a good thing. Well, of course, he does because he is a good and fair man who thinks hospitals, schools and social care are good things.

But there is a bigger thing here about power. The person who you pay your taxes to is the person who rules you. Taxes in Jesus' day were not quite like ours, they were more like a form of tribute. You could pay your money to the Romans who had conquered your land or to the religious/political elite who ran the Temple. Either way you are giving your money to a ruler who is oblivious of you as a person, you are being a servant or a serf.

There is something incredibly un-servant like in Jesus' reply, 'whose is the head on the coin?' Everyone in Jerusalem, including all the Temple, work hard to pay to and in effect serve the emperor. Jesus shows respect but clearly there is no deference in him. He seems to be above or at least quite detached from the Romans. He might hand over his coin but he is not subservient and he is certainly not going to hand over his soul. In Jesus' land it is God who is the emperor.

Soon after his conversion Bob Dylan captured the nature of human need to follow and serve.

> You may be an ambassador to England or France
> You may like to gamble, you might like to dance
> You may be the heavyweight champion of the world
> You may be a socialite with a long string of pearls
> But you're gonna have to serve somebody, yes
> Indeed you're gonna have to serve somebody.
> Well, it may be the devil or it may be the Lord
> But you're gonna have to serve somebody.
> You might be a rock 'n' roll addict prancing on the stage
> You might have drugs at your command,
> women in a cage.
> You may be a business man or some high-degree thief
> They may call you doctor or they may call you chief
> But you're gonna have to serve somebody, yes you are
> You're gonna have to serve somebody.
> Well, it may be the devil or it may be the Lord
> But you're gonna have to serve somebody.

In our selfie obsessed world it feels as though life is no longer about being part of a greater whole to which we have dues to pay or to political leaders to whom we owe allegiance. It all seems much more self-centred.

> I am me
> This is my life
> My space, my body, my time.
> I am free

I have my own opinions
No-one tells me what to do.

So what do we think TV adds, newspapers, conspiracy theories, social media and 'group think' are all about? When he became a Christian Bob Dylan discovered that actually everybody serves somebody, basically it's the devil or God. I think I'll choose God.

Jesus himself had spoken about making a choice between serving God or serving mammon i.e. money with all the false promises and stresses that it brings.

Matthew 6: 24

No one can serve two masters. Either you will hate the one and love the other, or you will be devoted to the one and despise the other. You cannot serve both God and money.

The big question is then obvious to us all: 'Am I willing to let Jesus be Lord of my life?'

Lord Jesus
May your breath be on my life.
May you be Lord
Of my heart,
Of my relationships.
Of my daily lifestyle
Of my money.
Amen

84. Bigger Living

Mark 12: 18–27

¹⁸ *Then the Sadducees, who say there is no resurrection, came to him with a question.* ¹⁹ *"Teacher," they said, "Moses wrote for us that if a man's brother dies and leaves a wife but no children, the man must marry the widow and raise up offspring for his brother.* ²⁰ *Now there were seven brothers. The first one married and died without leaving any children.* ²¹ *The second one married the widow, but he also died, leaving no child. It was the same with the third.* ²² *In fact, none of the seven left any children. Last of all, the woman died too.* ²³ *At the resurrection whose wife will she be, since the seven were married to her?"*

²⁴ *Jesus replied, "Are you not in error because you do not know the Scriptures or the power of God?* ²⁵ *When the dead rise, they will neither marry nor be given in marriage; they will be like the angels in heaven.* ²⁶ *Now about the dead rising – have you not read in the Book of Moses, in the account of the burning bush, how God said to him, 'I am the God of Abraham, the God of Isaac, and the God of Jacob'?* ²⁷ *He is not the God of the dead, but of the living. You are badly mistaken!"*

Death
Hades
Sheol
The Pitt.

Different names for the same thing.

Or as people of a certain vintage might remember, 'This parrot is dead, this is a dead parrot.' (Look up Monty Python if this allusion means nothing to you.)

The Sadducees were a very powerful and wealthy grouping or sect in the time of Jesus, more political than religious. They were close to the Temple but had a very shallow almost humanistic series of beliefs. They did not do the deeply spiritual and they certainly didn't do the supernatural, so angels and demons, resurrection and Heaven were all out of the picture. They would have been very unsettled by the thriving spiritual reformation and renewal that Jesus was leading and so they come, not so much with a genuine question but more of an anti-spiritual landmine for him to stand on. It is about a woman who marries her way through seven brothers.

'In the resurrection whose wife will she be? For seven had married her?'

The Sadducees had a very spiritless and grey 'everything finishes when your body packs up' view of life. Theirs was a small and short vision. Ezra Pound captures this small, this life only view of existence.

'And the days are not full enough
And the nights are not full enough
And life slips by like a field mouse
    Not shaking the grass.'

For the Sadducees, Ezra Pound, in fact most of us, life is all about the here and now. Jesus too thought this present life really important and that is why he reached out to so many to touch and improve their everyday lives. But he also looked through the window of this 'now' life to a bigger view, the landscape of eternity.

In the story Jesus never actually answers the Sadducees question. Instead he moves everything onto a higher level where the scriptures are opened, where the power of God is stronger than the power of death, where bushes burn without being destroyed and angels live without dying and where God is the God of the living.

When it comes to this life and eternal life I've got questions too. What about my parents, they became Christians in midlife. I was never kind enough to them in their later years so will I be able to say sorry to them when I get to Heaven? What about my daughter Zoe who cannot speak to me or understand what I say to her, will we be able to talk to each other in Heaven? What about me? What will it be like being me in Heaven with all my black spots, hard thoughts and bad tempers gone forever?

So here is the big question for all of us to think about, 'What will it be like being in Heaven?'

Lord God, Heavenly Father
You are the God of the living
Not of the dead.
Help me to live every day
Being fully alive
In you and for you.
And to bring me on my last day
Into my first day in Heaven
With you.
Amen.

85. A Generous Widow

Mark 12: 41–44

41 Jesus sat down opposite the place where the offerings were put and watched the crowd putting their money into the temple treasury. Many rich people threw in large amounts. 42 But a poor widow came and put in two very small copper coins, worth only a few cents.

43 Calling his disciples to him, Jesus said, "Truly I tell you, this poor widow has put more into the treasury than all the others. 44 They all gave out of their wealth; but she, out of her poverty, put in everything – all she had to live on."

> "Money makes the World go round"
> "Feed the birds, tuppence a bag"
> "Money, money, money in a rich man's world"

Simple song segments from *'Cabaret'*, *'Mary Poppins'* and *'Abba'*. Together they point to the importance, the desirability and the power of money.

Throughout English literature there is a running theme of money. People get it, lose it, marry into it and are desperate to hang on to it. Dickens, Trollope, Hardy, Austen they all inhabit this money dependent world.

No one saw it in clearer terms than Thackeray in his *'Vanity Fair'*, his name for the crazy 'money is everything' world of English 'high society'. Or as Harry Enfield put it a 'Loads-a-Money' society.

People often think of Jesus as always talking about good and bad, sin and forgiveness or heaven and hell but in fact money was one of his main subjects. He talks about rich men and poor men, big expensive banquets, loosing and finding treasure and of how 'Mammon' can become our master. The story of the widow's offering is a classic example. It is a story full of sadness at the state of the poor woman but also of admiration for her piety and reckless generosity.

A few years ago on a bright sunny Sunday morning the congregation of our church in Bradford was gathering for worship. There was a particular buzz amongst our young people who were all planning to go to Soul Survivor.

Today they were paying in the £120 to the youth leaders to pay for the trip. We were a fairly affluent church and most of the teenagers were simply handing in cheques written by their parents, except Charlie. Charlie was a financially struggling student, he had raised the money by a combination of skimping and odd jobbing and he was paying his costs in cash.

Five minutes before the start of the service Nick walked in. He had been part of our church before going off to be a youth worker in a poor part of East London and so I got him up to share with us all during the worship.

Nick told us how he was seeing some of his young people becoming Christians and that he was planning to take some of them off to Soul Survivor during the summer. However, none of his kids had much money and so they were desperately fund raising. At the end of the service Charlie told our youth team that he wasn't going to Soul Survivor after all, he withdrew his £120 from them and gave it all to Nick to aid his struggling East End teenagers. It was a 'widow's penny' moment.

When I was a young Christian my wonderful vicar at the time had a favourite saying, 'The last part of a person to be converted was their pocket'. Every time I heard him say this I sort of turned away because it hit the bullseye in my soul. I loved money and the things it could give me. My money was my money. I needed all of it to buy trendy clothes, music, books and to generally have a good time. I was a fully endorsed member of *'Vanity Fair'*. It was only years later through the natural and spontaneous generosity of my wife that I slowly and rather painfully discovered the joy of giving.

Now is the moment to stop and ask yourself the question about your own generosity. Are you giving out of your abundance or out of your poverty? How much do you give? And who do you give it to?

> **Lord Jesus**
> **Help me to hear this story**
> **And to be changed by it.**
> **May you reach your hand into my pocket**
> **And set me free.**
> **Amen**

86. All You Need is Love

Matthew 22: 34–40

> [34] *When the Pharisees heard that he had silenced the Sadducees, they gathered together,* [35] *and one of them, a lawyer, asked him a question to test him.* [36] *'Teacher, which commandment in the law is the greatest?'* [37] *He said to him, '"You shall love the Lord your God with all your heart, and with all your soul, and with all your mind."* [38] *This is the greatest and first commandment.* [39] *And a second is like it: "You shall love your neighbour as yourself."* [40] *On these two commandments hang all the law and the prophets.'*

In a moment of bloated arrogance John Lennon once said, 'The Beatles are more famous than Jesus'. He was even further off the mark when he said, 'Imagine there's no Heaven', but he was absolutely on the money when he sang, 'All you need is love'.

Surprisingly, Jesus did not say that much about love. Perhaps he simply preferred to see his whole life as a wordless proclamation or gift of love. The few things he did say about love however, are all golden nuggets. He calls us to love our enemies (Matthew 5: 43), he taught his disciples to love one another (John 13: 35) and teach those who follow him to continue in that love (John 15: 9). He saw himself as God's 'love-child', as his love gift to the world (John 3: 16).

In this story we see Jesus answering the testing question of a lawyer, 'Which is the greatest commandment?' The Pharisees were obsessed by commandments. They had rules and regulations to govern every part of their lives. Religion, food and drink, family, relationships, business-life, all were governed by rules, by a defining sense of right and wrong. They had religious morality in their blood. Still today we tie religion up with a sense of morality. As a vicar, people often bring their children to me for baptism or want them to enter our church school, many saying that they want them to grow up with a sense of 'right and wrong'.

The problem with morality is that it is often the midwife of guilt and failure. Rather than including people into a community of goodness it casts us out into a place of condemnation. Morality can be very judgemental, harsh and punishing.

Here we see Jesus rising above the rule book of morality and talking on a higher plain about something softer, kinder, and purer. He is talking about loving God, loving our neighbour and even loving ourselves (sometimes the most difficult of all).

I have lots of neighbours, friends, family and colleagues that I enjoy loving. I like them, they like me and return the love that I give them. The problems start when I try to love the ones who don't love me. The one who says things about me, who competes with me at work and has very different ideas than me in church. Is this where true love ends or is it where true love begins?

The sort of love Jesus talked about has a twin sister. She is called forgiveness. The only people we can ever forgive are those who take from us, tell lies about us and hurt us.

On the great hundred-day journey of finding, following and becoming like Jesus, love is a cairn. A great pile of rocks standing out on the hillside marking the path. If you are still trying to find him then his self-offering of love is a cairn to draw you on. If you feel you have found him or are getting close then his teaching about love will guide you in the next step of following. If you are following and wanting to become like him, then the great beacon like cairn of his love shows you how to do it.

> So where are you going to receive his gift of
> love today?
> So how are you going to walk in his love today?
> So who are you going to love today?
> Because all you need is love.
> Love is all you need.

Lord God
Help me to love you today
With all the fullness of my heart
With all the depth of my soul
And with all the conviction of my mind.

Help me also Lord
To love my neighbour
And to love myself
That love might grow
In me, and for me
And through me
Amen.

87. Apocalypse Now

Matthew 24:1–14, 28.

1 Jesus left the temple and was walking away when his disciples came up to him to call his attention to its buildings. 2 "Do you see all these things?" he asked. "Truly I tell you, not one stone here will be left on another; every one will be thrown down."

3 As Jesus was sitting on the Mount of Olives, the disciples came to him privately. "Tell us," they said, "when will this happen, and what will be the sign of your coming and of the end of the age?"

4 Jesus answered: "Watch out that no one deceives you. 5 For many will come in my name, claiming, 'I am the Messiah,' and will deceive many. 6 You will hear of wars and rumours of wars, but see to it that you are not alarmed. Such things must happen, but the end is still to come. 7 Nation will rise against nation, and kingdom against kingdom. There will be famines and earthquakes in various places. 8 All these are the beginning of birth pains.

9 "Then you will be handed over to be persecuted and put to death, and you will be hated by all nations because of me. 10 At that time many will turn away from the faith and will betray and hate each other, [11] and many false prophets will appear and deceive many people. [12] Because of the increase of wickedness, the love of most will grow cold, [13] but the one who stands firm to the end will be saved. [14] And this gospel of the kingdom will be preached in the whole world as a testimony to all nations, and then the end will come."

[28] Wherever there is a carcass, there the vultures will gather.

We call them 'Apocalyptic'. They are writings, visions or prophecies etc. that look to a doom- laden but eventually bright future. You can trace the apocalyptic thread through the Old Testament prophecies, especially Daniel, and on through Paul's writings. It climaxes in the book of Revelation which looks beyond the darkness to a glorious new beginning. Here then is Jesus' contribution to Apocalyptic Thinking'.

Forty years after his crucifixion the Jews rebelled against the Romans. Their rebellion led to a bloodthirsty siege of Jerusalem and the complete destruction of the Temple. Is this what Jesus was looking directly at in his future gazing? I suspect he was looking both at this and beyond at the whole unfolding of world history which reached its most destructive and cruel stages in our own, supposedly enlightened, times.

> The Killing Fields of 1914–18
> Adolf Hitler and Joseph Stalin
> Nagasaki and Hiroshima
> Pol Pot and Mao Tse Tung

Vietnam and the Middle East
Bin Laden and Isis.
Wherever the corpse is
There the vultures will gather.

Welcome to our world
And to the future.
So the Good News
Must be proclaimed.

It seems as though we have always been fascinated and drawn in by 'looking to the future' stories and predictions. Nostradamus, the return of King Arthur, the science fiction of H.G. Wells, Dr Who's time travelling and the terrifying future scenes of *Blade Runner* have all found a place in our shared imagination.

When Jesus looks to the future, however, he looks beyond the world of men and women to his own eventual return. No one knows when it will be. What we do know is that it will be, not so much an ending, as a new beginning.

So where does all this leave us? It leaves us in an in-between place, in a time zone called history, two thousand years after Jesus' first appearance with an unknown stretch of time before his second coming.

It leaves us in a post Covid19 world of plague, facing a future of environmental self-destruction. It leaves us in something rather like Narnia where it is increasingly winter all the time with fewer Christmases on the horizon. Yet we do know that Aslan will return and will bring with him a new spring time.

It leaves us in a world where nations and kingdoms still rise up against each other and yet the Kingdom of God is here and now. And when we remain faithful to Jesus the King and share his love and Good News we actually make it a better world.

Here then is a question for the in-betweeners who have not fallen away. What is the one thing we can do today to make our world a better place?

> **Lord Jesus**
> **As we live our lives**
> **In these strange and difficult times**
> **May you be with us every day.**
> **May we remain faithful to you every day**
> **May we serve our world**
> **And make it a better place**
> **Every day.**
> **Amen.**

88. The Last Supper

Luke 22: 14–20

> ¹⁴ *When the hour came, Jesus and his apostles reclined at the table.* ¹⁵ *And he said to them, "I have eagerly desired to eat this Passover with you before I suffer.* ¹⁶ *For I tell you, I will not eat it again until it finds fulfilment in the kingdom of God."*

> ¹⁷ *After taking the cup, he gave thanks and said, "Take this and divide it among you.* ¹⁸ *For I tell you I will not drink again from the fruit of the vine until the kingdom of God comes."*

> ¹⁹ *And he took bread, gave thanks and broke it, and gave it to them, saying, "This is my body given for you; do this in remembrance of me."*

> ²⁰ *In the same way, after the supper he took the cup, saying, "This cup is the new covenant in my blood, which is poured out for you".*

Shared meals are special times. I used to think a meal was simply a matter of sitting down, filling up and then moving on. Over time I realised that there is a lot more to it than this, it is a social get together and a slow experience, seeing and listening to the other people around the table, remembering what brings us together. Yes, it does include good food and drink but it is 'shared' food and drink.

The Covid19 lockdown was not a great time for shared meals. Nevertheless my wife, Maureen, and I managed two significant events. The first was my Brother Ray's 70th birthday party. Fewer than normal attended and we all had our time slots but the celebration of his life made it special. The second was a little garden party to which we invited a couple of old Christian friends and another couple of young 'searchers after Jesus' types. Here it was the conversation and spiritual depth, plus Maureen's baking that created the weight of the afternoon.

Jesus clearly loved the idea of meeting and eating together. The feeding of the five thousand was one such occasion and here the story of the Last Supper is another. This one is small, intimate, almost hidden away as Jesus and the twelve gather. Jesus realises what is unfolding but the disciples do not, although they may have had intimations that this was the last time they would meet before his death.

The tone is set by the first few words, 'When the hour came'. The meal was a looking back to the Passover when Jews, before escaping from Egypt, daubed the blood of a sacrificial lamb on their doorposts so that death would 'pass-over' and not touch their household. However, this will be a Passover like no other. Jesus will be the sacrificial lamb and his blood will be daubed on their lives. So in the silence of that upper room as they sit around a single table and, with the oil lamps burning and the shadows lengthening, these few poetic words become a reality.

> 'Loaf of bread
> Broken
> My body
> Given for you.
> This cup
> Poured out for you.
> New covenant
> In my blood.'

Today we call it the Eucharist, the Mass, the Lord's Supper, Love Feast or Holy Communion. In effect we have turned what was an intimate coming together with Jesus in the centre into a formal act of worship, a service. However, Jesus is still in the centre, we are still his disciples and it is still a Holy Meal. Whether we do it very formally with a robed priest and special music or informally simply passing the bread and wine to each other it is still what we call a sacrament. A sacrament is an outward physical enactment of a deeply inner spiritual truth. A sacrament is a 'sacred moment' and the inner truth is that Jesus is still here and feeding us.

You might like to look ahead to the next time you will celebrate the sacrament. Think also about the others you will be sharing it with. Then visualise Jesus being in the midst and actually offering you the bread and wine.

Lord God
Do not let me take this meal for granted.
Help me to remember
        to rededicate
        to repeat.
Fill me with your bread
Forgive me with your wine
And call me on to your Heavenly Kingdom.
Amen.

89. Love One Another

John 13: 31–35

> ³¹ *When he was gone, Jesus said, "Now the Son of Man is glorified and God is glorified in him.* ³² *If God is glorified in him, God will glorify the Son in himself, and will glorify him at once.*
>
> ³³ *"My children, I will be with you only a little longer. You will look for me, and just as I told the Jews, so I tell you now: Where I am going, you cannot come.*
>
> ³⁴ *"A new command I give you: Love one another. As I have loved you, so you must love one another.* ³⁵ *By this everyone will know that you are my disciples, if you love one another."*

Despite the face of Che Guevara being everywhere in our trendy, modern, cool world, Jesus is the one who should be seen as the greatest revolutionary of all time. If the effectiveness of a revolution is based on three indicators:

> How long has it lasted?
> How many people has it impacted?
> What qualities of human happiness and well-being has it brought?

Then who can compare with the man from Nazareth.

The essence of the Jesus revolution was, and still is, love. Jesus did not get his disciples to lead an uprising against the Romans or overturn the Jerusalem power base, he simply called on them to 'love one another as I have loved you'.

Perhaps more than anyone else in our modern age John Lennon captures the spirit of this Jesus revolution.

> There's love, love, love …
> Nothing you can do that can't be done
> Nothing you can sing that can't be sung …
> All you need is love
> Love is all you need.
> All you need is Love.

Jesus had already done quite a bit of teaching on love, both for his disciples and the crowds generally. Spiritually wrestling with the Pharisees in the temple, he compresses the whole of the Old Testament teaching and morality into two single commandments:

> *You shall love the Lord your God with all your heart, and with all your soul and with all your mind. This is the first and greatest commandment. And the second is like it! You shall love your neighbour as yourself.*

Jesus had regularly pointed out that most people are good at loving their friends but when asked about loving our neighbours he told them the Parable of the Good

Samaritan. This is a story all about loving people who we normally avoid and look down on. It is a story of crossing racial divides and rejecting prejudice. It is a story about love in action not in words. The whole life of Jesus can be seen as an acting out of the Good Samaritan story, so when he calls the disciples to 'love one another' he really is saying 'love as you have seen me love'. That is revolutionary; that is why the revolution has lasted, spread wide and touched so many lives.

Today the revolution lives on in us and in our loving of others.

> Easy to put into words
> Hard to put into practice.
> Easy to begin
> Hard to continue.
> Easy with those who love us
> Hard with the unlikeable.

Lord Jesus
As you lead, help me to follow
As you show, help me to copy
As you command, help me to obey.
To love the other
The other member of my family
Work colleague, neighbour
Brother or sister.
Lord
Help me to love as you have loved.
Amen.

90. In the Garden

Luke 22: 29–45

^{29} *Jesus went out as usual to the Mount of Olives, and his disciples followed him.* ^{40} *On reaching the place, he said to them, "Pray that you will not fall into temptation."* ^{41} *He withdrew about a stone's throw beyond them, knelt down and prayed,* ^{42} *"Father, if you are willing, take this cup from me; yet not my will, but yours be done."* ^{43} *An angel from heaven appeared to him and strengthened him.* ^{44} *And being in anguish, he prayed more earnestly, and his sweat was like drops of blood falling to the ground.*

^{45} *When he rose from prayer and went back to the disciples, he found them asleep, exhausted from sorrow.*

> A garden and moonlight
> Disciples asleep and one a betrayer
> Sweat and blood
> Olives and a cup.

Gardens are special places in the Bible. Genesis tells us that we were made to live in a garden, a serene place of fruitfulness and natural beauty where men and women could meet with God. At the end of the Bible, in the book of Revelation there is a new garden at the heart of the New Jerusalem. A river of life flows through it and a healing tree grows in it. Somewhere between these two we find Jesus, late at night, with his disciples in the garden of Gethsemane. It is here in this garden that we see Jesus at his weakest and saddest moment.

Most of us have a rather unbalanced view of Jesus' divinity and thus a reduced sense of his humanity. Without necessarily spelling it out we feel that it was almost easy for him to overcome problems, temptations and weaknesses because he was the Son of God and had extra powers and perceptions. We forget that he was also an ordinary, fleshy man with all the weaknesses and insecurities that come with it. In Gethsemane we see Jesus at his most vulnerable and human. His closest friends and supporters have fallen asleep on him, one of his disciples is leading an armed mob to hunt him down, looking ahead he sees the cross and here in his most desperate moment he almost snaps.

I once visited the Garden of Gethsemane and there I viewed an olive press. A sack of olives was thrown into a stone trough and a long beam of wood laid over them to squash them into pulp and force the oil out. When the oil stopped running a heavy stone weight was hung on the end of the beam to increase the pressure and squeeze more oil out. After a while the oil again stopped running so another stone was added and the pressure increased once more. I have always seen this as a picture of what happened to Jesus. He is being gradually almost crushed. The tears and sweat flow out of him like olive oil or blood. He calls out to his Father about removing the cup of suffering but his final words are 'yet not my will but yours be done'.

Jesus in the garden comes at the end of his ministry and it acts like a matching bookend to his time in the wilderness which came at the beginning. In both cases Jesus was completely alone, his humanity was tested to the extreme, he almost snaps but he eventually overcomes and keeps on the course set for him by his Father.

The Father laid out the road but it still needed Jesus to accept and to agree to walk it. It is a bit like Frodo's journey in *'The Lord of the Rings'*. As soon as he left the comfort of the Shire he was into the Wilderness of Weathertop and from there the road led to the threatening darkness of Mordor.

> 'But long ago he rode away,
> And where he dwelleth none can say:
> For into darkness fell his star
> In Mordor where the shadows are.'

If we are following Jesus are we willing to follow him into the garden?

What sort of pressure can we take?

How isolated is our isolation?

And what does it feel like when our friends fall asleep?

Lord God
As Jesus knelt before you in the garden
So I kneel before you now.
May you give me strength in my weakness
Your presence in my aloneness.
And the help of an angel
When my friends let me down
That I might be true to you.
Amen.

91. Judas and Peter

Matthew 26: 47–50 and 69–75

⁴⁷ While he was still speaking, Judas, one of the Twelve, arrived. With him was a large crowd armed with swords and clubs, sent from the chief priests and the elders of the people. ⁴⁸ Now the betrayer had arranged a signal with them: "The one I kiss is the man; arrest him." ⁴⁹ Going at once to Jesus, Judas said, "Greetings, Rabbi!" and kissed him.

⁵⁰ Jesus replied, "Do what you came for, friend."

Then the men stepped forward, seized Jesus and arrested him.

⁶⁹ Now Peter was sitting out in the courtyard, and a servant girl came to him. "You also were with Jesus of Galilee," she said.

⁷⁰ But he denied it before them all. "I don't know what you're talking about," he said.

⁷¹ Then he went out to the gateway, where another servant girl saw him and said to the people there, "This fellow was with Jesus of Nazareth."

72 He denied it again, with an oath: "I don't know the man!"

73 After a little while, those standing there went up to Peter and said, "Surely you are one of them; your accent gives you away."

74 Then he began to call down curses, and he swore to them, "I don't know the man!"

Immediately a rooster crowed. 75 Then Peter remembered the word Jesus had spoken: "Before the rooster crows, you will disown me three times." And he went outside and wept bitterly.

What a pair! One, the ultimate celebrity traitor in history and the other the most famous friendship denier of all time. They are the two who are closest to Jesus in his darkest hour. What was going on?

There are four places in the New Testament where we get a complete list of the twelve disciples. In each one Peter is top of the list and Judas is the bottom. Peter was the leader and Judas the betrayer.

There are lots of theories about Judas. One is that he was a political terrorist (hence the name Iscariot) dedicated to the overthrow of Rome. Another one is that he was a permanent outsider not very well accepted by the rest of the disciple gang. A third suggests he had a strong liking for money. Maybe he betrayed Jesus in order to provoke him into action. Luke's gospel suggests that he was taken over by Satan. At the end of the day

we don't really know why he did what he did, perhaps
he did not really know why either.

The final act here in the garden is not of Judas pointing
an accusing finger and shouting angrily but rather of a
gentle kiss of friendship and greeting.

The thirty pieces of silver weighed heavy in his
pocket. Judas ended up a bitterly disappointed man,
he repented of what he had done, gave back the
money and hung himself. The moment is captured
beautifully in *'Jesus Christ Superstar'*. As Judas's body
hangs from the tree a gentle, heavenly chant softly
rings out 'Poor old Judas, Poor old Judas'. Despite all
the bad feeling that has been poured on him over the
years I feel sorry for him. I like to think that he found
his way to Heaven and was welcomed into the arms of
his all-loving Father.

Peter was top of the list of the twelve and such a good
and strong leader that Jesus called him the rock.
In the early hours of that Friday morning whilst Jesus
was held in the High Priest's house, Peter was hanging
around in the courtyard. The rock turned to jelly, not
once but three times, as watchers and passers by simply
asked if he was part of the Jesus crowd.

> I do not know what you are talking about
> I do not know the man.
> Then he began to curse
> He swore an oath
> I do not know the man.

Judas and Peter pose two stark 'in your face' questions to all of us would be disciples.

Have you ever betrayed Jesus? When was the last time your rock turned to jelly?

> Father,
> Forgive me for I have sinned
> And am no longer worthy to be called your son.
> I have been a Judas
> I have been a Peter
> Father, forgive me.
> Amen

92. The Long and Winding Road

Matthew 27: 27–34

27 Then the governor's soldiers took Jesus into the Praetorium and gathered the whole company of soldiers around him. 28 They stripped him and put a scarlet robe on him, 29 and then twisted together a crown of thorns and set it on his head. They put a staff in his right hand. Then they knelt in front of him and mocked him. "Hail, king of the Jews!" they said. 30 They spit on him, and took the staff and struck him on the head again and again. 31 After they had mocked him, they took off the robe and put his own clothes on him. Then they led him away to crucify him.

32 As they were going out, they met a man from Cyrene, named Simon, and they forced him to carry the cross. 33 They came to a place called Golgotha (which means "the place of the skull"). 34 There they offered Jesus wine to drink, mixed with gall; but after tasting it, he refused to drink it.

The long and winding road
From the joyful crowds of Galilee
To the cursing soldiers of Jerusalem.
Gradually the words and the song changes

From the Beatles classic to the old Victorian
Hymn
'There is a green hill far-away
Without a city wall,
Where the dear Lord was crucified'.

I've always loved seeing God, faith issues generally, and in particular the Jesus story in popular culture. So I often find myself reading a book, listening to a song or watching a bit of telly and thinking, 'that's just like Jesus'. There are two great Beatles songs which for me light up Jesus' path to the cross and then the desolation of crucifixion.

From the moment of his arrest in Gethsemane Jesus is on Crucifixion Road. He is alone, deserted and getting closer to the top of the hill all the time. My Beatles song to go with his journey is *'The Long and Winding Road'*. Jesus began this road a long time before. It looks as though about a year or so into his wandering Galilean ministry the idea of the cross and of its inevitability began to form in Jesus' mind. At Caesarea Philippi he tried to share his 'premonitory' thoughts with his disciples but they never really caught on. For them the road to Jerusalem may have been something like a victory march but for Jesus it was the inevitable 'long and winding road' of destiny and his destiny was to be the ultimate sacrificial Lamb of God.

In the passage we see him on the last leg of the journey: from the Priest's house to Pilate's palace; from the Roman Governor to the Roman Soldiers; from reasonable debate to mockery. A scarlet robe, crown of thorns, rod of reeds and derisory 'Hail King of the Jews' are all part of the final twist on the way. Then out on the road to the cross, with the horizontal beam of the cross on his shoulders. He stumbles on the last bit of the long and winding road, Simon of Cyrene helps him along the way. A crowd including many women follow him, a young woman jumps out to mop his brow. On and on he goes, solitary, stumbling and sweat soaked.

> The long and winding road
> That leads to your door
> Will never disappear
> I've seen that road before
> It always leads me here
> Lead me to your door.

> The wild and windy night
> That the rain washed away
> Has left a pool of tears
> Crying for the day
> Why leave me standing here?
> Let me know the way.

> Many times I've been alone
> And many times I've cried
> Anyway, you'll never know
> The many ways I've tried.

At last he has reached the end of the road. Golgotha, otherwise known as the 'Place of the Skull', which just about says it all.

Question: 'What sort of road are you on? And where is it leading to?

> Dear Lord Jesus,
> You walked your road
> The like of which
> I cannot imagine.
> Today I have to walk my road
> May you accompany me, befriend me
> And lead me along it.
> Amen

93. Fool on the Hill

Matthew 27: 34–50

> ^{34} There they offered Jesus wine to drink, mixed with gall; but after tasting it, he refused to drink it. ^{35} When they had crucified him, they divided up his clothes by casting lots. ^{36} And sitting down, they kept watch over him there. ^{37} Above his head they placed the written charge against him: THIS IS JESUS, THE KING OF THE JEWS.
>
> ^{38} Two rebels were crucified with him, one on his right and one on his left. ^{39} Those who passed by hurled insults at him, shaking their heads ^{40} and saying, "You who are going to destroy the temple and build it in three days, save yourself! Come down from the cross, if you are the Son of God!" ^{41} In the same way the chief priests, the teachers of the law and the elders mocked him. ^{42} "He saved others," they said, "but he can't save himself! He's the king of Israel! Let him come down now from the cross, and we will believe in him. ^{43} He trusts in God. Let God rescue him now if he wants him, for he said, 'I am the Son of God.'" ^{44} In the same way the rebels who were crucified with him also heaped insults on him.

45 From noon until three in the afternoon darkness came over all the land. 46 About three in the afternoon Jesus cried out in a loud voice, "Eli, Eli, lema sabachthani?" (which means "My God, my God, why have you forsaken me?").

47 When some of those standing there heard this, they said, "He's calling Elijah."

48 Immediately one of them ran and got a sponge. He filled it with wine vinegar, put it on a staff, and offered it to Jesus to drink. 49 The rest said, "Now leave him alone. Let's see if Elijah comes to save him."

50 And when Jesus had cried out again in a loud voice, he gave up his spirit.

> Is dying the worst thing in the world?
> Is death the ultimate, unavoidable and
> inevitable end?
> Is deadness, nothingness?

Dylan Thomas captured something of its darkness in the poem he wrote on the death of his father.

> Do not go gentle into that good night,
> Old age should burn and rave at close of day.
> Rage, rage against the dying of the light.

There are four levels of suffering that Jesus experienced on the cross. They are like four depths of an ever-deepening dark night that he penetrates in his drowning in death experience.

- The physical pain of nails and struggling to breathe.
- The experience of rejection by the people he came to save
- Desertion by his disciples.
- And perhaps worst of all, the cutting of the umbilical cord which had always joined him to the Father.

It all comes bursting out in his final words from a broken heart, 'My God, my God, why have you forsaken me?'

> 'Day after day
> Alone on a hill
> The man with the foolish grin is keeping
> perfectly still
> But nobody wants to know him
> They can see that he's just a fool…'

I realise of course that the Beatles song *'Fool on the Hill'* is not actually about Jesus but to me it looks just like him. All alone, perfect stillness, up on a hill, nobody wanting to know him.

And for Jesus, the all-perfect, beautiful Son of God to do this, to allow others to do it to him no wonder St Paul talks about the 'foolishness of the cross'.

At the end he cries out to God and breathes his last.

So for me *'The Fool on the Hill'* will always be Jesus. And when they all say, 'he's just a fool' or maybe that I am a fool for believing in him, no matter. This Jesus was a fool to love me so much that he died for me, I am more than happy to be a fool for him, to want to find him, to follow him, to try and become like him.

A question for us all: If he was willing to be a fool for me, how much am I willing to be a fool for him?

> Lord Jesus
> You gave up your life
> So that my life might be
> Richer, deeper, fuller and longer.
> You gave up your life
> So that I might live eternal life
> Help me to find you
> Follow you
> And become like you.
> Amen.

94. Death Comes to Us All

Luke 23: 46–53

> *46 Jesus called out with a loud voice, "Father, into your hands I commit my spirit."-When he had said this, he breathed his last.*
>
> *47 The centurion, seeing what had happened, praised God and said, "Surely this was a righteous man." 48 When all the people who had gathered to witness this sight saw what took place, they beat their breasts and went away. 49 But all those who knew him, including the women who had followed him from Galilee, stood at a distance, watching these things.*
>
> *50 Now there was a man named Joseph, a member of the Council, a good and upright man, 51 who had not consented to their decision and action. He came from the Judean town of Arimathea, and he himself was waiting for the kingdom of God. 52 Going to Pilate, he asked for Jesus' body. 53 Then he took it down, wrapped it in linen cloth and placed it in a tomb cut in the rock, one in which no one had yet been laid.*

We are so used to tying the name of Jesus with concepts such as life, birth and eternity that it is difficult to think of him being dead. That is to say, a body with no movement or action, a brain with no thinking and a heart with no feeling. Jesus was supposed to be the light of the world. Death is the darkness of the world, the ultimate bottomless pit into which everything falls.

Since his death, Philip Larkin, the much-loved poet, has become a bit of a national treasure. Like many others I love his poems and, quite surprisingly, find most of them understandable. He was, however, a dour and melancholic thinker and his melancholia is nowhere darker than in his words on life and death.

> That this is what we fear – no sight, no sound,
> No touch or taste or smell, nothing to think with,
> Nothing to love or link with,
> The anaesthetic from which no one can come
> round.

Or as Jesus said, 'Father into your hands I commend my spirit.'

The centurion was moved, his followers watched from a distance and Joseph and Nicodemus step out of the shadows. They had both been rather 'hidden away followers' of Jesus. They lacked the courage to be out in public and both seem to have avoided the crucifixion but they found the strength from somewhere to step out and minister to Jesus in his death. (What a relief to know that we don't all have to be bold and courageous all of the time.)

They laid him in the tomb and wrapped his body in pure linen cloths, which is exactly what Mary did when he was born. So Jesus left this life as he had entered it. Finally the boulder is rolled across the tomb's entrance. Jesus is locked in, we are all shut out and no one then actually knows what goes on in that sealed space.

There is an old and wonderful idea that Jesus did not lie dormant but actually went to the place or the realms of death and set the dead free. It is called the 'Harrowing of Hell', the idea is of Jesus re-claiming lost people.

'The day is coming when all who are in their graves will hear his voice.' **John 5: 28**

'He went and made a proclamation to the spirits in prison, who in former times did not obey.' **1 Peter 3: 19**

In all of this the tomb is like a Tardis. It is bigger and with more happening on the inside than the outside. Time and space are seen to be relative and fluid, not absolute and standing still, Einstein would have loved it.

Here is the big question: When you think about death are you with Philip Larkin or with Jesus Christ?

Heavenly Father
You are Lord of the past, present and future.
You are the one who lights up the darkness
You are Lord of day and night
Of life and death
So may you help us to place our hope and trust in you
All our days.
Amen

95. Jesus the Glorious

John 20: 1, 11–16

¹ Early on the first day of the week, while it was still dark, Mary Magdalene went to the tomb and saw that the stone had been removed from the entrance.

¹¹ Now Mary stood outside the tomb crying. As she wept, she bent over to look into the tomb ¹² and saw two angels in white, seated where Jesus' body had been, one at the head and the other at the foot.

¹³ They asked her, "Woman, why are you crying?"

"They have taken my Lord away," she said, "and I don't know where they have put him." ¹⁴ At this, she turned around and saw Jesus standing there, but she did not realize that it was Jesus.

¹⁵ He asked her, "Woman, why are you crying? Who is it you are looking for?"

Thinking he was the gardener, she said, "Sir, if you have carried him away, tell me where you have put him, and I will get him."

¹⁶ Jesus said to her, "Mary."

She turned toward him and cried out in Aramaic, "Rabboni!" (which means "Teacher").

To my mind there is only one way to read the resurrection story or to begin an Easter Day service, and that is to listen to 'Fanfare for the Common Man' by Aaron Copland played at high volume. This is a light filled, magnificent and very loud piece of music. It begins with a piercing trumpet call coming out of the distance, suddenly the feel drops into a slightly more reflective 'valley of sound' before picking up the fanfare again and then hitting a massive wall of cymbals and drums.

Actually, I would rename the whole piece, from 'Fanfare for the Common Man' to 'Resurrection for the Son of Man'. Up to this point Jesus has actually been the common man, but as John's gospel has kept saying on his path to Jerusalem this is his glory time. Jesus the commoner has suddenly become Jesus the Glorious.

The Resurrection of Jesus can be seen as the second 'Big Bang'. A second act of totally unexpected and spontaneous creation of life. The first Big Bang happened about 13.8 billion years ago in complete nothingness, no time, no space, no universe yet suddenly it happened and then everything sprang into existence. In the tomb the spirit/humanity of Jesus is dead; he has fallen into a huge 'Black Hole' from where no light, life or hope can escape. Suddenly the completely unexpected and inexplicable miracle of life explodes. Just like the universe being born out of the Big Bang so all life beyond death is born out of this second Big Bang.

How wonderfully bizarre that the first witnesses to the resurrection and re-emergence of Jesus are women. In a Jewish culture and legal system no-one took the testimony or eyewitness account of a woman seriously. The only acceptable witnesses were men. The place of Mary at the centre of the story reminds us of how Jesus always turns the inherent sexism of his day upside down. To him, women are just as special and impartial as men. However, Mary being the first and biggest witness points to another important consideration. If Matthew and Mark, Luke and John had been making up this amazing story (as many have claimed over the years) they would never have invented a story where the main eyewitness was a woman, especially one with a dodgy background.

The Mary part of the story is both beautifully touching and also a powerful pointer to its truth. Since Mary, how many millions of us have experienced the light, joy and glorious impact of the resurrection of Jesus in our own lives?

Today Christians are under attack for believing in such a ridiculous and impossible story. Yet the story of the second 'Bang' is no more impossible than that of the first. Just because we cannot envisage let alone understand such events does not mean that they didn't happen. The place of Mary is just one of a whole string of incidents that point to the massive truth/probability of the resurrection story. We shall come across more of them in our next readings.

With a bit of creative imagination it is possible to work through Beethoven's nine symphonies and sort of fit them into the life of Christ. In this scheme the fifth with its momentous 'Da, da, da, daa' becomes Palm Sunday. Finally and most gloriously the ninth with its 'Ode to Joy' is the resurrection.

> 'Joyful, like a hero to victory.
> Joy, beautiful spark of the gods.'

Or as Charles Wesley put it:

> 'Thine be the glory
> Risen, conqu'ring Son
> Endless is the victory
> Thou o'er death hast won.'

The Glory Question for us all is then 'Where is the resurrection in my life today?'

Lord Jesus
As you rose from the dead
And conquered the power of death
May you help me to rise today
To overcome any adversity
And to bring glory to your name.
Amen

96. Answering the Doubter

John 20: 24–29

^{24} Now Thomas (also known as Didymus), one of the Twelve, was not with the disciples when Jesus came. ^{25} So the other disciples told him, "We have seen the Lord!"

But he said to them, "Unless I see the nail marks in his hands and put my finger where the nails were, and put my hand into his side, I will not believe."

^{26} A week later his disciples were in the house again, and Thomas was with them. Though the doors were locked, Jesus came and stood among them and said, "Peace be with you!" ^{27} Then he said to Thomas, "Put your finger here; see my hands. Reach out your hand and put it into my side. Stop doubting and believe."

^{28} Thomas said to him, "My Lord and my God!"

^{29} Then Jesus told him, "Because you have seen me, you have believed; blessed are those who have not seen and yet have believed."

We have seen how Jesus appeared on the first Easter Sunday morning to Mary. As the day progressed there were other appearances. First to two disappointed friends making their weary way back to Emmaus. They had expected so much from Jesus until the crucifixion. Then a third appearance story happens as the disciples are in hiding behind locked doors and filled with fear. These are failure and disappointment stories. Jesus' followers are not filled with optimism after Good Friday, quite the opposite, they think it is all over and they are fearing the worst. This, of course, is another big clue to the truth of the resurrection, how could such beaten people become world beaters?

My own favourite failure and disappointment transformation story is that of Thomas. The story of Doubting Thomas, as we now call him, works perfectly for me because I am a Doubting Robin. For some doubt is an intellectual thing, for others it is often more emotional, growing out of their temperament. And for some of us it is both.

I haven't always been a doubter. In fact when I first became a Christian I was filled, for several years, with overflowing confidence and belief, even certainty. Don't ask me where it has come from but as I have got older, experienced more of life and probed around more in the deep chambers of my rather melancholic 'inner me' doubts have become an ever-present reality. The doubts have entered my house of faith like a combination of rising damp and woodworm. I have all sorts of doubts. Does God exist? Did Jesus rise from the dead? Am I a true Christian? Is the church really on the right track?

I used to think it was a terrible thing for an evangelist and a vicar to be racked with doubt and I tried desperately to hide it away from people. Now I think, 'This is me'. 'This is who I am'. 'This is who God called'. Gradually I came to realise that my doubts were more about me than about God. God is a big God, he can cope with my doubts. So even as Doubting Robin I am still finding Jesus, still following him and still trying to become like him. Why, because I have discovered a 'knowing' and a devotion that is deeper than my doubts.

Jesus' response to the not quite believing Thomas is, 'Reach out and touch me', 'Try me out', 'Look at the evidence', 'Probe and search'. It is as if Jesus is saying, 'I know you think this is impossible, incredible but find out for yourself that it is true. Stop doubting and believe'.

This is not a theoretical story made up of ideas and hopefulness. It is rather a historical, made out of solid rock, observational story. It is tangible, you can feel its authenticity, you can reach out and touch its truthfulness. Who could have made it up and imagined it? It is a 'this is what really happened eye witness story'.

Many of us get frightened by our doubts, they feel like they are eating into the solidity of our faith. The result is we sweep them under the carpet, sing louder and pray longer. In my experience the best thing to do is to let them become like probing fingers. When we reach out to touch Jesus we find something for the brain and something for the heart. Firstly, for the brain or intellect, we find a bunch of rational and logical factors that have to be taken seriously. Secondly, for the heart, we find something or someone who is authentic, true. We find a living friend and leader. We intuitively know that death could not defeat this supremely good man. We reach out and touch the still living Jesus.

Today's question then is, 'What is the biggest doubt facing you about the resurrection of Jesus?'

> Lord Jesus
> Risen from the dead
> Full of glory, life and light.
> As I reach out to touch you
> May you speak into my brain with your truth
> And warm my heart with your living presence.
> Amen.

97. Disciples make Disciples

John 21: 1

¹ Afterward Jesus appeared again to his disciples, by the Sea of Galilee. It happened this way:

Matthew 28: 16–20

¹⁶ Then the eleven disciples went to Galilee, to the mountain where Jesus had told them to go. ¹⁷ When they saw him, they worshiped him; but some doubted. ¹⁸ Then Jesus came to them and said, "All authority in heaven and on earth has been given to me. ¹⁹ Therefore go and make disciples of all nations, baptizing them in the name of the Father and of the Son and of the Holy Spirit, ²⁰ and teaching them to obey everything I have commanded you. And surely I am with you always, to the very end of the age."

The resurrected Jesus moves on from Jerusalem to Galilee and the disciples move with him.

First he mysteriously appears on the beach to seven disciples who have gone back to fishing. He directs them to a great catch of fish and then cooks breakfast for them. Then he turns to Peter and turns his three

denials before the cock crowed into three affirmations
of love before they make a new beginning.

Then to the mountain. The last time Jesus and his disciples
stood on a mountain top together it had been the massive
shared spiritual experience of the Transfiguration. From
there it was downhill to Jerusalem and the cross. Here
they are back on top of the mountain again. Worship and
doubt are again joined like Siamese twins. We usually
think that the one drives out the other but they often seem
to live in the same house in Jesus' story.

Up to this point we have defined the disciples as those
who learn from and follow in the footsteps of Jesus.
Here we add a third element to the picture. From this
moment on disciples will also be those who do the work
of Jesus. Disciples do not just sit in Bible studies and
prayer meetings. Disciples make disciples. You need the
full colour spectrum to paint the discipleship picture
and the three primary colours are learning, following
and doing.

Disciples have a special relationship to Jesus, I always
think of the Celine Dion song as capturing its essence.

> You were my strength when I was weak
> You were my voice when I couldn't speak
> You were my eyes when I couldn't see
> You saw the best there was in me
> Lifted me up when I couldn't reach
> You gave me faith 'cause you believed
> I'm everything I am
> Because you loved me.

But it goes beyond this because it is not just about me and Jesus. It is about Jesus, me and the world.

Talking to various groups of Christians over many years I have discovered that this mark of going out and making disciples is probably the least popular aspect of following Jesus and becoming like him.

> Do I really have to?
> This is not my ministry or gift.
> I am not very good at this.

These eleven disciples/apostles were in effect called to be both evangelists (Good News Proclaimers) and discipleship makers. The two are part of the same work, baptising or helping people to find Jesus and then helping them to become like him.

These eleven were not the only ones sent out, they were the first ones. We are their children. I'm quite sure that they were as fearful and as self-doubting as we are and yet they went.

A question for all would be disciples, 'Can you think of three people you know that you could share Jesus with?'

> **Lord Jesus**
> **You went out**
> **You sent the disciples out**
> **Help me now to go out.**
> **Out to the people I already know**
> **And to talk with them**
> **About what I have found in you.**
> **Amen**

98. Power from on High

Luke 24: 44–49

> [44] He said to them, "This is what I told you while I was still with you: Everything must be fulfilled that is written about me in the Law of Moses, the Prophets and the Psalms."
>
> [45] Then he opened their minds so they could understand the Scriptures. [46] He told them, "This is what is written: The Messiah will suffer and rise from the dead on the third day, [47] and repentance for the forgiveness of sins will be preached in his name to all nations, beginning at Jerusalem. [48] You are witnesses of these things. [49] I am going to send you what my Father has promised; but stay in the city until you have been clothed with power from on high."

Now there is a bit of a problem with the ending of the Jesus story. Matthew and John end it in Galilee with the disciples being sent out into all the world. Luke's is a very different ending with the various disciples, followers and companions still in Jerusalem. No-one is exactly sure how to put the two endings together but for what it's worth here is my best guess.

After Jesus speaks the great commission to the eleven on top of the mountain I don't think it will have been the time and place for them to just set off into the great 'blue yonder'. I don't think they will have been in the right frame of mind either. Suppose they decided to first go back to Jerusalem, bring the others up to date and talk the whole thing through with them. There were about another hundred or so Jesus followers or 'companions' still in the city and it seems natural to me that the eleven would feel drawn back to them.

Then as the full company were gathered, talking and sharing, Jesus appears to them all. There in the midst of his people he again talks about proclaiming to 'all the nations' but he also tells them to wait.

The concept of power, once so appealing, has got difficult connotations today. The 'Black Lives Matter' movement points to power being used to supress and exploit black people. The environmental movement reminds us continually of how technological and economic powers are coming to destroy our world. We have a recent history of demagogues and dictators rising to power and then manipulating their power for evil doing.

However, power can be used for loving and good purposes. Love, truth, beauty and peace can be empowered. And it is this sort of power that Jesus talks to his followers about.

"You will be clothed with power from on high."

I have always had a great sense of mission in my life. I am not very good, however, at waiting and contemplating; at slowly, patiently receiving. I am really good at jumping up, rushing out and doing.

Jesus talks about a three-step process: pause, receive and go. I have a tendency to skip the first two and move straight to go. Others do a lot of pause and receive but never go.

I quite like listening to motivational talks. The Americans are especially good at this while we English are very restrained and buttoned up. My favourite is Oprah Winfrey, she has the power to encourage, to turn people to their 'good side' and to bring out all their hope and potential. This is all wonderful and empowering but it is basically operating on a human level. It is about me and my power.

Imagine a power, a Holy Spirit in fact, that can do all that I can do and then can add 'power from above'. Jesus is talking about the Holy Spirit, the one who can bring the heavenly level down to the human level and clothe us.

The story of Pentecost in Acts chapter 2 is the story of their being clothed – 'Suddenly, from Heaven, there came the sound like the rush of a mighty wind'.

Here then is the Holy Spirit question. How good are you at pausing and being clothed?

Lord Jesus
Help me to stay and wait
To hear the wind
To be clothed
To be empowered
And help me to go out.
Amen

99. The Big Story

Luke 1: 1–4

¹ Many have undertaken to draw up an account of the things that have been fulfilled among us, ² just as they were handed down to us by those who from the first were eyewitnesses and servants of the word. ³ With this in mind, since I myself have carefully investigated everything from the beginning, I too decided to write an orderly account for you, most excellent Theophilus, ⁴ so that you may know the certainty of the things you have been taught.

John 20: 30–31

³⁰ Jesus performed many other signs in the presence of his disciples, which are not recorded in this book. ³¹ But these are written that you may believe that Jesus is the Messiah, the Son of God, and that by believing you may have life in his name.

They are great stories. Moving, inspiring and motivating. In fact they are the greatest stories of the greatest human being who ever lived. But are they true? Was it really like this? Sometimes it seems like just too much to believe that Jesus was the Son of God, that wise men came and shepherds greeted him, that he cured the sick, cared for the poor, turned water into wine and rose from the dead.

At the beginning of his gospel Luke made it crystal clear that they were all true stories, known by those who were in the know.

> *"Handed on to us by those who from the beginning were eye witnesses."*
> *"So that you may know the truth."*

Here we are now. Almost at the end of the tale and now it is John's turn to make the key point, *"as they were handed on to us by those who from the beginning were eye witnesses"*.

We live in negative and often destructive times. Cynicism, fake news and conspiracy stories abound. The Media, TV documentaries, social networking and the new atheism seem to have come together in a grand alliance to discredit religious belief. Yet still these stories stand out alone as true, authentic and life-changing.

In 2016 I found myself talking about the resurrection to a room full of very bright sixth formers. Inevitably one of the loudest and most confident had established himself as a sort of group leader. In fact he was on the way to becoming a 'group think' former. These are the ones who tell us all what to think and stupidly most of us join in with the 'group think'. At a certain point in the discussion he strongly asserted, 'When you're dead, you're dead.' I could sense the room being influenced by him. Then it came to me and so I replied, 'Yes, when you are dead, you are dead, but when you are Jesus, you are Jesus.' Suddenly the 'group think' was not quite so tight and well-shaped. Later on when we asked the whole group to fill in a response sheet it was surprising to see how many had ticked the, 'I would like to find out more about Jesus' box.

Some time ago I read Anthony Beevor's account of the *Battle of Stalingrad*. It is a great book of compelling historical authenticity. I was so gripped that a couple of years later when a friend recommended *'Life and Fate'* by Vasily Grossman, a novel set in Stalingrad I read that too. There is always a big overlap between a historical novel and a historical account but they are not the same. Matthew, Mark, Luke and John are not historical novels. They are solid wall historical accounts made out of bricks, made out of eyewitness testimonies from lots of different people. It is vital that we all grasp this when we ask the big questions.

> Did it happen?
> Did he say that?
> Is this what happened?

These words at the beginning of Luke's and at the end of John's gospel are saying, 'yes it did and yes he did and yes it is' to all these questions.

These Gospel stories have been written that we might

Find him
Follow him
And become like him
That we might believe and have life.
Eternal life
Jam packed with peace and joy
Meeting lots of other people who have met him
Together changing the world.
And ourselves being part of the story.

So ask yourself, how are you reading the Jesus story?
And how deeply?

Lord Jesus
They met you
Listened to you
Were touched by you
And wrote the story.
Help me to read
Remember
Read again
And be changed forever by their truth.
Amen.

100. Ascension

Luke 24: 50–52

> *⁵⁰ When he had led them out to the vicinity of Bethany, he lifted up his hands and blessed them. ⁵¹ While he was blessing them, he left them and was taken up into heaven. ⁵² Then they worshiped him and returned to Jerusalem with great joy.*

Jesus ascends, departs. He leaves our world and returns to his. He goes ahead of us to prepare a place for us so that we can follow him.

He came, not so much in a miraculous way, more in an impossible to explain supernatural way, silently entering our world from another dimension, time, place, universe or whatever.

He left it in a similar way. One minute they see him, the next he is gone. Did he go up, down or just dissolve into the air? Is there a spiritual wormhole between his world and ours, a doorway, launch pad or trapdoor? The point is human words only really work when describing things that happen in the human world. The story of his Ascension, just like the accounts of his birth, is something that happens one third in the human world and two thirds in the Jesus world.

It's a bit like the Aslan story in the *Lion, the Witch and the Wardrobe*. One minute the great lion is there changing the world, defeating the darkness and breathing out his inner spirit and the next minute he is gone. Everyone misses him, and there is an empty place where he used to be, but the impact he had still lives on.

The disciples have lost their leader, their inspiration, their rock. How do they feel?

Jesus was born into my Robin Gamble world over forty years ago and he has never left it, he is still here with me. I try to conscientiously begin and end every day with him. In between I frequently forget him but he never forgets me. He lives in every moment and every experience. The good and the bad, my strengths and weaknesses, the best bits and the bits I am embarrassed by and ashamed of; he shares them all.

Not only that but the best is yet to come. You see, when I die he wants me to ascend, to pass from Earth to Heaven, from human lifespan to eternal life, from him living in my world, to me living in his.

> So take the imagined story of Aslan.
> Add Obi Wan Kenobi, Dumbledore, Dr Who and Gandalf.
> Throw in the disappearance of the last unicorn.
> And give it all a bit of historical reality.
> With the lives of Ghandi, Martin Luther King, Florence Nightingale and Nelson Mandela.

Let the whole crowd lift off and disappear in a
sort of God designed Tardis.
And imagine first Jesus and then yourself.
Ascending.

Jesus is no longer living in this earth world but he is
alive and well in Robin Gamble world and I have just
said I start each day with him. Every morning I sit down
and, over a big cup of tea, spend time with him. I pray
to him and read the gospels. Like Mary I ponder over
him and breathe him in. I attempt to become Jesus full,
to centre my being around him and to work out what
his mission is for me each day. In Robin Gamble world
he is my greatest source of peace, courage and joy. This
is not an emotional or imaginary experience, this is
a relationship; brain as well as heart, intellectual
conviction alongside emotional commitment. Not only
is he living in my world, I am living in his.

The last word goes to the great Freddie:

> Oh you're the best friend that I ever had
> I've been with you such a long time.
> You're my sunshine and I want you to know
> That my feelings are true.
> I really love you.

If Jesus had remained physically rooted in Jerusalem he
would have stayed as the best friend of a handful of
followers. Because he ascended above and beyond time
and place he can be best friend to all of us. Not as a
memory but as a reality.

> Oh, you're my best friend.

Lord Jesus
Risen and Glorious Lord
Ascended and now in Heaven.
May you live in my heart
And may I live in yours.
This day
And every day.
Amen

Jesus 100 Conclusion

I have read these Gospel tales time and time again. They still keep coming to me as fresh, all powerful, moving, inspirational and true eyewitness stories. Each time I read them I still hear and see and feel the real presence of Jesus. You might want to go back to the beginning yourself and read, not just my selection of 100 stories but the whole Gospels themselves. Or you could move on to the 'Acts of the Apostles', the next great chapter in the ever-continuing mega tale of Jesus, his people and his Kingdom.

Now as I finally reflect on these 100 stories of Jesus. As I think of myself as one finding him, following him and becoming like him, I am thinking of doors and doorways.

Doors are wonderful things because they open for us to enter new rooms, new houses and gardens and they often lead to us meeting new people.

My favourite doorway story is *'The Lion, the Witch and the Wardrobe'*. As with many other children, when I first read it I was desperate to find a wardrobe with a secret door into Narnia. It was much later that I realised that Jesus, himself, is the doorway, or the door opener.

ROBIN GAMBLE

"Ask and it will be given to you; seek and you will find; knock and the door will be opened to you.*"*
Matthew 7: 7

There is another and final doorway in the Jesus story. Except this time he is the one who is knocking on the door and I am the one, in fact the only one, who can open it.

Here I am! I stand at the door and knock. If anyone hears my voice and opens the door, I will come in and eat with that person, and they with me.
Revelation 3: 20

Who on earth would not want Jesus to come in and sit and eat with them?

All I have to do is open the door.

Biography

I live and work in the great northern city of Bradford. There I work away at helping the churches to grow and encouraging people to think again about Jesus.

When I am not doing this I am usually devouring books, walking the hills, painting pictures, listening to music or supporting Bradford City. All of this brings much joy, massive reflections and some frustrations.

I share this life with my life partner and fellow pilgrim, Maureen. She is my wife, my inspiration, my mentor and my lover. God has given us two children of which we are both so proud and utterly lost in admiration and friendship.

I had about four attempts at being a proper Christian. Eventually I made it thanks largely to the work of our vicar, Michael Savage. Frankly he rescued me and I have been rescuing others ever since.

So I have been trying to find Jesus, to follow him and become like him for most of my life; now it's over to you.

Acknowledgements

Producing this book seems to have taken ages and has depended on the tremendous support, reading, advising and continuous encouragement of various people. Mentioning, in particular:-

Jane Adams, without whom Jesus 100 would have been Jesus 10.

John Bromley and Sue Cooke for their careful reading and helpful comments.

Neil Short and Matt Woodcock for their willingness to test Jesus 100 on their congregations. In fact Neil has produced a series of group bible study notes and sermon guides to go with the book which you can find on the 'Leading your Church into Growth' website.

The congregation of St Wilfrid's Calverley for trialling Jesus 100 and Sue McWhinney and Toby Raistrick for making this possible.

My beloved wife, Maureen, who helped, cajoled and continually supported me.

How kind you have all been to me.

Also a big thank you to the 'Leading your Church into Growth' team for committing to sponsor this book.'

Lightning Source UK Ltd.
Milton Keynes UK
UKHW011858041222
413331UK00006B/166

9 781839 758331